M. CREON LEVIT

CHALLENGER

Books by Malcolm McConnell

Fiction

MATATA

CLINTON IS ASSIGNED

JUST CAUSES

Nonfiction

STEPPING OVER

INTO THE MOUTH OF THE CAT

THE ESSENCE OF FICTION

With Carol McConnell

FIRST CROSSING

MIDDLE SEA AUTUMN

THE MEDITERRANEAN DIET

With Johnny France

INCIDENT AT BIG SKY

CHALLENGER

A MAJOR MALFUNCTION

Malcolm McConnell

DOUBLEDAY & COMPANY, INC.
GARDEN CITY, NEW YORK
1987

All illustrations courtesy of NASA unless otherwise indicated.

Library of Congress Cataloging-in-Publication Data
McConnell, Malcolm.
Challenger: a major malfunction.

Includes index.
1. Challenger (Spacecraft)—Accidents.
2. Space shuttles—Accidents.   I. Title.
TL867.M36 1987   363.1'24   86-29170
ISBN 0-385-23877-0

To the crew of Challenger
and the men and women of NASA

CONTENTS

CONTENTS

vii

PREFACE

When civil servants carrying out public policy succeed, as they did during the Apollo moon landings, we all want to share the glory. Congress and the Executive Branch always receive their due credit.

But when policy fails, as it did in Vietnam and with the space shuttle program, we search for scapegoats. After the debacle in Indochina, the military was forced to accept an unfair portion of blame. Since the Challenger disaster, "NASA bashing" has become a national pastime. Congress, the Executive Branch, and the Press have been notably silent about their own roles in the tragedy.

The intention of this book is not to heap scorn on the civil servants of the National Aeronautics and Space Administration. In my opinion, the rank and file people in NASA are among the hardest working, most productive, and most talented employees in the federal government. They certainly gave more of themselves than other government workers during the long struggle to make the space shuttle an omnibus operational vehicle. And it must be remembered that they faced simultaneous budget shortfalls and technical problems of unprecedented complexity.

Nor is it the intention of this book to rethink the basic decisions that led to our manned space program. Although it is increasingly popular to ridicule the very concept of manned space flight, we should all remember that exploration is a fundamental human impulse, and that the history of civilization is also the history of human exploration. On a more practical level, we must never forget that the geopolitical realities of this century oblige us to match the achievements of the Soviet Union. For better or worse, we continue to be locked in a competitive embrace with the Russians. And it is clear that the Soviet Union has continuously placed great emphasis on manned flight since the early days of their space program. Therefore, it is simply inconceivable that the United States would abandon manned space flight while the Soviets make their slow, but undeniably impressive progress in this exciting, expensive endeavor.

Following the Challenger accident, however, the goals, shape and size of our manned space program must be the subject of intense and well-informed national debate. Perhaps my book will help those who participate in that vital debate.

This book's goal is to dissect a tragic policy failure, to reveal the political intrigue and compromise, the venality and hidden agendas that combined over almost twenty years to produce the disaster.

I wish to acknowledge the invaluable assistance I received from many men and women in NASA, particularly in Public Affairs, in researching this book. Although the material I uncovered was often painful for them, they never hesitated to meet their professional obligations.

However, I am sorry to report that NASA's Office of the General Counsel has been anything but forthcoming in answering my legitimate requests for information under the provisions of the Freedom of Information Act. Although I made my first written request in early August 1986, the agency's attorneys declined to acknowledge these requests until October 31, 1986, the last working day before my November 1 deadline, of which I had naively informed NASA earlier. The information I requested concerned the membership of the Source Evaluation Boards for the contract awards of the space shuttle solid rocket boosters and main engines. Even fourteen years after the event, NASA is apparently intent on keeping this information secret, contrary to the requirements of the Freedom of Information Act.

To my colleagues in the press who helped me, I offer my thanks for their support, and my admiration for the renewed diligence they showed after the accident.

Although this narrative dramatically reconstructs historic events, the book is not "New Journalism." All actions and conversations have been rigorously authenticated, either from sworn testimony before the Rogers Commission and interviews conducted by Commission and Congressional investigators, or from interviews by the author.

The staffs of several Congressional committees, the Information

Office of the Library of Congress, and members of the Rogers Commission were very responsive to my research needs. Professional researcher Brian Morgan was extremely effective at ferreting out many obscure but vital documents. Carol Emery McConnell spent hundreds of hours conducting and transcribing interviews, searching historical records, and editing multiple draft versions of the book on her word processor.

Malcolm McConnell
Washington

CAPE CANAVERAL

Challenger rose on a pillar of flame. Its engines split the cold sunlight, a rolling cacophony louder than massed artillery.

The Orbiter had the proportions of a child's drawing, squat body, stubby wings, a mottled skin of black and white tiles. It was dwarfed by the ocher bulk of the external tank and the columns of the solid rocket boosters.

Each second of its ascent the space shuttle burned ten tons of frozen gases and solid fuel. In eight minutes Challenger would be in space, her engines silent, falling through the chill vacuum of Earth orbit at seventeen thousand miles an hour.

Now, moments after lift-off, the onboard computers whispered and the aerosurfaces obeyed, rolling Challenger onto her back. A piston of blazing smoke thrust the space shuttle up the long trajectory.

In the crew cabin, seven men and women sat on two decks, strapped into padded seats, their backs to the ocean, their faces toward the sky. Clanging with vibration, the two-thousand-ton shuttle gained speed and altitude. As the vehicle clattered and swayed, the freight-train roar of the boosters pounded the cabin.

The crew was euphoric to be finally underway after so many delays.

"Looks like we've got a lot of wind here today," Pilot Mike Smith commented over the intercom.

"Yeah," Commander Dick Scobee agreed. He twisted in his seat. "It's a little hard to see out my window here."

Challenger passed Mach One, the speed of sound, at 19,000 feet.

The computers throttled back the three main engines to 65 percent of thrust, anticipating the stress that engineers call Max-Q, maximum aerodynamic pressure.

"Okay, we're throttling down," Scobee reassured his crew as the thrust dropped.

For fourteen seconds they swayed and jolted silently in their seats while the shuttle chopped through wind shear.

"Throttling up," Scobee called, watching the bright lines on his flight data screen.

"Throttle up," Smith confirmed from his own instruments.

"Roger," Dick Scobee formally acknowledged like a careful surgeon. They had performed this ritual so many times in the Houston simulators.

"Feel that mother go," Smith called, noting the violent surge of power. "Wooo . . . hooo!"

As Challenger climbed, its computers processed millions of bits of data, sifting, storing, routing ghostly digital pulses. A dozen telemetry channels beamed this data down to antennas at the Cape, where it was instantly retransmitted by satellite to the Mission Control Room at Houston's Johnson Space Center. Inside the quiet, air-conditioned confines of Mission Control, Jay Greene and his launch team sat intently at consoles, staring into their screens, listening to the faint satellite hiss on their headsets. They saw that Challenger's engines had returned normally to full thrust, that the ascent was proceeding perfectly.

CAPCOM Richard Covey hunched at his console, his face tight with concentration. "Challenger," he called, "go at throttle up."

On Challenger's noisy flight deck, Commander Scobee punched his transmit button and replied, "Roger, go at throttle up."

It was exactly seventy seconds after lift-off. The shuttle was near 50,000 feet, and most of Earth's turbulent atmosphere already lay below.

But in the next three seconds Challenger slammed through increasingly violent maneuvers.

Mike Smith voiced sudden apprehension. "Uh-oh."

In Mission Control, the pulsing digits on the screens abruptly stopped. At the top of each console screen, a frozen white *S* was now centered. Static, no downlink.

Challenger was dead.

*   *   *

Mission Control spokesman Steve Nesbitt sat above the four console tiers. For a long moment he stared around the silent, softly lit room. The red ascent trajectory line was stationary on the display screen across the room. Finally, he spoke: "Flight controllers here looking very carefully at the situation. Obviously a major malfunction."

PART I

YEARS OF INTRIGUE
AND AMBITION

REHEARSAL FOR DISASTER

On the overcast morning of January 8, 1986, the space shuttle Challenger stood on Launch Pad 39B of the Kennedy Space Center. Technicians in white coveralls worked on several levels of the massive service structure surrounding the Orbiter. In just over two weeks, Challenger was scheduled to fly its tenth mission. Now the workers were completing their checks and closeout lists, carefully verifying every system on the most complex machine ever made.

The Orbiter's skin of black and white heat tiles was almost hidden by the girders and piping of the Rotary Service Structure. From the Mobile Launching Platform on which Challenger stood, the space shuttle looked like a futuristic airliner that had somehow become entangled in the plumbing of an oil refinery. There was a ponderous, industrial quality to the scene, far removed from the gracefully powerful television image of the space shuttle in flight.

Challenger was mated to its huge apricot-colored external tank and its twin solid rocket boosters. Men crossing the launch platform were dwarfed by the assembly, like yard workers beside the awkward bulk of a dry-docked ship. The shuttle was roughly the length and weight of a World War Two destroyer. Challenger's external fuel tank alone was as large as a 1940s blimp, and its solid rocket boosters were bigger than many grain elevators.

To the men working on Challenger, the huge space shuttle often seemed more like a factory than a rocket ship. This morning, however, was different. People would enter the Orbiter and bring the ship to life. This was Countdown Demonstration Day, SOO17 in the ubiquitous NASA jargon heard around the Cape. Challenger's

3

crew was here from Houston; today all the separate systems aboard the shuttle, on the launch pad, in the Launch Control Center three miles away, and in the Mission Control Room in Houston would be tested for the first time with the flight crew aboard the Orbiter. This was a precise dress rehearsal, a delicately orchestrated procedure that exactly duplicated the actual launch countdown, right up to simulated engine start at the T-5 seconds mark.

A little after eight, the seven-member crew arrived, their shiny aluminum Astrovan driving up the concrete ramp, right to the base of the Fixed Service Structure. They wore sky-blue flight suits and black boots. They looked calm and rested. As they waited for the elevator, they joked and smiled. Four of the crew, Commander Dick Scobee and Mission Specialists Judy Resnik, Ron McNair, and Ellison Onizuka, had flown before, Scobee and McNair aboard Challenger itself. As longtime members of the astronaut corps, they had been to the Cape many times and had often clambered around shuttles on the launch pad. For the other three crew members, the mission would be their first flight. But two of them were familiar with the launch pad operation. Pilot Mike Smith, a former Navy test pilot, had been an astronaut for five years; Payload Specialist Greg Jarvis was an aerospace engineer who designed communications satellites that were launched aboard the space shuttle. The seventh member of the crew, however, Teacher-in-Space participant Christa McAuliffe, had only been to the Cape once before. During her training that fall, she had seen Challenger launched from the neighboring pad, 39A.

The crew was at the Cape during a period of intense and frustrating launch operations. On neighboring Pad 39A, the space shuttle Columbia stood beneath the low overcast; the attempt to launch it the day before had been canceled just nine minutes before scheduled lift-off, the third straight scrub in three launch attempts.

But Challenger's crew did not seem affected by Columbia's problems. They exchanged pleasantries with the pad closeout technicians and confidently predicted their own mission would fly on schedule. Ellison Onizuka kidded the NASA Quality Control technician, Johnny Corlew, because the closeout crew were not wearing Challenger's Teacher-in-Space mission patch on their

4

white coveralls: a breach of informal NASA protocol. Corlew had worked with Ellison Onizuka for several years and was used to his wry sense of humor. You all get yourself through the final simulator training on time, Corlew said, and we'll be sure to have our patches on launch morning.

Before filing through the wide door of the elevator that would lift them to the Orbiter access arm at the 195-foot level, the crew paused to take in the impressive bulk of their spaceship. From where they stood, the girders of the service structures and the gray steel flanks of the Mobile Launching Platform hid most of the Orbiter, but the orange external tank was clearly visible through the latticework of pipes. And the massive columns of the solid rocket boosters, SRB's in NASA jargon, towered above them, the largest solid-fuel rockets ever built, each as tall as a fifteen-story building, each carrying over five hundred tons of explosive fuel.

On launch day, when the external tank was loaded with liquid hydrogen and oxygen, the combined load of liquid and solid propellants would equal the explosive power of a small tactical nuclear weapon.

But as they confidently entered the elevator to begin the countdown rehearsal, Challenger's crew did not seem unduly worried by the proximity of the solid rockets. Throughout their collective years of training, they had been constantly reassured that the SRB's were among the safest and most reliable components on the space shuttle. The battered steel elevator door rumbled shut and the crew began their ascent to level 195. They had a busy and demanding morning ahead of them, and no one appeared preoccupied with potential explosive catastrophes.

The men and women of Challenger's crew could not see beneath the white steel skin of the SRB's into the tight tang-and-clevis connections known as field joints that linked the four massive cylindrical segments like giant tin cans. Each of these cylinders was over twenty-five feet long and twelve feet in diameter; each contained more than one hundred tons of fuel. On ignition the pressure inside the solid rockets' long flame tunnels would leap from sea level to hundreds of pounds per square inch in less than a tenth of a second. The cumulative stress of this so-called "ignition transient" equaled thousands of tons of gaseous pressure. These

5

superhot rocket gases expanded so violently that the entire steel rocket assembly would swell like a carnival balloon.

And the four circular field joints, hidden beneath a weather-protection band and locked together by 177 thick, steel pins, were the vital components that maintained the boosters' structural integrity against these fierce energies.

These field joints were designed to seal with "fail-safe" redundancy; they had long been considered one of the most reliable components of the entire shuttle system. They depended on the simple technology of pressurized synthetic rubber O-rings, not on notoriously unreliable hydraulic valves or delicate electronics. As far as anyone in the astronaut corps had been informed, there had never been a problem with the SRB field joints.

So, as Challenger's crew came out of the elevator at level 195 that morning and looked over the guardrail at the massive pillars of the SRB's just below, they had no way of guessing they were staring at the instrument of their destruction. To the astronauts, the space shuttle was a complex and sometimes overly sensitive system, but one they thought they fully understood.

Had the men and women of Challenger's crew somehow been able to see and understand the true nature of the solid rocket booster field joints, their cheerful confidence would have been shredded in an instant.

There was a fatal design flaw in the field joints hidden within the smooth white skin of the booster casings, a malignant knot that had already been diagnosed by the responsible officials at NASA's Marshall Space Flight Center in Alabama and by the engineers and managers at the company that had designed and built the boosters, Morton Thiokol's Wasatch Division in Utah. For almost a year these NASA and contractor managers had minimized the hazardous flaw and had successfully quashed outside investigation. Despite later denials, there is ample proof that Marshall and Thiokol officials recognized the catastrophic potential of the field joint problem. Almost half the first twenty-three space shuttle flights—including the second flight of the initial test program—had experienced partial failure of the booster field joints. The last five missions before Challenger's flight had been launched under a formal constraint stemming from partial field joint failures; unfortunately these constraints had been both issued and waived by the same Marshall Center manager, Lawrence Mulloy.

In January 1986 Morton Thiokol was involved in an ostensibly urgent field joint redesign effort to find a solution to the problem. That *urgent* effort had been underway almost a year. But before each mission, both NASA and Thiokol officials continued to certify that the solid rocket boosters were ready for safe flight.

Marshall Center managers tried to minimize the problem to protect their reputation within NASA's jealously competitive bureaucratic hierarchy, for fear of exposing past incompetence and losing scarce funding.

The motives of Morton Thiokol appear equally venal. Thiokol had gained the lucrative sole source contract for the solid rocket boosters thirteen years earlier, during a bitterly disputed award process that veteran observers have characterized as a low point in squalid political intrigue. At the time of the award to then relatively small Thiokol Chemical Company in Brigham City, Utah, both the newly appointed chairman of the Senate Aeronautics and Space Science Committee, Democratic Senator Frank Moss, and the new NASA administrator, Dr. James Fletcher, were insiders in the tightly knit Utah political hierarchy. This apparent Thiokol-Utah leverage has persisted over the years: James Fletcher was reappointed NASA Administrator following the Challenger accident, and the chairman of the Senate committee currently overseeing NASA's budget is Utah Republican Jake Garn, who rode aboard the shuttle in April 1985. By summer 1985, however—the year the catastrophic potential of the flawed field joints became obvious—Thiokol's monopoly position was under attack, and the corporation's executives were afraid to risk their billion-dollar contract by halting shuttle flight operations long enough to correct the faulty booster joint design.

In reality, as Challenger's crew smiled down from the launch pad catwalk at the massive white columns of the solid rocket boosters, they were looking at the final product of flawed policy and political corruption.

*   *   *

7

Most Americans, however, had a more romantic image of the space shuttle. To the public the Orbiter was a magical white bird, a nimble spaceliner that provided wholesome diversion on the evening news. The shuttle made them proud to be Americans; it gave them a warm sense of confidence about the country's high-technology future. In the past five years, press accounts had likened the gleaming Orbiter to a phoenix. The space shuttle had become the symbol of America's technological and political renaissance, a bold, successful gamble, the quintessence of this optimistic decade. The Orbiter rose beyond its own awesome fires, clean, powerful, high above the ashes of military defeat and political turmoil that had scarred the past twenty years. To millions of people, the space shuttle was a patriotic icon, the tangible symbol of what was best in American civilization, a product of daring scientific prowess, free-enterprise innovation, and insightful political leadership. The space shuttle had carried us back to the frontier and made us proud again.

That was the myth that surrounded Challenger as it stood on its launch pad in early January. The truth that lay beneath this myth was far less wholesome.

As the world was to learn in the months following the Challenger disaster, the mythical phoenix had been an unfortunate metaphor for the space shuttle. Another classic myth, "The Emperor's New Clothes," would have more accurately captured the essence of the program. Instead of merely involving a vain and senile monarch and a coterie of fawning sycophants, however, the myth of the "operational" space shuttle held sway over tens of thousands of NASA and contractor employees, the White House, Congress, and the American people. Certainly the Rogers Commission investigating the accident discovered a chasm of discrepancy between NASA's carefully nurtured image of an efficient, workaday space shuttle and the prevailing reality.

Simply stated, the space shuttle myth proclaimed that the vehicle had become the Free World's operational space transportation system. The omnibus shuttle would provide safe and economical routine access to low Earth orbit for scientific, commercial, and military cargos. And space shuttle operations would offer the profitability enjoyed by a well-run airline. According to NASA, the shuttle would soon pay its own way through internationally competitive commercial fees.

To accomplish this attractive goal, a variety of NASA officials and four presidents convinced themselves that space shuttles would fly as often as twice a month by 1988—down from the original projection of four monthly flights—using both the Kennedy Space Center and Vandenberg Air Force Base in California. Space shuttle flights would become so routine and reliable that the country could completely abandon the wasteful earlier generation of expendable launch vehicles. As the commercial advantages of routine shuttle operations expanded, an entire new space manufacturing industry would flourish to exploit the unique environment made accessible by the shuttle. A large, permanently manned space station would be in orbit by 1994, its components carried aloft in the shuttle's payload bay and serviced by regular shuttle flights. Before the end of this century, hundreds of astronauts and technicians would rotate to and from the space station.

In essence, the myth held, the space shuttle's innovative technology had liberated mankind from the planet's surface. The age of space exploration was giving way to the *exploitation* of space.

In retrospect, if an impartial analyst had scrutinized the space shuttle program in the months before the accident, he would have been either a fool or a charlatan if he persisted in the claim that the space shuttle provided safe, economical, and routine access to space.

*   *   *

In fact the shuttle's safety was precarious; over seven hundred separate pieces of flight hardware—including the solid rocket booster field joints—were listed as "Criticality 1," which meant that the failure of any *one* would result in the destruction of the vehicle and the death of the crew. These vulnerable items were built into every element of the space shuttle system, from the Orbiter to the external tank to the supposedly fail-safe solid rocket boosters. NASA engineers would later be obliged to testify that they did not actually understand the function or nature of several such key components.

The operational economy of the system was terrible. A space

9

shuttle flight cost over $200 million in January 1986, and less than half that amount could be recouped from paying customers.

Far from providing routine access to space, as the agency had predicted for years, flying shuttle missions taxed NASA and contractor resources to their limits. The managers, engineers, astronauts, technicians, and shift workers involved in this complex operation were nearing exhaustion as they prepared Challenger for its final flight.

* * *

The average person viewing Challenger on Launch Pad 39B would have perceived a technological marvel, the quintessence of this country's innovative scientific excellence. In reality, the vehicle—and especially its vulnerable and hazardous propulsion system—was the ultimate product of blatant Congressional pork barreling, bureaucratic duplicity, inexcusable corporate deception, and public ignorance.

As the Rogers Commission revealed, the Challenger tragedy was "an accident rooted in history." To understand what led to that fireball in the cold Florida sky, it is necessary to consider the events that preceded Challenger's rollout to the launch pad.

CERTIFICATION OF DECEIT

The afternoon of January 15, 1986, was sunny and mild. A light winter breeze stirred the saw grass on the dunes of Cape Canaveral. It would have been a perfect day to launch a space shuttle. But for the first time in weeks, the exhausted launch crew at the Kennedy Space Center did not have to think about the weather. They had finally launched Columbia on its 61-C mission just before dawn on Sunday the twelfth. This launch had experienced a record of three schedule "slips" and four actual launch pad "scrubs"; each of the scrubs had entailed a regular tanking of the vehicle with flight propellants and thousands of man-hours by the countdown team. But now all that grinding frustration was behind them; Columbia was safely in orbit, and the NASA and contractor technicians could devote their full attention to closeout of Challenger for its mission scheduled to begin January 23.

For a little while at least, these workers could step down from twenty-hour days to their more normal routine of twelve-hour workdays, seven days a week.

Cape Canaveral is the geological twin of Kitty Hawk, North Carolina, five hundred miles up the coast. Both are sandy barrier islands, separated from the mainland by tidal lagoons. They date from the end of the last Ice Age, when the ocean rose to drown the coastal marshes. Kitty Hawk has not changed much since the Wright Brothers flew their primitive airplane above the windy dunes.

But Cape Canaveral was radically transformed during the thirty-five years between the first test-firing of a captured V-2 rocket and the prelaunch activities of Challenger in January 1986. The ancient dunes have become the Kennedy Space Center, America's principal spaceport. A wilderness of palmetto and scrub pine has given way to expressways and cloverleafs, launch pads, workshops, and laboratories. Concrete causeways link the low islands. And the islands themselves have been sliced and shaped to yield barge channels and basins.

At the center of this altered landscape stands the Vehicle Assembly Building, the VAB, one of the most massive structures ever built. Like chips off the same gargantuan block, the smaller Orbiter Processing Facility and Launch Control Center squat beside the VAB. The building is so huge, so completely beyond normal human proportions, that it dominates the Kennedy Space Center emotionally as well as physically. It is a windowless monolith almost six hundred feet high, visible from twenty miles away, a gray cube, immutable, a modern pyramid.

The VAB symbolizes the pioneering bravado of the Apollo days, when the Cape was the focal point of the headlong race to the moon. With its painted American flag larger than a football field and its bright Bicentennial star logo, the VAB has become NASA's famous "can do" spirit made tangible. The vertical acres of gray aluminum evoke endeavors of heroic size and complexity. Here the massive Saturn V moon rocket was assembled, loaded on the monstrous, tracked "crawler," and trundled off to the launch pads.

Now the space shuttle uses the same facilities as the Saturn-Apollo hardware. But the heroic neoclassical élan of the moon race is gone. Now we have something called a "Space Transportation System." At an increasing rate in the past four years, a dark maw on the VAB's seaward side has opened and the lumbering crawler-transporter—wide as a city block—has emerged, bearing the improbable two-thousand-ton "stack" of the space shuttle toward Launch Pads 39A and 39B, three miles away.

Since 1981, the space shuttle has roared aloft twenty-four times from Pad 39A. Five of those flights landed back at the Cape, on the vast concrete landing field near the VAB. With those landings, the Kennedy Space Center became the homeport of the world's first reusable spaceship. Before the Challenger disaster, NASA seemed poised at the doorway to a bright future of science and exploration.

* * *

On this warm Wednesday, the Kennedy Space Center was busier than ever before in its twenty-five-year history. Nineteen eighty-six was to be NASA's most ambitious year of shuttle operations. There were fifteen flights scheduled in just over eleven months: fourteen from the Cape and the first mission from the new shuttle port at California's Vandenberg Air Force Base. In 1986 the shuttle was scheduled to launch nine communications satellites, two major probes of the solar system, three secret military payloads, and an assortment of Earth-monitoring experiments and space manufacturing equipment.

The Hubble Space Telescope would be put in orbit in October. This amazing instrument would allow astronomers to look fifty times deeper into space than was possible from the earth's surface —fourteen billion light-years—and backward in time to the violent infancy of the universe itself. Payloads such as this telescope and the European-designed Spacelab represented the best possible use of the shuttle. In these missions American astronauts could demonstrate the truly innovative technology incorporated in the vehicle. Unfortunately missions like these made up a minority of scheduled flights in the next decade.

Shuttle flights had now become so frequent that they required complex mission-designator numbers so that NASA planners could keep them straight. Beginning in 1984, flights were given one number to indicate the fiscal year in which they were originally scheduled ("5" would designate fiscal 1985) and a second number to indicate the launch site: "1" was the Kennedy Space Center and "2" was Vandenberg Air Force Base. Finally each flight was assigned a letter of the alphabet to designate its position in the fiscal year. Given the numerous delays the program had experienced in the previous year, however, one fiscal 1985 flight— the 51-L Challenger mission—actually flew after the 61-series fiscal 1986 flights had begun. NASA insisted that this system was not confusing and was needed to aid scheduling during the upcoming period of accelerated flight operations.

In addition to these scientific and commercial payloads, the shuttle was scheduled to carry some unusual passengers in 1986. The Columbia 61-C mission, originally slated for early December and launched a month late, carried a crew of seven, including an ambitious young Florida Congressman, Democrat Bill Nelson, who happened to be the Chairman of the House Space Science and Applications Subcommittee that approves NASA's budget. Later in the month, Teacher-in-Space Christa McAuliffe would fly aboard the 51-L Challenger flight, in time to coincide with President Reagan's State of the Union Message. Air Force Secretary Edward Aldrich would be an observer on the first shuttle flight from California's Vandenberg launch site that summer. And in September, a journalist would be on Challenger's 61-I crew when it lifted off Pad 39B.

This unusual collection of passengers was not without precedent. Since NASA had declared the space shuttle "operational" after only four test flights, a variety of individuals from outside the traditional Astronaut Corps had successfully petitioned NASA for berths aboard the vehicle. Probably the best known was Senator Jake Garn. But the roster of so-called "Payload Specialists" with influential backers also included a Saudi prince, a Mexican engineer, several aerospace contractor engineers, a French pilot, and a Canadian Navy officer.

With such a disparate group of nonastronauts flying aboard the shuttle, the public's perception of the system's routine reliability only increased.

As the program entered its busiest year, however, most experienced observers recognized that this ambitious flight schedule would severely test NASA's capabilities. There would probably be slips and perhaps some cancellations, but no one in the space press corps suspected that NASA would relax its famous "fail-safe" flight safety standards to get on with the year's busy schedule. The safety of manned space flight was the agency's hallmark, the enduring trait of our space program since the early days of the Mercury flights. The Soviets might risk a hapless woman and foreign "guest" cosmonauts aboard dangerous equipment to achieve propaganda coups, but NASA would never sacrifice safety for political gain.

NASA's most ambitious year, however, had started badly with the record delays of Columbia's launch, and the rigid launch windows of the spring scientific flights were rapidly approaching.

Now Columbia circled Earth every ninety minutes, its single satellite deployment completed. Columbia's secondary scientific experiment—a photographic scan of Halley's Comet, bearing the jaunty acronym CHAMPS—had failed, due to a dead battery. On Pad 39A, crews worked around the clock, refurbishing equipment blasted by Columbia's blazing exhaust. At the Shuttle Landing Facility, locally known as the SLF, crews prepared for Columbia's scheduled landing, just after dawn on Thursday, January 16. NASA's Mission Management Team had decided to bring Columbia home one day early, to make up for the multiple launch delays and gain a day in the processing of the Orbiter for its next flight, the more ambitious ASTRO mission to observe the comet, which was scheduled in early March, less than sixty days away.

Academic scientists had scornfully criticized NASA's meager effort to study Halley's Comet during its sweep through the inner solar system in the spring of 1986. These critics pointed out that the trouble-plagued shuttle had siphoned off so much of the agency's budget that America was reduced to taking an embarrassing and distant third place behind the Soviets and the Europeans when it came to observing Halley. Enlarging on this theme, respected astronomer James Van Allen had lambasted both the space shuttle and the planned space station in the lead article in the January *Scientific American.* The shuttle was an expensive, cumbersome luxury, he implied, which had diverted scarce funds from more legitimate space science while falling far short of its originally stated capabilities. In a prominent box in the article captioned "Slaughter of the Innocents," Dr. Van Allen listed seventeen major space science projects that had been cut from NASA's plans or greatly reduced due to the budget hemorrhage provoked by the expensive shuttle program.

Such criticism coming from a pioneering American space scientist rankled NASA officials. The agency had grown up in the forefront of innovative space science; NASA had taught the world how to build the equipment now being used by the Soviets and Europeans to explore the solar system. But the students were surpassing the teacher. Privately shuttle officials chafed at the criticism, labeling it distorted and unfair. The shuttle, they insisted, would soon prove to be the greatest tool in America's space science inventory. But the problems with Columbia were vexing. After the failure of the modest CHAMPS package, NASA was especially eager to get on with the more sophisticated ASTRO mission in March. Not only would this experimental package surpass CHAMPS, it would also give nice publicity to the role of *manned* space science as opposed to robot probes such as the Soviet Vega and the European Space Agency's Giotto spacecraft that would intercept Halley's Comet that spring.

In addition to appeasing American space scientists, NASA had an equally compelling motive in meeting the March 6 launch date for the Columbia-ASTRO flight. They wanted to scoop the Russians. The Soviet Union's Vega 2 spacecraft would encounter Halley's Comet on March 9, sending computer images back to Earth. If Columbia could be in orbit with live color television pictures of the diligent astronauts observing the comet, the importance of the more ambitious Soviet unmanned mission would be lost on the American public and their representatives in Congress.

But launching the March ASTRO flight on time would require a smooth turnaround for Columbia after the 61-C mission and a trouble-free Challenger flight late in January. Challenger was now scheduled for launch on Thursday, January 23, a date that had been slipped twice, as Columbia's December mission experienced scrub after scrub and spilled down the tightly orchestrated schedule into the second week in January.

The original purpose of Challenger's 51-L mission was the deployment of an important communications satellite, NASA's TDRS, the Tracking Data and Relay Satellite. The $120 million spacecraft would be deployed in low equatorial orbit; then an Inertial Upper Stage booster would carry it to geosynchronous Earth orbit, 22,300 miles above the equator, due south of Hawaii. This was the second of the two-TDRS system that NASA needed to communicate with its space shuttles and other orbiting spacecraft. The first TDRS had been deployed in 1982 and now provided a communications relay over half of Earth, from the mid-Pacific to the east coast of Africa. However, the deployment of the first

TDRS had almost failed when a faulty upper-stage booster malfunctioned. The first satellite was still not functioning at full efficiency, so NASA badly needed the second TDRS to complete its global relay system in anticipation of increased 1986 flight operations.

On the afternoon of January 15, technicians at the Cape were busy refurbishing Pad 39A and servicing Challenger on Pad B. Senior NASA officials at the Cape, in Washington, at the Marshall Space Flight Center, and at the Johnson Space Center in Houston assembled for a meeting that was an important milestone in the preparation of Challenger for its January flight and for the success of this busiest year in space. This was the Level I Flight Readiness Review, the management and engineering conference that would guarantee that Challenger was ready for flight. The "FRR" procedure, as these conferences were called, had been designed at the start of the shuttle program as a formal, disciplined ritual of certification. In this multistage process, all the government officials and aerospace contractors involved with the shuttle's subcomponents and payloads were required to present their evidence that the vehicle, its payload, and the ground-support equipment needed to launch and land the shuttle either were or were not ready for a safe flight.

The original rationale for these formal reviews was to create a logical, smooth flow of information, from the hardware engineers among the various contractors—"Level IV"—to the project offices in the NASA centers—"Level III"—to the center directors and the National Space Transportation System office that supervised all shuttle missions—"Level II"—and finally to the agency's senior management in NASA's Washington headquarters, "Level I." Challenger's January 15 Level I FRR was the culmination of this process; earlier meetings among contractors, shuttle component project engineers, and center directors had all determined that there were no major problems. Throughout this process there had been a series of formal, legally binding certifications, the equivalent of airworthiness inspections in the aviation industry. In effect the myriad contractor and NASA personnel involved were guaranteeing Challenger's flight readiness with their professional and personal integrity. Simply stated, they vouched that the Orbiter, its engines, external fuel tank, solid rocket boosters, satellite and scientific payloads, the crew, and the global tracking system and the abort landing sites around the world were all ready for launch.

It will be amply demonstrated below that this certification was an exercise in deceit.

The Flight Readiness Review on this Wednesday afternoon progressed smoothly. The meeting was a telephone conference, a "telecon" in NASA parlance. Over the years of the space program, the agency had perfected this form of communication to a fine art. Every NASA and contractor center was equipped with a sound-proof telecon room. These rooms held a large open square of tables on which highly sensitive four-wire speaker phones were placed between every two chairs. Some centers were also equipped with television cameras, so that slides and engineering charts could be beamed among certain participants. All this elaborate gear was necessary, given NASA's widely spread centers and contractors. With such equipment, space shuttle officials could conduct detailed engineering discussions with their colleagues around the country. The practice was so prevalent that some managers averaged at least one telecon a day.

On the afternoon of January 15, there was little need for complex chart presentations of difficult "open" problems. Every project official and center director who spoke was optimistic. Pending the "closeout" of some minor problems before the next formal review on the day before launch, there were no major areas of concern about hardware.

The discussion of the flight profile included a presentation of the predicted ascent and descent trajectories, anticipated engine performance, and fuel reserves. Once more, this phase of the flight did not seem to present any particular problems. The 51-L Challenger flight was a relatively straightforward mission: a simple satellite deployment, some payload-bay experiments, brief deployment and subsequent retrieval of the Spartan Halley's Comet observation package, and the televised lessons from space that Mrs. McAuliffe would offer on mission days four and five.

There was some discussion about the ideal orbital lighting conditions for the Spartan payload. The experiment was designed to observe the comet at its most active period, when it was closest to the sun and spewing forth the largest volume of gas and dust from its frozen nucleus. Ideally the Spartan experiment would require an afternoon launch, so that Challenger would be in the correct orbital position to launch the free-floating experimental package on flight day three. But an afternoon launch meant that the two Transatlantic Abort Landing sites would be in darkness, and only Dakar, Senegal, had lights; an afternoon launch would eliminate the security of the backup abort site, Casablanca. For the moment, NASA accepted the risk. If the flight were delayed well into the last week in January, the optimal Spartan observation conditions would be lost in any event, and they could always return to a safer morning launch.

Such discussions, of course, were closed to journalists. NASA was trying hard to maintain the image of routine shuttle operations that provided an equal opportunity for scientific, commercial, and military payloads without sacrificing flight safety. The dilemma at this particular FRR conference, however, involved a direct trade-off between optimal flight safety and optimal science. For the moment, the opportunity to salvage at least some of the Halley's Comet glory prevailed over conservative flight safety.

The priority of the TDRS payload also impinged on safety considerations. With this heavy payload and the fuel required to fly a nominal flight, Challenger would exceed the weight limits for two of the abort landing sites. A formal waiver of this constraint was submitted and accepted by the mission managers without discussion.

The officials at Houston's Johnson Space Center certified that the crew, led by Commander Dick Scobee and Pilot Mike Smith, would have successfully completed their required simulator training in time for launch. Johnson also certified that its Mission Control system was prepared for the flight.

Kennedy Space Center was in charge of all aspects of vehicle processing and launch countdown. Gene Thomas, the center's Deputy Director for Launch and Landing Operations, and Bob Sieck, the Deputy Director for Shuttle Operations, certified that KSC was ready for the mission, again pending solution of some minor remaining problems.

The Marshall Space Flight Center in Huntsville was responsible for the shuttle's propulsion system and the inertial upper-stage booster that would carry the TDRS to its high geosynchronous orbit. One by one the various Marshall project engineers who worked for Shuttle Projects Manager Stanley Reinartz spoke up to certify that Challenger's liquid-fueled main engines and its external tank were certified ready for flight. When Marshall's Solid Rocket Booster Project Manager, Larry Mulloy, made his presentation, he concluded that there were "no major problems or issues."

Before the meeting adjourned, the weather at scheduled launch time on January 23 was discussed as a potential problem area. January had already proved a month of unusual rainfall. Normally winter was Florida's dry season, but a record five inches of rain had fallen since Challenger was rolled out to Pad 39B just before Christmas. If the unseasonable rain continued, Columbia's return to Kennedy could be delayed and Challenger's launch might have to be slipped.

Here the NASA managers were powerless in the face of nature. Unfortunately the space shuttle, which had shown itself so versatile on so many missions, had several glaring weak points. Most vulnerable was its thermal protection system, the thousands of silicate tiles covering its skin that protected the Orbiter from incineration during the blazing heat of reentry. The shuttle simply could *not* fly in the rain. At speeds over 300 knots, raindrops acted like steel shot, shredding the delicate tiles. Launching or landing in rain could cause tile damage serious enough to destroy the Orbiter's lift and aerosurface control.

Therefore, if January continued rainy at the Cape, both Columbia's landing and Challenger's launch might be delayed. Columbia could always land at Edwards Air Force Base, but the delay entailed with an Edwards turnaround and the ferry trip back aboard the Boeing 747 shuttle transport aircraft would further complicate the Orbiter's inflexible mission schedule. Following its present 61-C mission, Columbia was slated to fly from Pad B only six weeks after Challenger. During the multiple delays that plagued the 61-C launch, Mission Management had grappled with this problem. If they could get Columbia launched by January 10 and landed back at Kennedy by the sixteenth, there would be no delays in Columbia's 61-E ASTRO flight, which had a rigid launch window on March 6. But this tight timing also meant that Challenger would have to be launched no later than January 26 in order to free Pad B for refurbishment.

From the conference room at NASA headquarters, Associate Administrator for Space Flight Jesse Moore polled his senior managers around the loop prior to the formal conclusion of the meeting. Everything looked good for a launch day of January 23. The consensus was relieved optimism. Columbia's protracted launch delays had been a nightmare, stretching through four launch-pad scrubs, which included some dangerous and entirely unforeseen mechanical anomalies. The project managers in the various conference rooms around the loop had all been at the Cape throughout the entire frustrating experience. They had been unprepared for such exhausting stress so early in this ambitious year. Maybe, one manager suggested, they'd gotten all the bad luck out of their system with Columbia. In any event Challenger would be ready on time, and NASA could press on with the year's adventurous schedule.

*   *   *

That afternoon, on the second floor of the Old Executive Office Building adjacent to the White House, presidential speech writers met to discuss various draft versions of President Reagan's upcoming State of the Union Message. At this stage of the drafting process, the Office of Communications had assembled the so-called "wish list" contributions of several cabinet members and independent agencies. The State of the Union speech was the administration's agenda; an agency that managed to gain prominent mention in the speech could be assured favorable presidential attention in the year ahead.

The theme of this year's speech was optimism about America's future. The Conservative Revolution would continue to reduce government's bureaucratic stranglehold on the American people, and innovative high technology, nurtured within a robust free enterprise system, would lead the country into the twenty-first century.

NASA's contribution to the draft speech included two suitably optimistic and exciting topics: plans for a suborbital aerospace plane, dubbed the "Orient Express," that would cross the Pacific at twenty-five times the speed of sound, and a vivid description of teacher Christa McAuliffe's Challenger flight. According to Shirley Green, NASA's Director of Public Affairs, ". . . we had suggested that the President restate his commitment to the completion of the Space Station by 1994; mention the initiation of the Aerospace Plane Research program; acknowledge the importance of space science; and comment on the flight that was expected to be in orbit at the time he was speaking. . . ."

Although the White House refused to release the actual draft contribution from NASA, which the agency hoped the President would read to the world, a Congressional source provided it. From this text it becomes clear that NASA, like many other government agencies, would have been very eager to hear its pet projects mentioned in such glowing terms:

"Tonight, while I am speaking to you, a young elementary [sic] school teacher from Concord, New Hampshire, is taking us all on the ultimate field trip as she orbits the Earth as the first citizen passenger on the Space Shuttle.

"Christa McAuliffe's journey is a prelude to the journeys of other Americans and our friends around the world who will be living and working together in a permanently manned Space Station in the mid-1990s, bringing a rich return of scientific, technical, and economic benefits to mankind.

"Mrs. McAuliffe's week in space is just one of the achievements in space which we have planned for the coming year, however. The U.S. Voyager spacecraft has just this week visited the planet Uranus and sent back striking images of this distant world after a two-billion-mile trip in space. Later, we will participate in a worldwide study of Halley's Comet, launch the Hubble Space Telescope, launch the Galileo spaceship on its way to Jupiter, and participate with our European partners in sending the Ulysses spacecraft to explore the poles of the sun.

"Our commitment to continuation of a strong civil space program through such projects as the Space Station, space transportation, space science, and the technology required for the programs of the 1990s is an investment in the future of America's greatness in space and in the young men and women of this nation who will be the leaders of tomorrow."

The speech was going to focus on the bright tomorrow that high technology would bring to increasingly stable and prosperous American families. Christa McAuliffe epitomized this optimistic theme. She was an attractive wife and mother and a talented educator. As a teacher, she had told the press, she was continually in touch with the future, which was literally embodied in her students. Clearly, Christa McAuliffe's flight dovetailed very nicely with the President's theme.

If NASA delivered this exciting mission, the White House speech writers were prepared to capitalize on such an unprecedented opportunity. In effect NASA's success in competing with rival agencies for the President's attention during the coming year of Draconian budget cuts would depend in part on the ability of the shuttle managers to launch the Challenger in time for the speech.

*   *   *

The fine weather of January 15 did not last through the night. Rain was falling at the Cape on the morning of Thursday, the sixteenth. Reluctantly the Mission Management Team for Columbia's 61-C flight ordered a "wave-off"; Columbia would remain in space one more day. Friday, January 17, was also overcast at Kennedy. Only seventeen minutes prior to the reentry burn over the Indian Ocean that would have necessitated a landing at the Cape, Flight Director Gary Coen in Houston told the crew to abandon the attempted landing at Kennedy and to prepare for a landing at Edwards on the next orbit. However, in an unusual step indicative of NASA's desperation to salvage the original March ASTRO mission schedule, senior management intervened, and ordered Columbia to stay aloft one more day and attempt a Kennedy landing then.

The press began to grouse that the Columbia mission truly was jinxed: "First NASA couldn't get it up, now they can't get it down."

On the night of the seventeenth, the weather at the Cape was solid overcast, but NASA managers were still hoping to squeeze in

23

the landing through a gap in the clouds. Once more, the tired astronauts had to prepare the Orbiter for a Kennedy landing, only to be waved off twenty minutes before the reentry burn. Flight controllers in Houston reluctantly issued the order to Columbia's Commander, "Hoot" Gibson, to bypass the Cape and prepare for a landing at the desert strip at Edwards Air Force Base. Thus NASA would lose almost a week getting the Orbiter processed out at Edwards and ferried back to the Cape.

Bad luck had plagued Columbia to the end. One former NASA official thinks the agency exacerbated its problems with this mission by allowing Bill Nelson, who had his sights on the Senate, to bully his way on board the flight in the first place. Nelson had lobbied NASA for two and a half years to get on board the shuttle. He allegedly saw the flight as a leg up in his political career; during training, his public relations staff bombarded local Florida newspapers with breathless diary excerpts. And as an indication of how important he considered his shuttle junket, he invited thirty-seven busloads of guests to view the launch of his mission. Courting his local constituency, which included Cape Canaveral, Nelson announced that he believed the Lord intended for him to travel into space. Apparently, what the Lord had intended, NASA was loath to put asunder. Bill Nelson would not be denied his orbital junket.

According to the former NASA official, if the Chairman of the House Space Subcommittee had not been on Columbia's crew, NASA would have simply canceled the mission after the first three launch scrubs, rather than jeopardize the intricate domino row of its 1986 flight schedule. The agency could easily have rescheduled the RCA satellite that was Columbia's principal cargo; they had done this many times in the past when the flight "manifest" had become too crowded. But they never before had to disappoint the ambitious Congressman who controlled their purse strings.

As things stood now, Columbia's multiple delays meant that Challenger was going to have to fly as close to its revised January 23 launch date as possible. Otherwise, Columbia's March ASTRO mission off Pad 39B might be jeopardized, and the shuttle's vociferous academic critics would have more ammunition. The impact of Columbia's launch problems definitely contributed to the urgency NASA administrators felt in launching Challenger; this relationship will be analyzed in more detail in another chapter.

But, even as Columbia landed on January 18, Challenger still was not fully equipped for its mission. There were vital "spare" parts aboard Columbia that hard-pressed NASA engineers needed to remove from that Orbiter and install on Challenger before the L-1 day Flight Readiness Review scheduled for the twenty-second. Despite NASA's ongoing official assurances that the operational shuttle was steadily progressing along its "maturity curve" toward routine operations, the increased flight rates of the previous six months had completely overpowered the inadequate logistics system.

After Columbia landed, Challenger's Kennedy Flow Director Jim Harrington arranged for the Astronaut Office in Houston to dispatch a T-38 jet trainer to Edwards. Late the next day, the sleek little jet landed at the Cape bearing vital parts that had been cannibalized from Columbia as soon as the Edwards ground crew had "safed" the Orbiter. These parts included a propulsion system temperature sensor, an important nose-wheel steering box, an air sensor for the crew cabin, and a general purpose computer, one of five needed for flight.

As soon as this equipment was unloaded from the T-38 at Kennedy's shuttle landing facility, a van rushed the gear to the launch pad where technicians immediately began the delicate and demanding task of installation. But even with this dramatic effort, it quickly became clear that Challenger was not going to be ready for the L-1 review on the twenty-second. Grimly mission managers met to discuss a formal slip of the launch. Congressman Bill Nelson's junket had kept the vital spare parts away from the Cape too long for NASA to make their deadline on the twenty-third. Such was the state of routine shuttle operations as the workers prepared Challenger for its final flight.

Veteran Astronaut Paul Weitz testified before the Rogers Commission about the inherent dangers of such spare parts procedures. Cannibalization, he stated somberly, "increases the exposure of both Orbiters to intrusions by people. Every time you get people inside and around the Orbiter you stand a chance of inadvertent damage of whatever type, whether you leave a tool behind or whether, without knowing it, step on a wire bundle or a tube . . ."

Commander Weitz did not add that the cannibalization process that Columbia and Challenger underwent in late January was especially hazardous. Columbia sat on the dusty desert runway at Edwards, hardly the filtered-air "clean room" environment of Kennedy's Orbiter Processing Facility. And Challenger was stacked on the launch pad, the Orbiter in a vertical position; this meant the installation of the heavy avionics boxes on the flight deck was an especially risky and taxing procedure.

No one in the space press corps, however (this author included), was perceptive or diligent enough to sniff out this ludicrous but commonplace aspect of the "operational" space shuttle program. Nor did the regular shuttle reporters fully realize that the Challenger Orbiter on the launch pad was, itself, a hybrid born of desperation. As the tired technicians struggled to mount the last spare parts on Challenger, shuttle flow engineers were making a final tally of the equipment from other orbiters Challenger would carry into space.

Challenger's wide body flap aerosurface had been removed from Atlantis. Its bulbous orbital maneuvering system (OMS) pods had come originally from Columbia; Columbia, itself, had borrowed Discovery's OMS pods for its latest mission. And from Discovery, Challenger had received the three vital main engine heat shields and several important avionics boxes.

At this time NASA press releases were talking bravely about their four-Orbiter "fleet" of operational space shuttles. But the public affairs spokesmen did not discuss the harried T-38 flights to pick up cannibalized Orbiter parts in California. In January 1986 NASA had fifteen missions scheduled for its four Orbiters in the first eleven and a half months of the year. Discovery—the source of most of the cannibalized spares—was set for permanent basing at Vandenberg in July, so it would have to be brought back up to flight specifications before leaving the Cape. Thus the Orbiter Discovery, the main supplier of spare parts, would become a competitor for these scarce items. In effect, NASA had missions scheduled for four Orbiters but only enough parts for two of them to fly.

Horace Lamberth, the Kennedy Center's Director of Engineering, testified about this problem before the Rogers Commission. If the Challenger accident had not halted flights, he stated, "we would have been brought to our knees this spring" by the spare-parts shortage.

What led up to this unfortunate situation reveals a great deal about our country's erratic space policy over the past fifteen years.

A DECADE OF COMPROMISE

On July 4, 1982, the Orbiter Columbia landed on the concrete runway at Edwards Air Force Base in California's Mojave Desert after seven days in space. This mission was the final of four test flights, and the first to be launched with no schedule delays. On hand to greet Columbia's astronauts were President and Mrs. Reagan.

The President used the occasion of Independence Day as an opportunity to delineate his administration's space policy. Now that the space shuttle had successfully completed the test flights, Mr. Reagan announced from the flag-decked rostrum, it was ready to assume operational tasks. "The United States Space Transportation System is the primary space launch system for both national security and civil government missions," the President stated. The shuttle program's first priority, he added, was to become "fully operational and cost-effective in providing routine access to space."

His words were warmly welcomed by NASA leaders, even though the speech was drafted in their own public affairs office. With this clear statement of U.S. space policy, the agency had a mandate to proceed with operational shuttle flights at all practical speed. Despite the Supply Side tax cuts enacted that year, and despite subsequent budget deficits, NASA felt confident that it had the backing of the popular new President, who would continue to charm adequate appropriations from Congress. With this budgetary security, NASA could subsidize shuttle flights, offering bargain launch rates to its new clientele of commercial satellite operators.

Later that year NASA announced its projected five-year flight schedule and invited commercial customers worldwide to sign up for launch space. Backpedaling from the wildly unrealistic estimates of the early 1970s, NASA nevertheless projected an optimism that matched the country's prevailing mood. There would be twelve flights scheduled in 1984, fourteen in 1985, and seventeen each in 1986 and 1987. Nineteen eighty-eight would see full commercial and national defense operations of twenty-four flights from both Kennedy and Vandenberg.

The actual flight rate achieved in 1984 and 1985 was much lower: five in 1984 and eight in 1985.

And worse than not meeting its own ambitious goals, this record coincided with the demise of the Supply Side Revolution, the rise of annual federal budget deficits in the hundreds of billions, and the birth of the Gramm-Rudman-Hollings deficit reduction law. NASA could no longer count on Congressional bounty to subsidize the shuttle operations that the agency had so long promised would eventually pay for themselves.

Why, Congressional critics began to ask, was NASA unable to meet its "routine" flight obligations? Why were there so many delays and cancellations? If the shuttle was operational, Congressional critics declared, let it operate at a profit. The shuttle, NASA officials testified, was in fact operational, but there had been certain problems endemic to any massive and complex development program. By next year, if the agency's budget was kept adequate, the space shuttle would be flying on a regular schedule.

In July 1984 NASA Administrator James Beggs testified before the House Subcommittee on Space Applications. Each space shuttle launch, he said, presently costs between $150 and $200 million, of which a maximum of $71 million could be recouped in commercial fees.

Republican Congressman Robert S. Walker posed a hard question to Mr. Beggs: "The $80 million difference is in fact a subsidy?"

"I would prefer to phrase it differently," Beggs answered. "It's a continuation of our policy to recover our costs over a period of time."

NASA planned to raise its launch fees by 30 percent later in the decade, he added, when there would be a steady rate of twenty-four shuttle flights a year.

But, Walker persisted, would launch costs *ever* drop below $100 million and approach the break-even point?

"You bet," Beggs replied jauntily.

Congress, however, was no longer lenient. In July 1985 the House cut $375 million from NASA's Fiscal 1986 appropriation, thus freezing the agency's budget at the 1985 level of $7.51 billion. Unfortunately for NASA, its appropriation was the first Fiscal 1986 budget to go to the House floor for a vote, and the agency found itself a test case in the debate over the implementation of the Gramm-Rudman-Hollings law.

To compensate for the five percent budget cut, Congress allowed NASA to raise the price cap on its shuttle launch services earlier than expected. In 1986—if the agency could find the customers— NASA could begin charging up to $105 million per flight, depending on the payload carried. The significance of these Congressional actions was clear: If NASA wanted to make ends meet, the shuttle truly had to begin paying its own way. And to accomplish that goal, the shuttle simply had to start delivering the routine cost effectiveness of dependably regular operations of which the President had spoken on the Fourth of July at Edwards Air Force Base.

But nagging questions about the space shuttle's fundamental reliability were increasing in such disparate quarters as the National Academy of Science and the Pentagon.

Defending its space shuttle as an innovative (yet dependably operational) technology, the space agency continually stressed that the vehicle would soon live up to its inherent potential, as if the shuttle's design were a paradigm of excellence on which there could be no improvements. Once more myth prevailed over reality. The space shuttle's final design did not, in fact, represent the innovative excellence of America's best scientists and engineers. It was a compromise that had been shaped more by economic considerations and hidden political maneuvering than by technical limits.

* * *

Nineteen sixty-nine was NASA's greatest year. That summer the agency sent the first two astronauts to the moon. And there were plans and hardware available for eight more lunar landings over the next four years. NASA's swollen budget and payroll initially seemed secure under the administration of Richard Nixon, a President who had long favored the space program, especially when so many lucrative aerospace contracts benefited his home turf in Southern California.

One of President Nixon's first official acts was the creation of the Space Task Group, under the leadership of Vice President Spiro Agnew. This body was to chart America's post-Apollo future in space and offer the President a clear choice of policy priorities and realistic estimates of their implementation cost. Joining Agnew on the body were the new NASA Administrator Thomas O. Paine, Presidential Science Advisor Lee A. DuBridge, and Air Force Secretary Robert C. Seamans.

They took their job seriously and worked fast. Less than four months into their mandate, Agnew spoke for the Task Group when he announced the creation of a new national goal: a manned landing on Mars before the year 2000. Agnew made his speech on July 16, 1969, the day Apollo 11 blasted off from Cape Canaveral, en route for the first moon landing.

Two months later, the Task Group made their official report. The manned landing on Mars could be accomplished by any of three operational plans. The first called for a massive effort that would dwarf the Apollo program and put Americans on Mars by 1983. The second plan was less intense and placed our astronauts on Mars in 1986. And the final option proposed a landing in the 1990s.

Each of these ambitious endeavors entailed building a large, permanently manned space station in low Earth orbit, where the Mars vehicle would be assembled and whence it would depart on its interplanetary voyage. The plan also required a large reusable space shuttle that would ferry crews and supplies to and from the space station.

NASA's Paine was the most outspoken enthusiast for this bold policy of exploration. Former NASA historian, Duke University

31

Professor Alex Roland, has described Paine's attitude as "swash-buckling."

The problem with the Task Group's options was cost. By even the most conservative estimates the budget for the Mars mission would far exceed the $24 billion expense of the Apollo moon landings. Nixon was flabbergasted by the cost of the proposed project. His much-touted "secret plan" to end the war in Vietnam showed no promise of succeeding. And American casualties and war costs continued to rise. Meanwhile social unrest and disenchantment with the government—*any* government—was peaking. The Democratic-controlled Congress took advantage of the overall unrest to snipe at the Republican administration. Congress clamored to save Great Society social programs and scornfully derided the proposed space spectaculars. Even as the Apollo astronauts walked on the moon, leading Democrats were openly declaring the program a shameful waste.

Clearly this was not an auspicious time for Nixon to support the ambitious Task Group recommendations. With practiced political aplomb, he gave the goals vague endorsement and left his staff to supervise the bureaucratic trench fighting over what, if any, future manned space program would follow Apollo.

Without strong presidential leadership, Paine and his Mars mission enthusiasts had to retreat. In quick succession, the goal of a Mars landing was shelved and the space station was put on hold. Finally, the only aspect of the Task Group's grandiose venture that remained even remotely affordable was the reusable space shuttle. Lacking a space station departure port for the Mars mission to service, the space shuttle was, in effect, without an assignment, an orphan technology even before it was born.

The only justification for the shuttle NASA could invent to satisfy the rebellious Democrats in Congress was cost effectiveness, the quintessential panacea of the 1970s. In Vietnam at this time, American commanders had to answer elaborate cost-effectiveness surveys on ordnance use. Simply firing at the enemy was no longer justification for expending expensive artillery rounds. A brigade commander's ammunition allowance for the next fiscal quarter might depend on how artfully his subordinates played the game of cost-effectiveness.

NASA was not exempt from this process. The agency quickly learned that its institutional survival no longer depended on flamboyant and adventurous exploration of the space frontier, but rather on developing an inexpensive and efficient reusable spacecraft. Clearly the romantically heroic cachet of Projects Mercury, Gemini, and Apollo was no longer appropriate. NASA would now develop a national "Space Transportation System," a rugged space truck that could be launched like a rocket, work efficiently in orbital space, and fly back like a cargo plane to land at commercial airports, then be resupplied for another flight within two weeks. That was the type of program Congress found attractive in the long winter of Vietnam discontent. And that was what NASA promised to deliver.

The myth of the omnibus space shuttle was being forged in the committee rooms of Capitol Hill.

But Thomas Paine and his "swashbucklers" in NASA still envisioned a space shuttle that could eventually serve as the springboard to the Space Station and interplanetary exploration. Therefore they initially proposed what Professor Roland has aptly called a "Cadillac" space shuttle. This two-stage system would be based on two manned, fully reusable components: a huge, winged rocket booster and a smaller, winged orbiter. Each vehicle would have a flight crew, and each would return for landing at the launch site and be quickly refurbished for the next mission.

This shuttle concept represented engineering daring on a scale beyond the bold sweep of the Apollo-Saturn program. The winged booster that would carry the orbiter piggyback would be larger than the Saturn V moon rocket. Using the booster's monstrous belly as a fuel tank, the dual vehicle would blast off from Cape Canaveral and accelerate to transonic speeds at an altitude of fifty miles, where the smaller craft would continue into orbit and the booster would loop back to the landing field beside the launch site. Paine envisioned an orbiter large enough to carry the heavy modules of the eventual space station and the components of the projected interplanetary spacecraft. Only cryogenic propellants—supercold liquid hydrogen and oxygen—were powerful enough to lift this gigantic ship. But even the Saturn's cryogenic engines would not be strong enough for the thrust requirements. So

NASA's Marshall Space Flight Center in Huntsville, Alabama, was assigned the initial feasibility studies on a huge new cryogenic engine to be used in both the booster and the orbiter.

Among outsiders, Marshall had a reputation as a hardworking, no-nonsense engineering shop that thrived on challenge. The center had grown out of the old Redstone Arsenal during the Apollo glory years, when Wernher von Braun was its director. The people at Marshall were proud of their skills; they saw themselves as the heirs to von Braun's visionary engineering excellence. If anyone could perfect the revolutionary engines for the shuttle, it would be the Marshall engineers. Some engineers at other NASA centers saw Marshall's Teutonic confidence as arrogance; they went so far as to christen von Braun's old fiefdom "Hunsville." It was not until after the Challenger accident, however, that a much more somber perspective emerged on the true situation at the Marshall Space Flight Center. But in the early seventies, the men at Marshall were still ebullient from their fantastic successes in the Apollo program. Their "can do" confidence seemed well justified. If any engineers could design a revolutionary new rocket engine, they could.

In March 1971 the Marshall center issued a Request for Proposal (RFP) for the design of the new engines. The RFP called for a two-stage shuttle with a twelve-engine, crewed, reusable booster stage, and a piggyback orbiter stage that would carry two of the same cryogenic engines. The winged booster would transport the orbiter to an altitude of fifty miles where the orbiter would break free to complete the flight. Both vehicles would land at the launch site for a quick turnaround for the next mission.

Although such a heroically scaled space shuttle would have very high development costs, NASA assured Congress and the Office of Management and Budget (OMB) that the actual operational costs would be low. NASA estimated that the fully reusable two-stage system would cost just over $10 billion to develop but could be flown for under $4 million a mission. Using a 1969 study by Associate Administrator George Mueller, the agency projected that its planned shuttle could place 50,000 pounds into low Earth orbit for as little as five dollars a pound, an incredible saving over the $1,000-per-pound cost for expendable launch vehicles. The fact that Mueller based his figures on an unrealistically large fleet of space shuttles that would be fully utilized did not seem to bother the NASA enthusiasts.

This innovative "Cadillac" system would cost $10 to $14 billion and would be ready for flight by 1975, according to NASA projections.

Congressional Democrats were outraged. Led by Senators Walter Mondale and William Proxmire (neither of whom had a home state aerospace industry), both the Senate and the House attacked the program as the thin wedge of a wasteful space "extravaganza" that would cost taxpayers more than $25 billion before it was over. It is very interesting to note, however, that the often shrill cries of outrageous indignation from these two senators grew fainter as largesse slopped from the Congressional shuttle pork barrel. When Minnesota's 3M and Honeywell corporations (and a host of smaller firms) and several Wisconsin heavy equipment and electronics companies received lucrative shuttle contracts, the voices of liberal concern from Mondale and Proxmire became less plaintive.

In the face of the initial Democratic resistance, however, NASA was forced to retreat. During subsequent consultations, OMB indicated they could live with a development cost of approximately $5 billion. So that's what NASA promised to deliver. As former NASA development engineer Sam Beddingfield described this belt-tightening process, NASA was not used to designing under budgetary constraints. "For the first time in our space effort," he wrote in a history of the shuttle, "it became apparent that cost parameters would need the same considerations as the usual design parameters of weight and performance." In other words, NASA no longer had a blank check and a presidential mandate to "swashbuckle."

When the agency returned to Congress, it promised a space shuttle that would cost approximately $5 billion to build and that would definitely earn back its development costs within ten years. By making these incredible promises in 1970 in order to squeeze an initial trickle of start-up funds from Congress, NASA became committed to designing a space shuttle with both a low development cost *and* the certainty of dependable routine operations.

35

At the time NASA was making these clearly unrealistic promises, much of what they said closely matched the ethos of the period. The Vietnam War was a draining wound in America's side; Great Society entitlement programs had institutionalized exponential growth in the civil sector budget; and the burgeoning environmental movement produced a clamor for redressing the monumental problems of pollution. Clearly space was a low national priority. However, NASA's managers skillfully played on several of the prevailing buzz issues to elicit support for the shuttle program. A *reusable* space shuttle would not waste precious national resources, nor would it be as environmentally harmful as throwaway rockets. The tremendous savings inherent to such a system would liberate funds for entitlement programs. The innovative Earth resource monitoring projects planned for the shuttle would allow us to better conserve our forests, farmlands, and oceans. The list went on.

In retrospect, this commitment to a cost-effective reusable space transportation system solidified the eventual myth of the operational space shuttle. And NASA—a traditional engineering research and development institution—also committed itself to the unprecedented role of a profitable space freight transport organization. It is now blatantly obvious that NASA executives in the early 1970s had pledged their agency to perform the impossible. NASA's own shuttle design studies stressed the high development cost but low operational cost of the completely reusable vehicle, versus, the low R & D budget, but higher per-flight cost of the partially reusable compromise shuttle they eventually built.

But Congress and the OMB had forced the agency into an unfamiliar corner. After years of unprecedented generosity, NASA was presented with a dilemma: either build a truly cost-effective space shuttle within the spartan development budget OMB would approve, or get out of the manned space flight business. Now, of course, many critics contend that NASA simply should have faced reality and abandoned the costly shuttle concept, perhaps to focus on less ambitious follow-ups to the Saturn-Skylab project already in development. But NASA's leaders were fighting to save the bureaucracy's life; there were tens of thousands of civil service jobs at stake in the shuttle decision. Abandoning the project would have been tantamount to self-mutilation; NASA needed the shuttle to save jobs. Therefore, the agency was willing to promise almost any outlandish performance of the eventual vehicle—including a ridiculously short turnaround time and low per-flight cost—just to keep its people employed.

In the first ten years of the manned space program, NASA had been blessed with luxurious budgets, the clear goal of the moon landings, and decisive, dedicated leadership. Sadly, it was to lose each of these advantages as it struggled to build the space shuttle during its second decade.

* * *

Physics and its subdisciplines of aerodynamics and astronautics are rigidly absolute sciences. Simply *wishing* for a cheap space shuttle that would also fly an efficient operational lifetime of fifty or one hundred missions does not overcome the imperatives of nature.

Compared with the difficulties of the space shuttle design, the Saturn-Apollo system was child's play. Despite its size, the huge Saturn V booster was really just an enlarged ballistic missile with cryogenic upper stages. The blunt bullet of the Apollo command module was not required to perform routine round-trips from Earth to space. This module used an ablative heat shield to absorb the friction of reentry and parachutes to soften its ocean splashdown. Even Apollo's truly innovative lunar landing module was not obliged to operate in the complex turbulence of the Earth's atmosphere.

But the space shuttle would have to perform as both an airplane and a spacecraft; it had to stand up to the worst extremes of transonic atmospheric flight and the harsh orbital environment, and it had to prove robust enough for routine operations with short turn arounds between missions.

To complicate the already horrendous design problem, NASA found itself committed to further difficult specifications imposed on it by the Air Force. For the Air Force to endorse the shuttle for eventual use on polar-orbit missions from Vandenberg Air Force Base, the orbiter needed a thousand-mile horizontal, or "crossrange," capability on its reentry glide path. In ninety minutes of orbital flight, the Earth would have turned that distance, and the orbiter had to cross this range for a safe return to its launch site field. The Air Force also locked NASA into its overly optimistic large-payload concept: a sixty-by-fifteen-foot payload bay, capable of carrying up to twenty-two tons into a polar orbit with a respectably high apogee.

Accepting these Air Force requirements, however, did not guarantee future Defense Department funding for the space shuttle. But NASA felt obliged to incorporate the Air Force wish list in the hope for eventual military support. The Air Force's own manned space program, the Manned Orbital Laboratory (MOL), had recently been scrapped by Congress. This program would have used off-the-shelf hardware—Gemini capsules and Titan launch vehicles—and would have given America a military space capability similar to the Soviet's Soyuz-Salyut space station system, which was primarily a military program, despite the shrill denials of Soviet propagandists. Some NASA officials felt confident that the Air Force would become an enthusiastic backer of the NASA shuttle, once the generals saw the Soviet progress with Soyuz-Salyut and realized the shuttle was the only game in town.

Unfortunately for NASA, this gamble would come back to haunt the shuttle program. By lobbying hard for Air Force involvement in the shuttle, the agency committed itself ever more firmly to the concept of a dependable heavy-lift space freight service. And, as will be seen, the Air Force had plans for such a service in the 1980s; if the shuttle could not deliver the goods, the generals would seek other systems that would. They were not bound by bureaucratic loyalty or the romantic dreams of space exploration.

All these requirements, however, had a direct bearing on the design of the shuttle's propulsion system and the orbiter's airframe. Obviously the orbiter had to be built around a large, cylindrical payload bay. The original NASA concept had called for a slow, straight-winged glider that could not meet the thousand-mile cross-range requirement. So NASA bit the bullet and approved a high-speed, delta-winged orbiter. In order to glide one thousand miles either side of its reentry track, the chunky delta-wing orbiter had to employ an unprecedented twenty-two-degree glide slope—

seven times as steep as commercial aircraft—and it had to land fast: as any fighter pilot can attest, delta-winged aircraft do not loiter well at low speeds.

Another problem with the delta-winged orbiter that would haunt the space shuttle program for years was the weight inherent in this design. According to space shuttle expert Professor John Logsdon of George Washington University, the delta-wing design required much higher reentry maneuvering speeds. "Maneuvering during high-speed reentry," Logsdon has noted, "also exposed the shuttle to high temperatures for longer periods of time than a 'straight-in' approach; this doubled the weight of the thermal protection system required. These increases in orbiter weight made it difficult to meet payload weight-lifting requirements and placed extra demands on the shuttle's propulsion systems."

Still worse, weight restrictions soon forced NASA to remove the air-breathing jet engines originally intended to give the orbiter a "go around" capability; they were now committed to a heavy, fast, low-lift space glider that had to descend from orbit to the runway with absolute precision, to land on the first—and only—approach, regardless of the weather, on *every* flight. At this point, the heat tiles' vulnerability to rain was not suspected. It was assumed the shuttle's fast descent would incorporate advanced computer guidance and navigational aids. These would be needed, as the landing phase would be especially hazardous. Lacking atmospheric engines, there could be no margin for error provoked by electronics or flight control failures, not to mention orbital emergencies requiring a sudden, unplanned reentry.

The safety implications of this divergence from the original design were glossed over by NASA engineers. Given the prevailing mood, it is easy to understand how these same designers removed the launch-abort rocket escape system from the orbiter's original design. All previous manned American spacecraft had carried small, solid-fuel escape towers that would extract the crew capsule from a failed booster during the critically dangerous early moments of a mission. But once more, weight restrictions forced NASA designers to abandon the prudence they had shown in the moon landing program. In 1971 these designers seemed confident that enough safety could be engineered into the space shuttle's propulsion system to obviate the need for escape rockets.

And it was in the boost-stage propulsion system that NASA was forced to make its most serious compromises on the original shuttle concept. Without the option of the giant reusable winged booster of the "Cadillac" shuttle, NASA had to depart radically from proven technology and venture into truly uncharted regions of design. The agency had to somehow develop an unmanned booster stage that could be retrieved and refurbished for multiple flight.

So, by 1972, NASA developed a *partially* reusable design that called for multiple cryogenic engines on the orbiter (which further reduced its weight-payload ratio), a huge expendable external fuel tank to feed these engines, and two strap-on reusable boosters to provide the bulk of lift-off thrust.

At this stage in the design definition process, NASA had not yet decided on kerosene-oxygen or cryogenic engines or solid rocket motors for the strap-on boosters. After additional design calculations, however, it became clear that liquid-rocket boosters would never meet the stringent rapid-turn-around requirements of an economical commercial space freight shuttle. Any strap-on boosters would have to descend by parachute after use; if they fell into the sea, they would require extensive renovation, and there was no way to cushion the complex plumbing of liquid boosters for a safe parachute descent to land.

Therefore, having eliminated a winged and piloted booster vehicle, NASA designers were left with the option of solid rocket fuel boosters. Once more compromise drove fundamental design. NASA's engineers had been forced to choose a composite shuttle design that would appear to be *mostly* reusable. They decided that the strap-on solid fuel boosters would be equipped with large parachutes to carry them to a soft water landing one hundred miles downrange from the launch site after their fuel was spent. The huge external tank would be sacrificed after use. But the orbiter would glide back to a shuttle landing field near its launch site, be mated with a new fuel tank and refurbished solid rocket boosters, and be ready for flight again within two weeks.

The concept of cost-effective reusable solid rocket boosters thus became central to the myth of the shuttle's ability to pay for itself. The burden of these boosters' cost-effective reusability increased as the program matured and it became apparent that the reusable orbiter's highly touted main engines were anything but reliably cost-effective.

Once the basic design was chosen, the agency's budget analysts studied the proposal and announced that it could be developed for well below $10 billion. Furthermore NASA intended to convince Congress and the OMB that this design could turn a profit as an operational system. The agency commissioned the Princeton research firm Mathematica to study the proposed shuttle's cost effectiveness. Mathematica cooperated, using optimistic data from the very aerospace contractors who hoped to land lucrative shuttle contracts. If the shuttle flew as *few* as thirty flights a year, their report stated, the system would actually pay for itself.

This and subsequent optimistic cost-effectiveness analyses and projections did not discover serious design flaws.

However, the compromises NASA was forced to accept created problems that have haunted the system from its first test flights. The designers intended to solve the problem of reentry heat through an ingenious system of lightweight silicon tiles that would radiate the frictional heat-energy back into the atmosphere as the orbiter decelerated. The original orbiter design concept of a short fuselage with straight, high-lift wings lent itself well to this innovative solution. But the complexly curved geometry of the delta-wing design was another matter. The tiles not only offered thermal protection, they also provided the orbiter's lift and aerosurface control. The cambers and curves of the delta-winged orbiter created unusual combinations of stress and vibration harmonics. Keeping the more than thirty thousand uniquely shaped tiles properly glued to the orbiter's heat-sensitive alloy skin eventually proved to be a frustrating burden.

The main propulsion system was equally vexing. In the original concept of two piloted vehicles, the bulk of the thrust was provided by twelve clustered engines on the huge booster craft. This meant that the orbiter could be equipped with only two similar engines that would place the vehicle in final orbit and provide the deceleration of the de-orbit reentry burn. However, in the compromise design, the orbiter carried a total of three cryogenic engines, as well as two orbital maneuvering engines in their separate, complex OMS pods. Thus the weight of the orbiter's total on-board propulsion system steadily increased over the original design. But there were ultimate limits to the weight. So these main engines had to be lighter and deliver more thrust than the Saturn V moon rocket's workhorse J-2 upper-stage engines, the most powerful cryogenic engines built up to that time. Whereas the Saturn's upper stages had required five J-2 engines, each producing 232,000 pounds of thrust, weight restrictions on the orbiter meant that its propulsion would be limited to three much lighter but much more powerful engines. The propellant turbopumps of such power plants would have to operate reliably at speeds exceeding thirty thousand revolutions per minute, for up to fifty consecutive flights, a specification that has come back to haunt NASA's shuttle program.

The fragility inherent in these design compromises was not lost on early critics of the program, both in and outside of government.

But President Nixon finally gave the shuttle his full support because he saw it as a popular program he could flaunt on the 1972 campaign trail, especially in the newly Republican Sun Belt, where most aerospace contractors were located. As we shall see in the next chapter, scrutiny of the contributions to the scandal-ridden Committee to Re-elect the President reveals just how attractive the space shuttle was to the giant Sun Belt aerospace corporations.

To NASA's great relief, two of the shuttle's potentially strongest opponents in the first Nixon administration, OMB Director George Schultz and his deputy Caspar "Cap the Knife" Weinberger, had obviously received their marching orders from the White House. They gave the shuttle their full blessing late in 1971. So the extended process of design compromise ended on January 5, 1972, when NASA's once and future Administrator James Fletcher joined President Nixon in San Clemente to pose for pictures with a shuttle model, while the President announced his approval of the project. The space shuttle, Richard Nixon promised, would "take the astronomical cost out of astronautics."

Administrator Fletcher agreed completely. The space shuttle

would give America "the means of getting men and equipment to and from space routinely, on a moment's notice, if necessary, and at a small fraction of today's cost."

Neither man mentioned giant space stations or landings on the planet Mars.

Professor Alex Roland has accurately summarized the political wrangling and the results of this compromise. The space shuttle project, he wrote in *Discover* magazine, produced a protracted war of wills that tugged NASA, the Congress, the Air Force, and the White House in different directions. And the shuttle design that emerged from this political battle pleased nobody. Certainly NASA had not received the Cadillac shuttle that Thomas Paine had envisioned. "Instead of a horse," Roland stated, "NASA got a camel—better than no transportation at all and indeed well suited for certain jobs, but hardly the steed it would have chosen."

*   *   *

And that stable of compromise camels eventually included the Orbiter Challenger. In mid-January 1986, Challenger was certified ready for Space Transportation System mission 51-L, the twenty-fifth space shuttle flight. Challenger stood mated to its external tank and solid rocket boosters on Launch Pad 39B, a hybrid machine created by a series of political compromises that the world had long forgotten.

Certain aspects of this political process, however, have never been brought to light. And they have a direct impact on the decisions that led to Challenger's launch on the record cold morning of January 28, 1986.

THE POLITICS OF PROCUREMENT

The process of awarding the prime contracts for the space shuttle's principal elements—the main engines, the orbiter, the solid rocket boosters, and the external tank—occurred during that period of political turmoil we remember as the Watergate years. Therefore the unprecedented controversy and divisiveness that three of these contract awards provoked was largely eclipsed by the broader and more sensational scandal that eventually encompassed the President and his men. It is interesting to speculate, however, on whether NASA would have persevered with its choice of prime contractors, despite the official protests and unofficial grumbling these choices engendered, had the wrath of Congress not been focused on more important matters.

And it is equally interesting, but certainly more somber, to speculate on the relationship between these controversial contract awards and the Challenger accident.

In 1971 Richard Nixon was nearing the end of his first term. The war in Vietnam still dragged on, and the resulting inflation, economic dislocation, and domestic discord were shaping up as possible obstacles to his reelection campaign the next year. In retrospect, of course, only a President with a monumental lack of self-confidence, such as Richard Nixon, would have felt seriously threatened by George McGovern's muddled campaign. But given the scale of Mr. Nixon's unorthodox and often illegal campaign efforts, he obviously took the threat seriously.

His chief domestic advisor, John Ehrlichman, correctly believed that securing a Republican majority in the Sun Belt was essential to Nixon's reelection. McGovern's policies wouldn't play well in either the Old South or in the traditionally conservative Southwest. And Nixon could probably guarantee a Republican sweep of the Sun Belt if he could take credit for economic growth in the region. Certainly Ehrlichman and other key White House strategists were well aware that the aerospace industry was vital to the Sun Belt's economy. But in 1971 cutbacks in military contracts and the phasing down of the Apollo moon landing program had hurt the industry badly. Ehrlichman undoubtedly recognized the potential windfall the $5 billion space shuttle program presented the depressed Sun Belt aerospace industry. Ehrlichman later told Professor John Logsdon just how seriously the Nixon White House viewed the political impact of the aerospace industry's prosperity. "When you look at employment numbers," Ehrlichman explained, "and key them to battleground states, the space program has an importance out of proportion to its budget."

Although the political significance of a revitalized aerospace industry in the Sun Belt was a major factor in Nixon's decision to approve the space shuttle, the cold war propaganda value of the project was also a strong consideration. The President saw the shuttle, like the Apollo moon landings, as a clear demonstration to the world of America's technological superiority over the Soviet Union. To Nixon this was no small matter, as he faced the deteriorating situation in Vietnam.

While the White House and the OMB debated NASA's plans for a space shuttle, aerospace contractors lobbied for approval of the project. NASA actively encouraged the contractors in these efforts, which often took the form of feasibility and economic impact studies. And one company, North American Rockwell (later to become Rockwell International), was especially active. Rockwell had been the prime contractor for the Apollo project and needed a big shuttle contract to guarantee the survival of its civilian aerospace operations.

Naturally the company has never made public the exact nature of its strategy, but the scope and importance of the effort has emerged from subsequent events. One of the first priorities was securing a position of influence within the NASA bureaucracy where the contract decisions would be made. In 1970, when it became clear NASA was pressing ahead with the shuttle project, Rockwell intensified its lobbying efforts at the White House. That year the company managed to place Dale D. Myers, the Vice President and Manager for the company's Space Shuttle Program, as NASA Associate Administrator for Manned Space Flight. Next to the Administrator, James Fletcher, Mr. Myers would have the most power in awarding contracts. A hungry fox was thus installed in the middle of the henhouse.

The names of Dale Myers and Dr. James Fletcher resonate throughout the sad, sometimes squalid history of the space shuttle.

With this inside track, Rockwell next set about to solidify White House support for the program. According to Berkeley historian Walter A. McDougall, Rockwell was an active lobbyist. "After North American Rockwell provided exaggerated estimates of the employment it would stimulate," McDougall wrote in his seminal study of space politics, *The Heavens and the Earth,* "Nixon and his adviser John Ehrlichman approved of the Space Transportation System [the shuttle]."

But Rockwell's strategy was not limited to securing just *one* prime contract. The company wanted the same dominance it had enjoyed in the Apollo program; this meant that Rockwell had to secure the lucrative but uniquely demanding contract for the development of the main engines. Because the main engines were classed as the "pacing" technology, NASA decided to award the engine-development contract even before the shuttle project itself was officially approved by the White House. On March 2, 1971— with former Administrator Thomas Paine no longer in office and Administrator-designate James Fletcher not yet on board—the agency tendered a formal Request for Proposal (RFP) to the three leading rocket engine contractors: Aerojet General, of Sacramento; Pratt and Whitney, of West Palm Beach, Florida; and the Rocketdyne Division of North American Rockwell, Canoga Park, California.

Even though Rocketdyne had built the cryogenic engines of the successful Saturn boosters, industry experts considered Pratt and Whitney the most likely candidate for the contract. As New York *Times* science writer John Noble Wilford described the engine contract competition, Pratt and Whitney's advantage was undeniable: With NASA and Air Force support, the company "had developed and tested essentially all the components for a high-pressure engine that already met shuttle requirements; the other two companies had not."

But industry experts may not have taken into account Rockwell's determination or its degree of influence with the Nixon White House and within NASA. The agency called for a submission deadline of April 21, and Rockwell was able to present a very impressive submission.

Over the next eight weeks, teams from a formal Source Evaluation Board (which, the reader interested in historical accuracy might wish to note, had been handpicked by Associate Administrator for Manned Space Flight Dale Myers) met in secret to consider the bids. This confidential process was traditional with NASA; ostensibly it protected the competitive proprietary trade secrets contained in the bidding contractors' proposals. But the secret process would also allow the NASA Administrator (or his associates) to stack the board with sympathetic members.

*   *   *

Following the Challenger accident, the author submitted a formal Freedom of Information Act request to obtain the membership list of the Source Evaluation Boards for the space shuttle main engines and the solid rocket boosters. NASA took almost three months to acknowledge this request, and when they did, they stated such information fell into a "gray area," which was usually excluded from the provisions of the Act. At the time this book went to press, NASA had still not furnished the membership of these Evaluation Boards. It should be noted, however, that there have been persistent allegations that employees of the Thiokol Chemical Corporation took positions at the Marshall Space Flight Center during the period in question, and served on the SRB Selection Board. NASA's inability to meet its statutory obligations and provide this information in a timely manner does little to lay this troublesome issue to rest.

*   *   *

In July 1971 new NASA Administrator Fletcher announced that he had made his choice. The Rocketdyne Division of North

American Rockwell would develop the space shuttle's main engines, under a program to be administered by the Marshall Space Flight Center. Rocketdyne had come from behind to defeat Pratt and Whitney.

But Pratt and Whitney did not take the announcement passively. They vented their shock and outrage in a formal protest of the award, an effort that resulted in a review of the selection process by the General Accounting Office (GAO), the official watchdog agency of Congress. Later that year, the GAO made its report. NASA's Source Evaluation Board had found the three competitors very close in technical and engineering excellence. But Pratt and Whitney had submitted the lowest proposed cost, probably as a result of the extensive development work it had already carried out on high-pressure cryogenic engines. In a less politicized atmosphere, perhaps Pratt and Whitney would have prevailed.

However, the board did not make the final choice; it could only offer its recommendation to the Source Selection Official: Administrator James Fletcher. He opted for Rocketdyne. When the GAO reviewed the Pratt and Whitney protest, they determined that "the procurement was conducted in a manner that was consistent with applicable law and regulations and was fair to all proposers." However, the GAO did not investigate the possible influence of Dale Myers (a once and future Rockwell executive) on the Source Evaluation Board. This was Washington government contract hardball at its toughest, and Rockwell simply knew how to play the game better than its competitor. Dr. James Fletcher would soon demonstrate just how skillful he himself was at this form of hardball. Pratt and Whitney's protest and appeal process dragged on for almost a year; in the interim, NASA awarded Rocketdyne a series of ninety-day contracts, which allowed the company to entrench its position.

When the appeals were exhausted, Rocketdyne was home free with a contract worth a minimum of $450 million.

The next item on NASA's (and Rockwell's) agenda was the big one, the prime contract for the space shuttle orbiter. In May 1972 NASA tendered RFPs for the orbiter to the four major competitors: Grumman Aerospace of Bethpage, New York; Lockheed Missiles and Space Company of Sunnyvale, California; North

American Rockwell's Space Division of Downey, California; and McDonnell-Douglas Corporation's Astronautics Company of St. Louis.

Once more, industry experts considered Rockwell an outsider. During the so-called Phase B design definition period, Grumman had led the development of the eventual shuttle configuration of delta-winged orbiter, strap-on boosters, and external fuel tank. They had proved their mettle in the Apollo program by designing and building the innovative and highly reliable Lunar Excursion Module, the legendary LEM that had permitted Americans to beat the Russians in the moon race. Now Grumman executives were confident they would be tapped to develop the shuttle orbiter.

But Grumman was based in Democratic Long Island, smack in the middle of the anti-Nixon East Coast. This entire region was considered hostile by the White House; it certainly formed no part of the Sun Belt strategy.

On July 26, 1972, James Fletcher announced his choice: Rockwell. The contract was worth a total of $2.6 billion over six years. Officially Grumman accepted the choice with good grace. But privately one Grumman official voiced his company's outrage. "We were screwed," he exclaimed.

Although the McDonnell-Douglas Astronautics orbiter proposal did not score high in the engineering competition, it must be noted that this design incorporated a practical abort capability that would have protected the shuttle crew during all phases of the mission, including initial ascent. Their proposed orbiter carried a small solid rocket abort motor, tucked between the main engines. Combined with a system of thrust termination for the big solid rocket boosters that had already been developed for the Air Force Manned Orbiting Laboratory program, the McDonnell-Douglas orbiter would have been able to separate from the "stack" and safely glide back to the shuttle landing site.

Incredibly, the McDonnell-Douglas proposal actually anticipated the cause of the Challenger accident. Their abort system provided for a "burn through wire" that would have sensed "O-ring leakage," then triggered booster thrust termination and the orbiter's abort rocket escape system.

However, this system added several thousand pounds of weight to the orbiter in the thrust neutralizer, the abort rocket, and airframe reinforcement so that the orbiter could withstand the stresses of the abort sequence. And NASA in the early 1970s was not about to trade weight for insured safety.

According to Tom A. Brosz, the highly respected editor of *The Commercial Space Report,* "It is inconceivable that any competent designer of an aerospace flight system would create a vehicle which lacked the capability for safe abort during the most critical part of the launch." But, when NASA chose the Rockwell design, that was exactly what the agency did.

* * *

Once the fine print of the multibillion-dollar orbiter and main engine contracts had been hammered out and Rockwell was settled into building the hardware, Dale Myers straightened out a few other items, then resigned his political appointment as NASA's Associate Administrator for Manned Space Flight. He then rejoined Rockwell.

* * *

In 1974 a Congressional committee examining election fraud in connection with the larger Watergate investigation interviewed President Nixon's private secretary, Rosemary Woods. She was obliged to turn over a confidential list of major corporate donors that had secretly contributed to Nixon's reelection war chest before the Federal Election Campaign Act came into effect on April 7, 1972. Among the aerospace contractor donors on this list there were two—McDonnell-Douglas and North American Rockwell— that had competed for major shuttle contracts. But North American Rockwell had clearly outspent its competition in this dubious area as well. Rockwell had made a secret donation of $98,278, a tidy sum back in 1972—almost three times McDonnell-Douglas's secret contribution. The eventual contract return of over $3 billion certainly justified the original expenditure.

* * *

In September 1986, eight months after the Challenger accident, President Reagan announced his choice for a new Deputy Administrator for NASA, who would assist the newly appointed Administrator, Dr. James Fletcher, in the important work of rebuilding the agency after the disaster. The President came up with a familiar name: Dale D. Myers.

*   *   *

In mid-March 1972, Dr. James Fletcher wrote to a committee of political leaders from Utah to inform them that NASA had chosen solid rocket motors for the space shuttle's reusable boosters. As the president of the University of Utah from 1964 until he took up his duties as NASA Administrator in 1971, Dr. Fletcher was well acquainted with most of the men on the committee. He understood their eagerness about the booster decision: one of Utah's leading industries was the Wasatch Division of the Thiokol Chemical Corporation in Brigham City, sixty miles north of Salt Lake City. And Dr. Fletcher was also well acquainted with Thiokol; his wife came from Brigham City.

Over the years, Dr. Fletcher's supporters have implied that his connection to Utah and to the leadership of the Church of Jesus Christ of Latter-day Saints, the Mormons, is at best tenuous. This is a smoke screen. According to Dr. John Heinerman, a Salt Lake City anthropologist and the coauthor of *The Mormon Corporate Empire*, an authoritative study of the Church, Fletcher was a key member of the Utah Mormon hierarchy. Dr. Heinerman stated that Dr. Fletcher was a "very active, very devout Mormon," a member of the high council of the Los Angeles stake—analogous to a Roman Catholic archdiocese—and regional representative of the church's First Presidency (the church's executive office). Dr. Heinerman also maintains that Fletcher's appointment as NASA administrator in 1971 fit a pattern of Mormon outreach to positions of political and financial leadership beyond Utah. This policy, Heinerman said, can be traced to the ascendancy of Nathan Eldon Tanner to the position of Second Counselor in the church's First Presidency, the triumvirate equivalent to the Catholic Holy See. It should be noted that President Nixon's influential Secretary of the Treasury, David Kennedy, was also a devout Mormon and also influential with the church hierarchy. About the time President Tanner's expansion policies were being implemented, he and Dr. James Fletcher were named to the board of directors of a corporation called Pro-Utah, Inc. This organization's stated goals included:

"1. To promote and encourage the economic, commercial, financial, industrial, agricultural, and civic welfare of the State of Utah.

2. To promote and encourage the development and retention of businesses, industries, and commerce within the State of Utah and the development and utilization of the natural resources of the State of Utah.

3. To promote, encourage and attract businesses, industries, and commercial activities to locate within the State of Utah for the betterment of the economy of the state. . . ."

Having noted these facts, Dr. Fletcher's subsequent actions during the solid rocket booster contract award become more understandable.

After the Challenger accident, however, Dr. Fletcher told a reporter who questioned the administrator's allegiance to Utah, "I had no commitments to Utah."

Thiokol was a medium-sized contractor with experience in munitions, military pyrotechnics, and missile solid rocket manufacture. Their expertise in boosters included work on the Minuteman and Trident missiles' solid rocket motors. But they were by no means the industry leaders in producing *large,* sectional solid rocket boosters. That title had to go to United Technologies' Chemical Systems Division in Southern California, the maker of the huge Titan-III strap-on boosters that stood over ninety feet high and weighed almost three hundred tons.

Thiokol, however, did have other advantages than just the active interest of Administrator Fletcher. One of the company's strongest supporters was Utah Democratic Senator Frank E. Moss. In 1973 he somehow managed to have himself named Chairman of the Senate's Committee on Aeronautical and Space Sciences, the committee that had oversight of NASA policy and budget, even though he was not previously a committee member. Clearly Senator Moss was a pivotal figure in guaranteeing future Senate support for the space shuttle.

After Dr. Fletcher announced NASA's intention to use solid

rocket boosters on the shuttle, he gave Senator Moss a briefing on the subject. Then Moss told the press that this decision could bring his state a contract for a billion dollars. Moss had confidence that NASA Administrator Fletcher would not forget his friends back in Utah when he chose the SRB contractor. In this regard, it should be noted that Utah Senators Wallace F. Bennett and Frank Moss lead the witnesses in supporting Dr. Fletcher's nomination before the Senate Space Committee in April 1971. In Senator Bennett's prepared remarks he described Fletcher as "one of our state's outstanding citizens." He also noted that he had known Fletcher for twenty-five years and that one of Dr. Fletcher's brothers was the senator's son-in-law. Obviously Dr. James Fletcher had, indeed, an entree to the inner corridors of power among the tightly knit Mormon hierarchy in Utah.

In Senator Moss's remarks he noted that Dr. Fletcher was one of the "most able administrators in the state." Despite later disclaimers, Dr. James Fletcher clearly had an abiding personal interest in seeing Utah prosper.

Senator Frank Moss would not be disappointed in his hopes for Dr. Fletcher's appointment. And in July 1973, NASA announced RFP's for the solid boosters from Thiokol, United Technologies, Aerojet Solid Propulsion Company, and Lockheed Propulsion Company. With the exception of Thiokol, the bidders were all based in California.

A Source Evaluation Board of thirteen members (the membership of which NASA still keeps secret) met for three months and carefully considered the merits of the four proposals; that fall the Board made their presentation to the Source Selection Official, once more Dr. James Fletcher. Using the complex set of selection criteria delineated in the RFP, the board rated the competing contractors numerically as to overall mission suitability. But first they judged the four competing designs purely on their engineering merits. By this criterion, Aerojet, a leading contender, was considered the safest because its one-piece booster casing "precluded the potential failure modes associated with joints." However, contractor management and the cost effectiveness of the entire production proposal package were also judged.

Out of a possible 1,000 points, they scored:

Lockheed – 714
Thiokol – 710
United Technologies – 710
Aerojet – 655

On November 20, 1973, NASA announced that Administrator James Fletcher had chosen the Thiokol Chemical Corporation to build the largest solid rocket boosters ever designed. In his Selection Statement, Dr. Fletcher defended his choice by stating there had been a virtual "standoff" among the three top-rated competitors, but that Thiokol's superior scores in the management area and the lower total cost of their proposal made the selection inevitable. "Any selection other than Thiokol," Dr. Fletcher wrote, "would give rise to an additional cost of an appreciable size."

After the Challenger accident, Mark Thompson, a national reporter for Knight-Ridder Newspapers, investigated Fletcher's connection to Thiokol and to Utah. Thompson tracked down Senator Moss's former top aide, Kem C. Gardner, who was working as a Mormon missionary in Massachusetts. This was Gardner's comment on the question of Fletcher's motives in the decision. "There's no question that one of the main reasons Thiokol got the award was because Senator Moss was chairman of the aeronautical and space sciences committee and Jim Fletcher was the administrator of NASA." Kem Gardner also told Thompson that there had been a "furious battle" among the competing contractors and their Capitol Hill supporters. Although Fletcher was initially so noncommittal and aloof from Moss's lobbying that Gardner was "frustrated," he felt that Moss's position as chairman "gave us major clout in lobbying for it." He added that this effort influenced NASA's subjective judgment process. "That's where I think our lobbying paid off; that's how those decisions are made."

When this author contacted Kem Gardner for comment, he stated that he had been misquoted by Thompson, that he now felt Senator Moss had not had sufficient clout to influence Fletcher's decision. Gardner added that since Thompson's story had run, he had been called by a number of people who were unhappy with Gardner's comments.

Mark Thompson stood by his story and the accuracy of the

quotes. He explained that he always tape-records interviews, and that he drew Gardner's quotes from such an interview tape. Thompson won a Pulitzer Prize in 1985 and is widely known in Washington press circles as a hard-working and honest reporter.

It is ironic that the Source Evaluation Board and Fletcher noted Thiokol's excellence in management when the company had experienced a disastrous explosion at one of its munitions plants in Georgia only eighteen months earlier in which twenty-nine employees were killed and more than a score were maimed. Federal investigators had already determined that ineffective management of the Thiokol plant was at least partially responsible for the explosion.

Soon after the announcement of the Thiokol contract award, Lockheed lodged a formal protest, which—as in the case of the main engine contract protest—triggered a formal review by the GAO.

Lockheed's protest contended that NASA had unreasonably and unfairly judged their proposal. They charged that NASA's decision had been "marred by plain mistakes, inconsistency, arbitrary judgements, and improper procedures." Among other charges, Lockheed contended that NASA had overestimated the projected costs of the Lockheed production plan, and *under*estimated Thiokol's probable costs. No one mentioned the influence of an old-boy network of Utah political leaders, perhaps because such charges might have provoked countercharges of anti-Mormon prejudice. But among aerospace industry insiders, the nature of the decision was clear. According to a former senior project engineer at the Marshall Space Flight Center, the Thiokol contract was the result of pressure from "the Mormon Mafia," of which Dr. Fletcher was a leading member.

These are serious charges that raise the ugly issue of religious bigotry. In the case of the Mormons, the issue is further colored by the unpleasant background of brutal intolerance that the church suffered in its early years. However, a reasonable observer of religious influence in American secular affairs will see that organized religions throughout the country have long lobbied the political leadership to obtain specific secular goals. The Roman Catholic Church with its large ethnic Irish membership in the Northeast has consistently pressured the White House and Congress to intervene in favor of Catholics in Northern Ireland; this pressure has resulted in actual granting of asylum to convicted IRA terrorists. Jewish religious organizations in greater New York have been active in shaping America's policy toward Israel and its Arab neighbors. And Christian fundamentalists throughout the Bible Belt have lobbied long and hard for specific legislation on their pet issues: pornography, abortion, etc. Of course, the role of black religious leaders in the civil rights movement is legend. Therefore an examination of Mormon influence on the American space program falls in the purview of legitimate historical investigation, not under the ugly cloak of bigotry.

Naturally the GAO review of Lockheed's protest did not address allegations of unfair Mormon/Utah influence. Instead, the agency carefully analyzed the two companies' proposals, comparing each element of the submissions with the findings of the Source Evaluation Board. The GAO report made clear that the responsibility for the final decision had always rested with the Source Selection Official (Dr. Fletcher), and that its role was neutral review of the selection process.

The detailed ninety-eight-page report is difficult reading, and the GAO is careful to maintain its neutral perspective. However, the GAO analysis does produce certain unequivocal conclusions:

Although the board found that Thiokol's probable costs amounted to projected savings of $122 million over Lockheed's probable cost projections, the board mistakenly underestimated Thiokol's projections for ammonium perchlorate fuel supplies by $68 million.

Therefore the *actual* project cost difference between Thiokol and Lockheed, the GAO stated, fell within a range of uncertainty that negated the economic advantages of Thiokol's submission.

The GAO also made a point of noting that Dr. Fletcher had dismissed a similarly uncertain cost advantage held by Pratt and Whitney in the disputed main engine contract competition (where the three leading competitors were also classed as essentially equal in technical excellence).

Concluding its report, the GAO asked publicly, and no doubt rhetorically, that Dr. Fletcher reconsider his decision. "We recognize," the GAO stated, "that the selection remains the function of the SSO. Our role is to test the reasonableness of the result. However, the circumstances appear to call for the SSO to determine whether the net significant decrease in the probable cost difference between the proposals of Thiokol and Lockheed, in light of the four-point difference in mission suitability scoring, calls for a reconsideration. In the event the SSO determines that a reconsideration is called for, the proposals of each should be considered as they and the attendant circumstances existed as of the time of the original selection decision except for the above-stated difference in probable cost."

Within this thicket of thorny bureaucratic prose there lay one glaring fact: the "significant" economic advantage of the Thiokol proposal no longer existed. A reasonable, neutral administrator, therefore, would have thrown open the competition once more. Comptroller General Elmer B. Staats, head of the GAO, went out of his way to oblige Dr. Fletcher to reconsider his decision. In Staats's transmittal letter sent to Fletcher with the GAO report, Staats writes: "Your attention is invited to the conclusions reached in our decision. Please advise of the actions taken with respect thereto." In other words the Comptroller General officially requested that Dr. Fletcher act on the conclusions; and these conclusions called for the NASA Administrator to reconsider his contract award.

Fletcher did not interpret the GAO report this way. His choice of Thiokol was solidified into a formal cost-plus-fee contract that eventually brought the Utah company revenues of over one billion dollars.

The GAO noted that NASA consistently refused to give Lockheed's protesting officials Selection Board estimates of probable cost differences between the submissions. This created the impression that NASA might have been more arbitrary than it wanted to admit in its cost-probability analyses. In other words Thiokol seemed to enjoy some kind of special relationship with the NASA leadership.

Lockheed's protest also contended that Thiokol was chosen partially because of its ability to build the boosters using its own plant facilities in Utah. However, the RFP called for a multiphase contract, the third phase of which would be open to competitors in the 1980s. But if Thiokol locked up the manufacturing process within its own plant, Lockheed charged, such eventual competition would be meaningless. Lockheed proposed to construct the boosters in a newly built government plant at NASA's Mississippi Test Facility, where the shuttle's external tanks would be processed for barge shipment to the Cape. Dr. Fletcher dismissed these objections. In so doing, he effectively buried the issue of any monopolistic advantage gained by Thiokol. However, the question of this sole-source advantage returned to obsess the company's leaders in the weeks before the Challenger accident.

Dr. Fletcher also found Lockheed's barge transportation plan less efficacious than Thiokol's proposed rail-shipment system. However, one of the Rogers Commission's findings on the contributing causes of the Challenger accident was that the lower segment of the shuttle's right-hand solid rocket booster might have been damaged during rail shipment from Utah. The GAO also found that NASA's overall consideration of Lockheed's transportation plan was "inconsistent." Yet NASA defended its choice, thus strengthening the impression that the agency's leadership was closely identified with every aspect of Thiokol's submission. In the 1980s the inherent inefficiency of this plan became evident: booster segments shipped in a horizontal position on railcars often required difficult processing to bring the distorted segments "back to round." The Lockheed plan would have shipped booster segments in a vertical position on the barges.

Another contractor, Aerojet, had proposed to eliminate the segmented casing altogether and to build the solid rocket booster as a single, "monolithic" case. However, their proposal required the construction of a new plant on the intracoastal waterway in southern Florida, so the board correctly assessed the cost of this design to be beyond the very limited shuttle development budget. Had the White House and the OMB given NASA a realistic development budget, the board might have looked more favorably at Aerojet's proposal.

Probably the most significant aspect of this dispute as it affected the booster design and the eventual accident was Dr. Fletcher's strong defense of Thiokol's engineering excellence. In his formal

Selection Statement, Administrator Fletcher singled out Thiokol's casing field joint design as an example of such excellence: "The Thiokol motor case joints utilized dual O-rings and test ports between seals, enabling a simple leak check without pressuring the entire motor." Fletcher described this design as an "innovative" feature that offered great operational economies, for which Thiokol was to be commended.

Dr. Fletcher thus went out of his way to officially endorse the Thiokol field joint. He remained Administrator until 1977, during the initial period of solid rocket booster testing and certification. When Marshall engineers began to question the fundamental reliability of the Thiokol design, they may well have remembered the bitter Lockheed contract dispute and recalled their Administrator's strong endorsement of Thiokol's innovatively excellent field joint design. It is not unreasonable to assume, therefore, that the Thiokol design acquired something of a sacred cow status, given its high-level patronage. For whatever reasons, the Marshall Space Flight Center never seriously challenged Thiokol on the booster field joint design until the hardware itself began to present alarming evidence of design flaws during operational shuttle flights. Even then, however, the aura of protective patronage seems to have shielded this engineering malignancy from vigorous examination until the fatal accident.

As we shall see, Thiokol was clearly reluctant to initiate a major redesign of its booster's field joints during the year preceding the disaster. This reluctance might well have stemmed from their long-held sensitivity about the bitter contract-award dispute of 1974.

In any event many NASA engineers might have concluded that Thiokol continued to enjoy high-level patronage throughout the operational shuttle program. When Dr. Fletcher left the agency in 1977, the Utah connection was maintained through Senator Jake Garn, who soon took over the chairmanship of the Senate subcommittee on independent agencies, which had direct oversight of NASA's budget. Viewed in this light, Thiokol can be seen to have consistently benefited from highly placed Utah patrons: Senators Wallace Bennett and Frank Moss, Dr. James Fletcher, and Senator Jake Garn. And this patronage has stifled both competition and any impetus for Thiokol to improve the flawed booster. According to Donald E. Day, a Senior Associate Director of the General Accounting Office, Senator Jake Garn was among several Congressmen, including Florida's Don Fuqua and Bill Nelson, who have "gotten too close to the agency and have been less objective than they should have been." Mr. Day noted that auditors' warnings on safety mismanagement, which included problems with Thiokol's booster, have been consistently ignored by key Congressional committees, including Garn's subcommittee. "Even though we bring things to the Congress," he complained bitterly, "there is this shield. They say, 'Thank you, GAO, for your work,' and then ignore it."

Former Comptroller General Staats went even further. He noted that NASA's leadership became much more political and less open after Administrator James E. Webb left office. "Mr. Webb was a good manager," Staats said. "He put together a good team. But afterward there was less openness, less willingness to listen to the kind of challenges we were making."

*　　*　　*

The fallout from the disputed contract awards continued up to the very day of the Challenger disaster. In the winter of 1985 NASA finally succumbed to Congressional pressure and agreed to consider competitive bidding on the pending contract renewal for production of solid rocket boosters, thus seriously threatening for the first time Thiokol's (by then Morton Thiokol, Inc.) thirteen-year monopoly. Through the first three weeks of January 1986, NASA and Thiokol conducted negotiations over a new one-billion-dollar contract. And there was an important negotiation teleconference scheduled for Tuesday, January 28—the day after Thiokol managers made their recommendation to proceed with the launch, the day Challenger was destroyed.

*　　*　　*

The squalid legacy of the space shuttle's design compromises and contract awards is apparent in other aspects of the program. As in the case of the underfunded spare parts system, the vehicle's terrible operational inefficiency—its so-called "turnaround time" —became a semipublic scandal. The human toll of the increased flight rate was becoming more obvious during the months before the accident.

THE HUMAN TOLL

In March 1985, NASA Administrator James M. Beggs spoke about the problems confronting the space shuttle program as the agency struggled to meet its increasingly ambitious mission schedule, the so-called "flight manifest."

"The next eighteen months are very critical for the shuttle," he told *Aviation Week and Space Technology*'s Craig Covault. "If we are going to prove our mettle and demonstrate our capability, we have got to fly out that manifest."

Mr. Beggs was not exaggerating. The shuttle program faced unexpected competition from abroad and mounting criticism within the U.S. Government.

Foreign competition centered on Arianespace, the commercial satellite launch consortium organized by the European Space Agency, ESA. Flying the Ariane launcher developed by ESA, Arianespace took advantage of the equatorial launch site at Kourou in French Guiana. At the equator, a lower-thrust launcher could successfully challenge the larger space shuttle, which had to cross twenty-eight degrees of latitude from Cape Canaveral before reaching the injection point for the Earth-stationary orbit favored by most commercial communication and weather satellites.

And of course, Ariane had another major advantage over the shuttle. Using an unmanned, expendable booster, an Ariane mission cost only a fraction of a shuttle flight. The manned space shuttle—with all its heavy and expensive life support system and its elaborate complex of worldwide landing sites—was much less efficient at satellite launching than the smaller Ariane. On several shuttle missions, the Orbiter was a terribly expensive, virtually empty van transporting a single commercial satellite to its equatorial injection point, a task that had often been performed by expendable launchers at a quarter of a shuttle flight's cost. Nowhere was the fabric of the Emperor's New Clothes thinner than on these missions.

The French had been instrumental in fostering this space-launch system, so that Europe could be independent of both the United States and the Soviet Union. In the late 1970s, however, few Americans considered the Ariane serious competition for the space shuttle. After all, the Ariane prototype was a small expendable rocket, powered by seemingly obsolete kerosene-oxygen engines, which did not seem to offer the operational economy of the shuttle. But ESA had planned for an incremental upgrade of Ariane that would move steadily toward higher performance from the same basic vehicle. With the addition of cryogenic upper stages and strap-on boosters, Ariane would gradually increase its thrust and payload. In this regard, Ariane was similar to contemporary Soviet launch vehicles; in 1986 several standard Russian launchers were simply upgraded variants of the vehicle that launched the first Sputnik twenty-nine years before.

While NASA concentrated on the revolutionary space shuttle, the ESA plodded along with mixed success, developing the evolutionary Ariane launch system. Well funded by ESA, the Ariane program slowly advanced. And by the mid-1980s, NASA found itself with serious competition for the lucrative international satellite trade. In 1984 Arianespace launched four commercial and scientific satellites. The next year Arianespace moved up to a more powerful model of their basic rocket and successfully launched seven satellites. Several of these missions were dual-satellite launches to geosynchronous Earth orbit, a clear indication of the consortium's competitiveness.

Even more serious from NASA's point of view, ESA's continued subsidy of Arianespace meant that the consortium could offer very competitive launch fees to its growing international clientele. Arianespace advertised dual-communication satellite launches for a total mission cost of $58 million, while the lowest rate NASA could quote was $34 million per satellite on a fully commercial shuttle mission. Business gradually shifted toward Arianespace. By May 1984 the Europeans had firm orders for twenty-eight launches, representing a hefty $813 million in fees.

To exacerbate NASA's problems, Congress was intent on trimming the agency's shuttle-flight subsidies, just when Arianespace was taking commercial advantage of its own.

And NASA was threatened from other quarters of the government. The Air Force, which ironically had dictated the shuttle's fundamental capabilities and design, was now the leading critic of its operational performance. In June 1984, during the middle of a difficult year for the shuttle, the Air Force asked Congress for hundreds of millions of dollars to develop and build ten new large expendable launch vehicles, "ELV's," for placing heavy military satellites in polar and geosynchronous orbits. According to the Air Force, national security concerns required that the military be able to launch satellites—especially sophisticated reconnaissance satellites—on short notice, with a strong assurance of mission success. Given the shuttle's poor reliability record to date, the Air Force claimed, NASA met neither requirement.

The Air Force request hit NASA hard. If the service acquired its own fleet of ten ELV's, the agency would lose at least ten paying cargoes. Worse, this pattern might mean a gradual abandoning of the shuttle by its most reliable launch customer and establish a pattern to be emulated by other agencies. NASA feared that the National Oceanic and Atmospheric Administration (NOAA) might seek its own independent launch capability. And, later that year, NOAA confirmed these fears by ordering advanced Tiros weather satellites that were not shuttle-compatible, which it planned to have launched on old-fashioned Atlas rockets. Less than two years after President Reagan's optimistic message from the flag-draped rostrum at Edwards, the space shuttle was in danger of losing its most-dependable "national security and civil government" customers.

NASA cried foul and went to the President for help. Mediating the dispute between NASA and the Air Force, the White House offered a compromise: the Air Force would get funding for ten upgraded Titan 34D ELV's, but the service would guarantee to use at least one third of shuttle-payload capability after 1988—

about eight flights a year—when the shuttle was "fully operational" and flying twenty-four missions a year. The White House did not, however, resolve the growing dispute between NASA and NOAA. Instead, the issue was left to the two agencies to work out between them.

All of this unforeseen competition and criticism put NASA in an extremely difficult if not impossible position. In order to keep the confidence of its commercial, civil-government, and military customers, NASA would have to fly the shuttle dependably on an increasingly ambitious launch schedule. But the very nature of this schedule created pressures and engendered conditions that threatened launch-schedule reliability, to say nothing of flight safety. But the agency had been pushed into a corner. By the spring of 1985, less than a year before Challenger's 51-L mission, NASA's credo had become: "Fly out that manifest."

If NASA could not meet its 1985 schedule, the cascading domino effect of major delays would threaten the even more ambitious 1986 manifest. NASA's 1986 launch schedule called for three long-planned scientific missions with rigid launch windows. Columbia's ASTRO-1 flight in March would be America's most serious examination of Halley's Comet, and the country's international space-scientific reputation would ride with this mission. In May NASA would launch two major probes of the solar system: the Ulysses international solar-polar flight on May 15 and the Galileo Jupiter Orbiter on May 21. These probes would be the first demonstration of the shuttle's deep-space launch capability and would involve cryogenic Centaur upper-stage boosters and a plutonium nuclear-electric generator in the payload bay for the first time, mission elements many safety experts felt exceeded reasonable risk standards. (These hazardous missions were among the first major flights to be taken away from the shuttle following the Challenger accident.)

Failing to meet this schedule, Beggs told *Aviation Week,* "we will give all our friends and enemies an excuse to say 'You really can't depend on the shuttle.' That issue has now become very important. We are going to fly about every month and sometimes twice a month in the next eighteen months, so it's very ambitious."

According to Beggs, the shuttle processing and launch operation at the Kennedy Space Center was the key to this ambitious schedule's success. "We will have to demonstrate a very good and effective turnaround operation," Beggs said. "I think that we can do it, but it will be a demonstration that will show really how good we are."

*　　*　　*

Following the Challenger disaster, the Rogers Commission investigated the nature of this relentless drive to achieve an effective turnaround operation at Kennedy. The commission found that this effort took a toll on the labor force and managers faced with the challenge. Under the pressure to meet the manifest, shift workers, engineers, and project managers were forced to work increasingly long hours. These long hours often lasted for weeks and sometimes for months of consecutive workdays. It became clear to the commission that many key shuttle workers had been worked to beyond reasonable limits.

And the effect of this increased pressure on shuttle processing personnel was inevitable: fatigue bordering on exhaustion, which produced errors in judgment that led to accidents and an eventual breakdown of safety standards.

To get a space shuttle off the ground, you can't just check the oil and kick the tires. An extremely complex operation precedes every launch, a process called the "shuttle flow."

Before the space shuttle, the Kennedy Space Center only processed spacecraft for one-way travel: from the assembly buildings to the launch pad and into space; manned capsules completed the trip by parachute descent and ocean splashdown, but none returned to Cape Canaveral for reuse. With the advent of the shuttle, however, this relatively straightforward process was complicated by several orders of magnitude. The requirements of vehicle assembly still prevailed; the space shuttle's components, consisting of the orbiter, external tank, solid rocket boosters, and the various payloads had to be brought together in an exact sequence. But inspection, refurbishment, and repair—plus the vital process of flight certification of used components—became the added responsibility of KSC's work force.

And these additional duties extended to the multimission schedule of a four-Orbiter fleet. In the past workers and technicians at the Cape could concentrate on one mission at a time. Although flight preparation had been broken into separate flow teams for each Orbiter, certain key technicians and all of the senior management were not able to benefit from this division of labor. By January 1986 these workers and managers were actively involved with the preparation of at least three missions. Plans for the 1986 launch schedule called for parallel operations on Launch Pads 39A and 39B, and a steady "flow" of Orbiters through the Orbiter Processing Facility and the Vehicle Assembly Building. This was the turnaround operation that James Beggs said would demonstrate NASA's mettle.

For the first two years of shuttle operations, this flow was a rather stately procedure, directly supervised by senior NASA managers. But the luxury of slow-paced, management-intensive processing did not fit expanded flight operations. In 1983 the Lockheed Space Operations Company won the contract to manage the entire shuttle processing responsibility, and thus became the central coordinator of the dozen or so prime contractors and sub-contractors involved with space shuttle operations. These original contractors—Rockwell for the Orbiter, Morton Thiokol for the solid rocket boosters, etc.—still carried out their specialized operations, but Lockheed managed the overall process. Efficiency and cost-effectiveness were the goals of this new managerial program; one result of this change was a net reduction of NASA quality control and safety inspectors. Another was a marked increase in overtime, as fewer people struggled to perform more work.

According to Bob Huddleston, a veteran NASA quality control specialist, the situation had become serious before the accident. "I think we tried to push the shuttle into the operational phase so fast that the quality control suffered," he told Bob Drogin of the Los Angeles *Times*. "People were working a couple of months sometimes without a day off, ten and twelve hours a day, and that has to take an effect. That's where quality suffers."

Although both NASA and contractor official statements on shuttle processing spoke in typically optimistic terms that stressed a smooth flow and a meticulously organized "interface," the workers actually involved with this hectic process faced another reality.

The major effort of shuttle processing occurred at five locations: the twin-hangar Orbiter Processing Facility (OPF), the Vehicle Assembly Building (VAB), the KSC Industrial Area, the Launch Control Center, and Launch Pads 39A and 39B.

When an Orbiter landed at the Kennedy field, either from orbit or ferried in from Edwards, it was towed along a concrete taxi road to the squat gray OPF, beside the Vehicle Assembly Building. Inside one of the two so-called high bays the Orbiter was surrounded by intricate scaffolding and the process of postflight inspection was begun. This task involved much more than opening a few inspection panels and checking a handful of items in the main engine compartments, as unrealistic early shuttle advocates had suggested. Every step of the inspection process had to be documented in writing and with a photographic record. NASA's boasts about the operational system notwithstanding, shuttle managers realized they still had a lot to learn about the normal wear and tear on an Orbiter during a shuttle flight.

Almost every inspection revealed unforeseen problems. Technicians found damage to the Orbiter's fragile landing gear brakes and steering system, especially after Kennedy landings increased. Routine ferry operations from Edwards produced costly and time-consuming heat-tile damage. And the intricate plumbing of the main engines soon proved much less robust than earlier predictions. Rocketdyne's troubles with the main engines went back to the beginning of the program. Perhaps because Rockwell had less experience than Pratt and Whitney with the high-pressure turbopumps needed to effect the engine's extreme weight-to-thrust ratio, the years of development were littered with the expensive wreckage of multiple test explosions. Failure of the engines to pass flight certification—and the chronic tile problem—delayed the first shuttle flight by several years. Later, during the regular flight schedule, the high-speed turbopumps simply did not live up to expectations. Ironically Pratt and Whitney's original protest was vindicated fifteen years later. On August 13, 1986, NASA announced that the company had been awarded the contract to produce an alternate and more efficient turbopump, a task it should have been given in the summer of 1971.

Rockwell's problems were not limited to the Rocketdyne main

engines. Cost overruns and delays plagued the development of the Orbiters at Rockwell's Palmdale assembly plant. And according to Dr. Howard Frankel, the former plant physician, drug and alcohol abuse were rampant among workers there while the Orbiters were being assembled. He said that the aerospace union to which the employees belonged protected them from dismissal despite chronic substance abuse and related absenteeism. Heroin, cocaine, and hallucinogens were readily available on the shop floor, he said, as was alcohol. He had to treat one individual working on the Challenger Orbiter who had passed out at his assembly station. The man was "semistuporous" and had a blood-alcohol level of 0.35, more than three times the legal intoxication point.

The company's problems also extended to its subcontractors. NASA audits reveal that one metal fabricating subcontractor had falsified weld X-rays for components of Challenger's airframe. An executive of another subcontractor, Metal Service Center of Atlanta, was convicted in 1984 of substituting ordinary stainless steel for an exotic alloy to be used in an advanced engine.

Although there is no indication of such widespread substance abuse or of fraud among Kennedy workers, there is evidence that safety standards were slipping under the unrelenting pressure. Inspecting and repair—and all too often cannibalizing the shuttle's main engines—accounted for much of the prolonged overtime work in the OPF. One local attorney handling worker compensation cases, David Faherty, described the impact of this demanding work. "There's a common complaint of seventy-five to eighty-hour work weeks," he told the Washington *Post.* "They work around the clock in the Orbiter Processing Facility. There's a lot of overtime pay for people who would like to see a little daylight outside the job and spend some of their overtime money."

And, as Bob Huddleston noted, safety and quality control suffered. In March 1985, a few days before Administrator Beggs spoke about efficient turnaround times, tired, inexperienced workers in the OPF dropped a heavy personnel access crane onto the Orbiter Discovery's payload bay doors, causing $200,000 damage and a launch delay of several weeks.

In the echoing vastness of the VAB, workers soon discovered that the ostensibly straightforward task of "stacking" the solid rocket boosters was an exhausting and frustrating procedure. The booster sections arrived on special railcars from the Morton Thiokol plant in Brigham City, Utah. Each steel casing segment was loaded with 150 tons of explosive rocket fuel. Despite the assurances in Thiokol's contract proposal thirteen years before, the 2,500-mile journey on America's decaying rail system often jolted the huge booster cylinders so badly that workers had considerable difficulties fitting the sections together into a vertical column. And in the nearby solid rocket booster shipment facility, men who had put in excessive overtime also experienced problems handling the refurbished booster sections. In November 1985 a crane operator tried to lift the heavy shipment ring from one of Challenger's booster segments. But the crane's digital strain gauge—a vital piece of equipment for the operator—failed at a crucial moment and the segment fell several feet. The booster section was damaged enough to require its replacement—not an easy task, since the reusable sections were all required to contain solid propellant that had been mixed in the same batch, so that burn would be uniform. Eventually, however, the swap was made, and only a few days of processing time were lost.

In the postmishap investigation, NASA discovered some revealing information. Contrary to regulations, the agency's Quality Control Officer was not at his post during this delicate phase of the operation. The men at the lower end of the operation were not watching the lift in progress. Technicians were distracted, pulling shipping pins from another segment as the booster section was coming down. And the vital Emergency Stop operator was absent from his post.

NASA described this snafu as "a lack of task discipline."

Although NASA did not specifically address the problem of worker fatigue, this factor should have been obvious. The men on the floor were simply numb. What the report did reveal, however, was a sense of fatalism and dejection among the tired workers. "It appears to be nearly unanimous that the Thiokol and Lockheed technicians conceive the cranes to be unreliable," the report added. In other words, the men didn't trust the equipment, but they were too tired and fed up to do anything about their fears.

On the launch pads, preflight inspections of the shuttle's propulsion, flight control, and auxiliary power systems often revealed hardware problems of varying severity. On several occasions the entire vertical assembly of the composite space shuttle, bolted to its massive Mobile Launcher Platform, had to be returned to the VAB, so that repairs could be made within the building's controlled environment.

To exacerbate these problems, NASA was continually modifying flight hardware to reduce weight or improve efficiency and safety. These "mods," as they are called in aviation parlance, often arrived unannounced from Houston or the Marshall Space Flight Center. And the complicated job of inserting the required modification into the tight processing schedule always seemed to fall on the same overworked technicians and managers. To further complicate matters, there was the common annoyance of payload changes brought on by problems with upper-stage satellite boosters or, in some cases, by design problems with the satellites themselves.

Similar growing pains plague airlines, trucking companies, or even city bus operations when new equipment is introduced. But the space shuttle was not a jumbo jetliner or a new air-conditioned bus. The shuttle employed energies far beyond the realm of aviation or surface transportation. The thousands of systems and subsystems of the Orbiter, external tank, and solid rocket boosters, had to achieve a perfect level of reliability under extreme conditions, dependability that truly was "fail-safe." NASA's Flight Critical rating system for hardware components was based on harsh realities: items classed as Criticality 1 simply had to work correctly every flight; there was no backup system. If such a component failed, the results were "catastrophic loss" of the space shuttle and its crew. And in every composite vehicle of the Orbiter, tank, and boosters there were over 700 such Criticality 1 items.

Therefore a stringent system of maintenance-safety accountability involving voluminous documentation was established before the first shuttle ever flew. And for a time during the relatively slow flight schedule between 1981 and 1984, Kennedy's work force was able to meet the demanding requirements of this safety-oriented maintenance. But the flight schedule did not stay slow very long.

And the maintenance and modification load increased in proportion to the number of missions.

According to NASA estimates quoted in the Washington *Post*, every minute of a shuttle mission required three man-years of preparation, and much of this burden fell on the 14,000 contractor and NASA workers and managers at the Cape. More specifically the bulk of this responsibility was shared by a handful of key workers, technicians, and project managers. As the pace of operations increased, team leaders and key technicians found themselves involved in nightmare paper chases, trying desperately to "close out" the detailed work certifications that were the core documents of the maintenance safety system. If a damaged heat tile was replaced, the job itself might take an hour, but acquiring the scores of requisite inspection stamps to close the task's "open paper" might take days.

And much of the actual hardware processing was sequential: the external tank could not be attached to the solid rocket boosters until the boosters themselves were stacked. Therefore days of boredom might alternate with weeks of twelve- or fourteen-hour days.

One KSC engineer who wished to remain anonymous summarized this situation with bitter insight. "The marvelous 'shuttle flow' everybody was crowing about was the worst damned bottleneck I've ever seen in an industrial setting." Reflecting on his own situation, he added this telling remark: "The only dependable *flow* around the OPF was gastric acid . . . big-time Ulcer City."

Although this engineer might have suffered somatic damage from the prolonged stress, this was not the norm among Kennedy workers. The Occupational Medicine office reports no statistically significant increase in stress-related physical afflictions during the increased flight operations in the two years leading up to the Challenger accident. However, according to Bill McGuire, the clinical psychologist who manages the employee counseling program at the Cape, there was a twenty-five percent increase in the number of workers and managers who sought counseling for the effects of stress. But McGuire cautions that this situation might not be related to overwork; the increase coincided with an organized effort on his part to reach out to supervisors and foremen, alerting them to be watchful for signs of stress among their subordinates.

This overwork was not limited to shiftworkers on the hangar floors. Hundreds of NASA managers routinely put in eighty-hour work weeks in the month preceding a mission.

In this stressful atmosphere mistakes and mishaps were bound to increase. And we may never know just how many such processing errors and accidents actually occurred. According to the analysis of Kennedy operations performed by the Rogers Commission, the original lenient accident-reporting policy, under which a worker would not be punished for reporting accidental damage to the Orbiter, was eroded to the point that many technicians feared for their jobs if they admitted damaging the shuttle during processing.

This strained processing operation did not escape the attention of the shuttle's biggest customer, the Air Force. In a classified October 1985 report, the Air Force painted a dismal picture of ground-support efficiency at Kennedy. The document stated that hundreds of maintenance requirements were being skipped, that record-keeping was slipshod, and NASA's spare parts program was a shambles. According to the Air Force, there was also an overall shortage of qualified engineers and technicians at Kennedy to reverse this trend.

On January 6, 1986, only four minutes before the scheduled lift-off of Columbia on the delay-plagued 61-C mission, a console operator in the Launch Control Center misinterpreted a computer message and inadvertently drained off 18,000 pounds—almost twelve percent—of the Orbiter's liquid oxygen propellant. Luckily the draining oxygen triggered a temperature alarm and the launch was scrubbed. NASA's report on the incident states blandly, "Had the mission not been scrubbed, the ability of the Orbiter to reach defined orbit may have been significantly impacted."

In other words the error might have provoked a dangerous in-flight abort.

The Rogers Commission found that operator fatigue was a major factor in the mishap. The men in the Launch Control Center had been on duty for eleven hours, on the third straight twelve-hour night shift, preparing for the mission. To this day, however, senior shuttle officials at Kennedy maintain that an operator should be able to work such shifts without impairment. They point out that this particular console operator had just come off a two-week vacation and was therefore hardly worn to a frazzle by extensive overtime. But according to Dr. Paul Buchanan, director of Kennedy's Biomedical Office, three consecutive twelve-hour night shifts will disorient anybody, *especially* a person who has had two weeks of a normal sleep cycle.

The overworked Kennedy technicians got a respite between the Columbia scrubs of mid-December and the Christmas-New Year holiday. After the first of the year, however, the schedule intensified once again. In January there were a total of five launch pad scrubs and two launches involved in the Columbia and Challenger missions. Three scrubs occurred on weekends. *No* important shuttle technician or manager at Kennedy had a day off in the twenty-seven days preceding Challenger's flight.

Inevitably the pressure took its toll.

Since the Challenger accident, some press reports have created the impression that workers and NASA officials at the Cape were both duplicitous and negligent in the performance of their duties. Ironically the reverse is true. Thousands of men and women charged with the impossible task of flying out the manifest worked themselves beyond exhaustion. If a person did not follow the proper sequence in a complex hardware assembly operation, there was neither malice nor conscious negligence involved. These people were simply tired and their judgment was affected.

Dr. Buchanan stated that overall worker efficiency at the Cape was affected by extended overtime and rotating shift work. Workers who were assigned long stretches of night work before a launch, then were shifted back to days to prepare for the next mission suffered the equivalent of "jet lag" disruption of their circadian rhythms. And the judgment of managers, the experienced men who made the vital launch decisions, was also affected by protracted overtime, Dr. Buchanan stated. The consecutive runs of twelve- to sixteen-hour days, which Kennedy shuttle managers and engineers all stated came with the job, had a definite impact on decision making. "I would think any kind of decision would suffer," from such overwork, Dr. Buchanan said. Cumulative lack of sleep, as occurred before both the Discovery 61-C flight and the Challenger launch, was a subtle enemy of sound judgment. The managers might *feel* in control, Buchanan said, "but that does not mean you are functioning at anywhere near your optimal capacity. You more than likely are not. And it can affect the decisions you make."

But NASA managers remained optimistic right up to the violent termination of Challenger's flight, that frigid January morning. Nineteen eighty-six, the press releases all proclaimed, was going to be the agency's most ambitious year.

PART II

COUNTDOWN

THE "SPELLBOUND" PRESS

Thursday, January 23, was a day of bright sun at Cape Canaveral. A mild sea breeze moved across the lagoons; the sky was wide, cloudless. This was winter Florida at its most benevolent. On such shirt-sleeve January afternoons, it was hard for the reporters assembling at the Cape to remember the brown slush and frozen potholes they had left behind in the North. Everything looked perfect for the launch on Saturday.

But the journalists arriving at the press mound that afternoon were greeted with disappointing news. The Challenger flight, which had been delayed twice in the past week—from the twenty-third to Saturday, the twenty-fifth—had been slipped yet again. The new launch date was now Sunday, January 26, at nine thirty-six in the morning. The NASA press release on the latest slip cited bad weather forecasts at the Kennedy launch site on Saturday, and at the primary Transatlantic Abort Landing site, the so-called "TAL." A weather front was expected to pass through the Cape on Saturday, bringing rain, but better conditions were predicted for Sunday morning.

The reporters milling around the geodesic dome that was KSC's futuristic press site accepted the news with varying degrees of equanimity. There was a mix of old space hands and new people covering this Teacher-in-Space mission. The oldtimers bantered back and forth in NASA jargon, exchanging bewildering acronyms such as "RTLS" and "TDRS deploy" just to keep the newcomers suitably impressed. The press corps might have been mildly irritated by the delay. But none of the experienced reporters (this author included) doubted the veracity of the Public Affairs press release. The press was in the habit of believing NASA, a pattern that went back twenty-five years for the most experienced reporters. They had no way of guessing that there were other, more pressing, concerns than threatened sandstorms at the West African TAL abort site shaping the decision to delay Challenger's launch yet again.

Months later the Rogers Commission would give the actual reasons for the delays: "On January 22, 1986, the Program Requirements Change Board first slipped the launch from January 23 to January 25. That date subsequently was changed to January 26, 1986, primarily because of Kennedy work requirements produced by the late launch of mission 61-C."

The "Kennedy work" of which the Commission spoke was the cannibalization of the Orbiter Columbia out at Edwards and the installation of these used parts aboard Challenger. Had the launch date not been slipped, the Mission Management Team never could have successfully completed the mandatory flight readiness checks at the formal L-1 review. But as we will see, NASA Public Affairs was not accustomed to volunteering such embarrassing information, and the veteran space press corps was not used to asking probing questions.

*   *   *

On the KSC press mound, the Mission Clock silently flashed through the forty-three-hour countdown. There would be twenty-eight hours of planned hold time in the countdown process. And after these holds, if the weather forecast was accurate (and the harried last-minute installation of spare parts was successfully completed without damaging Challenger as she stood on the launch pad), the countdown would resume Saturday night at the T-11 hours mark. Lift-off was scheduled for 9:37 on Sunday morning, although the Public Affairs office was quick to point out that that was just the beginning of the three-hour launch window.

The chronic flight delays of the past year had been popular sniping targets for the media, so now NASA made less of a fetish of "on time" lift-offs. Actual scrubs and mission cancellations, of course, were another matter. The KSC Public Affairs people were sensitive about the record number of scrubs and delays that had plagued Columbia's Bill Nelson junket two weeks earlier. Once more the media had derided NASA's operational ability: first the launch was delayed six times, then the landing was scheduled and canceled on three successive days. Such unpredictability upset magazine editors and television news producers, and the KSC officials were convinced that these news executives had allowed their ire to color the tone of the coverage.

But the 61-C mission was finally over, and the countdown to the Challenger Teacher-in-Space flight appeared to be proceeding well. Public Affairs now began its standard ritual of media events, photo opportunities, and press briefings designed to focus national attention on the upcoming flight. Over the course of twenty-four successful space shuttle missions, NASA's Public Affairs professionals had perfected this process to a fine degree of orchestration. NASA always brought in an extra complement of Public Affairs officers from Washington and Houston and assigned agency retirees to assist the KSC press office in catering to the assembled media.

The press site offered a very efficient photo and videotape reproduction service. Public Affairs provided a variety of guided tours of the launch pad and VAB areas, and the Xerox machines behind the Press Dome counter buzzed with a steady stream of news updates, most conveniently long enough to be read verbatim in a forty-second stand-up TV spot. On T-1 day, Public Affairs always scheduled an elaborate series of press briefings that detailed every aspect of the mission and culminated in the formal Prelaunch Briefing at which the reporters met with Jesse W. Moore, the Associate Administrator for Space Flight, the launch directors, and an Air Force meteorologist. These briefings were broadcast by the agency's own satellite television network to all the NASA centers, so that reporters across the country could also question the experts.

This was high-tech press agentry and it worked. Covering a shuttle flight, you always felt vaguely *managed,* especially when you stopped to consider that NASA ground rules forbade reporters from scheduling their own interviews with the actual "program" people. All such contact had to be scheduled by Public Affairs. The elaborate security system at the Cape also made unauthorized meeting with engineers, managers, and technicians next to impossible; a reporter simply could not drive up to the center headquarters building or the VAB and button-hole a program person. The press depended on the good faith of NASA to spread the word.

The agency's reputation for openness was unique among government bureaucracies. And the bewildering technical nature of the shuttle program, combined with the undeniable record of success, had convinced most reporters that the shuttle's operational development was proceeding more or less on schedule, without insurmountable hardware or management problems. Most important, few journalists questioned the space shuttle's fundamental safety. After years of briefings and press releases, they truly did believe that the shuttle's redundant systems had produced "fail-safe" reliability.

Even thoroughly professional veterans such as John Noble Wilford, Pulitzer Prize winning science writer of the New York *Times,* were gullible supporters of the agency. "There is no question that the press was somewhat lulled by the many successes of NASA," Wilford later admitted. "The press somehow came to believe that NASA was pretty-nigh infallible and took the shuttle program too much for granted. I plead guilty to that."

For what it's worth, so does the author of this book.

Indications of this general press credulity could be seen in both the print and electronic media, ranging from public broadcasting, to network television, to the country's leading magazines and newspapers. The average journalist working the space beat was seduced by the glamor of the program and apparent candor of NASA officials.

The shuttle's obvious technical growing pains, such as the chronic tile problems, hazardous landing gear malfunctions and unpredictable performance of the main engines, had been widely reported, but these reports were always tempered by the optimism of the shuttle managers. And none of these reports prompted a single follow-up investigation. In many ways the press had become a NASA cheering section.

In a harsh but accurate analysis of the NASA-media relationship in the *Columbia Journalism Review* (appropriately entitled

"NASA and the Spellbound Press"), William Booth details the media's infatuation with the space shuttle, which lasted over a decade. He correctly points out the difficulty reporters faced trying to investigate a complex technical problem without the aid of whistle-blowers in NASA or among the contractors.

Booth also focuses on the media's love affair with the man-in-space adventure. Shuttle flights were, in fact, thrilling to observe; the press began to see itself as *participants* in the adventure. And the undeniable success of twenty-four shuttle flights eclipsed the near disasters that almost befell several. "Dazzled by the space agency's image of technological brilliance," Booth wrote, "space reporters spared NASA the thorough scrutiny that might have improved chances of averting a tragedy—through hard-hitting investigations drawing Congress's wandering attention to the issue of shuttle safety."

But perhaps Booth has not fully considered the role of NASA's bureaucratic evasiveness, often reaching duplicity, in the overall issue of press credulity. In retrospect it now becomes obvious that NASA officials were often as devious with the media as they were with Congress. A prime example occurred in the Postlaunch Press Briefings following the 51-D and 51-I launches in April and August, 1985. Both these missions were launched in marginal weather conditions, with overcast and rain in the area. Discovery's 51-D flight carried Senator Jake Garn on the first Congressional space junket in April; and Discovery was also the Orbiter for the August 51-I mission. Both flights had been delayed: the April mission by the embarrassing crane accident in the Orbiter Processing Facility and the summer flight by a weather scrub and a frustrating last minute computer failure. Both missions occurred during the period Administrator Beggs had declared vital to proving NASA's mettle: its ability "to fly out that manifest."

Obviously NASA management was eager to get these two missions launched. But no one at the Press Site expected Discovery to fly on the threatening morning of April 12, 1985. There was a solid overcast above the Cape and the assembled reporters could hear Chief Astronaut John Young report rain, as he flew the prelaunch weather runs with the Shuttle Training Aircraft. Yet with just fifty-five seconds remaining in that day's launch window (and NASA's impatient Administrator James Beggs aiding the "team" decision in the Launch Control Center), the countdown was resumed and Discovery was launched through the overcast.

At the postlaunch briefing, the press at the Cape and "on the loop" in Houston relentlessly probed Launch Director Bob Sieck about the weather conditions. Had NASA, the reporters demanded, stretched its famous fail-safe flight rules; had they bent the sacred Launch Commit Criteria to get this mission off despite the rain? Sieck and Shuttle Operations Director Tom Utsman fielded each question with aplomb, often escaping into technological culs-de-sac to avoid direct answers, leaving the reporters stymied.

The questioning focused on the rain's impact on a Return to Launch Site Abort, the so-called "RTLS." Viewed from the press grandstand, it was obvious that NASA was launching the Discovery into a menacing and turbulent overcast. Worse, there was moderate rain in the area that would have damaged the Orbiter's delicate heat tiles in the event of an RTLS abort. Theory held that such an abort would save an Orbiter that lost power in one or two main engines early in the flight. In this emergency procedure, the commander jettisons the external tank after the fuel is expended and flies back to the Kennedy landing field. But most astronauts admitted that an RTLS was a demanding—perhaps too demanding—piece of flying that would require optimum conditions to pull off safely.

And the shuttle's crew simply could not carry out the tricky maneuver in the rain; nor could the shuttle be safely launched through rain clouds. Rain damage to the Orbiter's "TPS" or Thermal Protection System—could so badly pit the soft tiles that the shuttle might be out of service for weeks. At those speeds the raindrops struck the silicate tiles like steel shot. If the shuttle were exposed to rain for a long period, the eroded wing and control surface tiles would render the Orbiter unflyable; it would crash far short of the landing field. This remained a major concern on each shuttle mission.

So the press corps probed and harried the two complacent managers. Would the rain in the area have precluded a safe RTLS? Sieck and Utsman admitted that there would have been "some" heat tile damage, if Discovery had had to abort and return to Kennedy. But Sieck dismissed out of hand the possibility of an unsafe RTLS. The launch decision had been a "judgment call," influenced only by "how much tile refurbishment you're willing to take at the end of the mission." In other words there was a cost consideration, but no true safety issue.

The two managers repeatedly referred to John Young's weather reconnaissance report as the true indication that no rules had been broken or safety standards compromised. The implication was clear: Young, the crusty old Chief Astronaut, who had flown every type of spacecraft since Gemini days, would never make a call that would jeopardize one of his crews in any way whatsoever. But under pressure Sieck admitted that John Young actually did not make the final launch-weather decision himself but had only one of "several inputs."

The press grilling went on for thirty-five straight minutes, and the two NASA officials continued to stonewall. Finally this reporter asked Sieck if he would have permitted a scheduled *landing* in the weather conditions that had prevailed at launch. Obviously an RTLS and a landing amounted to the same thing. Sieck hedged. That, he said, would have been a "tough decision," dependent on many factors.

Four months later Discovery was launched under even more threatening conditions. Again the press grilled Bob Sieck on the safety issue, once more focusing on the question of RTLS capability. As in April, Sieck maintained the facade that no flight-safety compromises had been made. The press pushed hard, but at the end of the day, the media only had its collective judgment versus the seemingly frank assessment of an experienced senior shuttle manager.

After the Challenger accident, however, the press had other, more honest sources. John Young eventually discussed the actual weather conditions for the 51-D launch. Captain Young described flying through "pinhead type" rain at the bottom of an overcast that went from twelve to thirty-two thousand feet. If there were bigger raindrops and stronger turbulence in that overcast, both the ascent and the RTLS capability would have been seriously compromised. He reported these conditions to the weather team on the ground and was assured that the overall weather situation permitted a launch.

But Young was still unhappy. "So then I got back," he explained, "and asked the weather people, 'How did you know those drops were going to stay small?' And they said, 'We didn't.' To me, that was a *very* risky situation. If I had it to do all over again, I would have scrubbed."

And Young was even more damning in his reassessment of the 51-I launch decision, in which he was once more the weather observer. During the bitter fallout from the Challenger disaster, Young wrote a scathing memorandum on the lax flight safety generated by launch pressure. His summary of problems was entitled "Examples of Uncertain Operational and Engineering Conditions or Events Which We 'Routinely' Accept Now in the Space Shuttle Program."

The second item on his list concerned the Discovery launch of August 1985. There was rain and turbulence in the two cloud decks above the RTLS runway, Young stated. Aerodynamic drag resulting from tiles damaged in this rain could have severely limited Discovery's ability to maneuver in the storm's turbulence. This could have caused the loss of the "vehicle and the crew."

Once more Young was ignored by the weather team, and once more the shuttle was launched through less than marginal conditions. A wild gamble had been taken and the press was cynically deceived.

There were no whistle-blowers. Before the Challenger accident, John Young kept his information about flight safety to himself. No one understood the increasingly dangerous risks being taken as the flight rate increased in 1985. Reporters still included such bromides as "routine access to space" in their stories; they dutifully cut-and-pasted the NASA press releases into their work. So mundane had shuttle flights become that most of the veteran space shuttle press corps was not even at Cape Canaveral for the Challenger Teacher-in-Space mission. They were out at the Jet Propulsion Laboratory in Pasadena, covering the story of the Voyager spacecraft's Uranus flyby. Ironically a supposedly pedestrian unmanned planetary probe had upstaged the glorious space shuttle.

For the first time in twenty-five shuttle missions, the three big television networks had no plans for live coverage of the launch.

But the touchstone of press credulity lay in their own eagerness to fly aboard the shuttle. To a person, every reporter (including this author) regularly covering the space shuttle had applied for the Journalist-in-Space project. Each one wanted to be the journalist who climbed aboard Challenger that coming September and rose above the column of flame into the black mystery of space, dreams of Pulitzers and Emmy Awards dancing in his head.

In all the millions of words the media devoted to the space shuttle over fifteen years, there is no mention whatsoever of dangerous field joints or eroded "O-rings" in the solid rocket boosters. Like the public they ostensibly served, they had been seduced by the myth of the operational space shuttle.

*　　*　　*

That afternoon NASA offered a doubleheader media event at the nearby Shuttle Landing Facility: the return of the Orbiter Columbia from Edwards atop its 747 carrier aircraft, and Astronaut Arrival, a standard milestone on the shuttle crew's ritual progress toward the launch. Like kids on a field trip, reporters assembled at the press site and filed aboard school buses for the short ride to the field.

No one on the buses appreciated the bitter irony of the situation; no one then knew how desperately NASA managers had fought to prevent Columbia from landing at Edwards, so that its precious spares could be easily transferred to Challenger, and Columbia herself could begin the round-the-clock turnaround race in the OPF for the March ASTRO mission. Nor was anyone aboard the crowded school buses aware that Columbia's brakes had been damaged during the supposedly routine landing on the long Edwards runway. Had Columbia actually landed at the shorter Kennedy field, the slumbering press corps might have had a terrible demonstration of why the brakes were classified "Criticality 1."

The Shuttle Landing Facility, the "SLF" in NASA jargon, was a giant slab of grooved concrete surrounded by subtropical wetlands. Public affairs escorts always announced to tour groups that KSC was a wildlife refuge and that the vast runway had to be checked for sunning alligators before every shuttle landing. That particular bit of lore had appeared in scores of newspaper and television stories. The irony of the Jurassic reptiles menacing the futuristic orbiter was perfect for the gee-whiz journalism that comprised the bulk of shuttle reporting, this author's included. But no reporter was astute enough to note that there had only been five such landings at Kennedy and that each had occurred in the chill dawn, when it was highly unlikely any alligator would be seeking sun. Nor had these complacent reporters followed up on the full reports of a hot internal debate that pitted the Astronaut Corps against the shuttle program managers over the issue of Kennedy landings. The astronauts wanted to stick to Edwards landings until the bugs were removed from the landing gear and brakes; the managers insisted on landing at Kennedy, so that the precious manifest could be met. While the debate raged, the press wrote about sunning reptiles.

The buses deposited the reporters at the end of an asphalt road, near the wide runway. And they waited. Covering any space shuttle activity entailed unpredictably long waits, and the return of Columbia was no exception. The Boeing 747 shuttle transport aircraft was in itself a dependable workhorse, not prone to delays. But the weather between Southern California and Central Florida was the problem. When the Orbiter rode piggyback atop the big jet, it moved through the atmosphere at speeds up to five hundred knots. And the atmosphere often contained rain clouds. However, with Edwards landings the Orbiters had to be returned to Kennedy for refurbishment and launch. So there was always the danger of tile damage.

The Kennedy Space Center is on the coast of Central Florida, an area renowned for its thunderstorms. The region has one of the highest lightning fatality rates in the country. And this was the shuttle's principal base of routine operations.

While the crowd of reporters and cameramen waited in the drowsy sunshine, several wandered over to inspect the shuttle landing caravan, the fleet of specially equipped vehicles that surrounds the Orbiter at the end of its landing roll. This equipment had often been described as the working hardware of a spaceport. There were covered mobile staircases, generators, cherry-picker hydraulic arms with high-tech "sniffers" to sense leaks of toxic gas from the Orbiter's reaction control jets, and even a huge mobile fan to disperse such leaks. At close quarters, however, it became clear that this equipment was hardly the gleaming Star Trek gear one would envision.

Like many of the simpler elements of the overall shuttle operation, the landing caravan had been assembled years before the spacecraft ever flew. The equipment had been ready in the mid-1970s, and was in effect fifteen-year-old technology, frozen in time, stuck out on this giant landing field, waiting for the space shuttle to reach its operational promise. The harsh sun and salt air of Cape Canaveral had had their way with the old flatbed trucks and pickups of the landing caravan. There were rust and dents, blistered paint and frayed, bleached-out duct tape. The surrounding concrete was ringed with ancient oil stains.

The caravan evoked a volunteer fire department, not the Free World's spaceport.

*   *   *

Columbia finally arrived around three. With ponderous grace the massive transport plane touched down at the end of the runway and rolled right past the assembled press. Columbia was perched high on the Boeing's back, like a hawk with folded wings stealing a ride on a dull and plodding goose. Certain of the photographers in the crowd voiced earthier analogies involving barnyard miscegenation.

This was the first Orbiter to fly, the grandmother of the fleet, but its checkerboard tile skin looked new, unpitted. There was no sign that it had just been ferried back from California after eight days in space. Nor were there clues that it had undergone emergency surgery out in the desert, when the harried technicians from Kennedy had removed the vital spares to be rushed back to the Cape for last-minute installation in Challenger. Once more, the press was seduced by the spectacle and failed to look beneath the surface.

"Hope this weather holds," a photographer said, replacing a

long lens in its battered leather scabbard. "You couldn't ask for better flight conditions."

The reporters nodded, smiling agreement. It was a great afternoon. Soon the crew would arrive, and there would be plenty of sun for the cameras.

THE POLITICS OF SPACE FLIGHT

On this Thursday afternoon, tired men worked inside the Orbiter Challenger installing the final cannibalized parts that had arrived on the T-38 from Edwards. But there were no close-up lenses on the sweating faces of technicians as they performed their awkward surgery. The only television cameras showed the shuttle from a distance, serene, white, seemingly invincible. From this angle the composite stack of Orbiter, external tank, and solid rocket boosters would have been familiar to television viewers around the world, a stock image, the phoenix poised for flight. Few people would have recognized that the shuttle on Pad 39B was a hybrid machine created by a series of political compromises the world had long forgotten.

At three that afternoon Challenger's unusual crew—itself a product of more recent political compromises—joined their spacecraft at the Cape.

The Public Affairs escorts had grouped the press herd at one end of the Mate-Demate tarmac where Columbia sat atop the massive transport aircraft. Like school children the reporters were instructed to stay outside the area cordoned off with yellow rope. Microphones marked the place where the crew would assemble, and there was the normal jostling for position among the still photographers and TV crews.

While the news media waited, a green Huey clattered in to land near the shuttle transport jet. In the helicopter was KSC Security's Reaction Force, an antiterrorist team reputed to be among the best trained and equipped in the country, given that the space shuttle offered such a tempting sabotage target. The first trooper to emerge from the Huey's door was a burly, brush-cut fellow in flak jacket and web gear, clutching a wicked Colt assault rifle. He would have looked at home at Fort Bragg. The team's second member was a strikingly attractive young woman with long blond hair. Although she was armed and equipped like her male colleagues, her unexpected presence intensified the stagey charade ambience that had been building all afternoon. At the yellow cordon, a local photographer grunted. "Wouldn't mind getting a body search from *her.*" A nearby television camerawoman glared in disgust.

This female SWAT team trooper seemed appropriate to the occasion. Two of Challenger's crew were women, another was black, and one was Japanese American. This mix might appear normal today, but only three years before, Dr. Sally Ride had made headlines as the country's first woman in space. In the eyes of millions of Americans, the space shuttle represented an unprecedented opportunity for women and minorities to demonstrate their potential. Before the shuttle, the Astronaut Corps had been the exclusive preserve of the white, male test pilot, made famous by Tom Wolfe. Now almost a third of the shuttle Mission Specialists were women, and several were mothers.

NASA often said that the shuttle would carry America into the bright new future of the twenty-first century. And the American public now accepted minority and women astronauts as a given. The selection of high school teacher Christa McAuliffe to be the first average citizen to fly aboard the shuttle had provoked considerable public interest. Yet few Americans could name any of the women astronauts to follow Sally Ride and Judy Resnik, and the black, Asian, and Hispanic members of the Astronaut Corps were equally obscure.

This anonymity presented a problem for NASA. The more routine the space shuttle became, the less public interest there was. To assure support for the program, NASA was obliged to accept blatant political manipulation of crew assignments that severely upset the carefully orchestrated training schedules. Under Congressional and White House pressure, the Astronaut Corps had been expanded to include bizarre junketeers: the Teacher-in-Space, a senator and a congressman, a Saudi prince, and all the others. People even spoke seriously of singer John Denver being offered a ride.

Still, few reporters (and fewer editors) seemed inclined to investigate the growing scandal of the Payload Specialists, as these guest astronauts were called. Editors wanted human interest and good visuals. NASA was happy to comply.

The quiet afternoon was interrupted by the snarl of jets. Three lean T-38 trainers peeled off to land in close formation on runway 15, then taxied in an arrowhead pattern toward the waiting press. Behind them, NASA Two, the Gulfstream executive jet, set down and trailed the smaller planes. The ritual of Astronaut Arrival had begun.

The T-38s taxied smartly onto the tarmac, their dual canopies open at a jaunty angle, so that the photographers could snap the standard shots of the astronauts in "Right Stuff" flight helmets and parachutes.

The press watched with reverent attention as the crew climbed from the cockpits. Commander Dick Scobee piloted the lead plane, with Mission Specialist Ellison Onizuka in the back seat. Judy Resnik flew behind Shuttle Pilot Mike Smith. The photographers' motor drives whined as Dr. Resnik removed her helmet and her dark hair fell to the shoulders of her blue flight suit. From the third jet, Mission Specialist Ron McNair climbed down with athletic grace. Chief Astronaut John Young remained in the front cockpit of this jet, meticulously writing in his logbook.

This gave the five Challenger crew members the chance to link up and join their two colleagues, Christa McAuliffe and Greg Jarvis, who had flown from Houston aboard the Gulfstream. Now the crew was complete. They formed a loose procession toward the microphones, and the Nikon motor drives whined louder. Astronaut Arrival was a photo opportunity rivaling a royal visit. And certainly no space shuttle crew had ever offered such tempting "visuals."

One of the photographers grinned. "Looks like a war-movie propaganda platoon," he muttered. "Got one of everything."

Only a few people in the crush of eager reporters were old enough to remember the World War Two films in which every bomber crew seemed to embody America's ethnic melting pot.

This was about as heterogeneous a group of Americans as could be assembled aboard the space shuttle. As they waited to speak their brief comments at the microphones, one couldn't help noting just how much these astronauts exemplified the sweeping social changes that had gripped the country during the fifteen years since the shuttle project began.

Dick Scobee, Mike Smith, and Ellison Onizuka were undeniably military aviators; they bore that quiet and precise confidence which comes with years of disciplined effort in an exciting and exacting profession. Unlike earlier generations of astronauts, however, both Scobee and Smith had served combat tours in Vietnam. Their presence on this crew symbolized America's acceptance of its Vietnam experience and of the long war's veterans. Lieutenant Colonel Onizuka's status as a Mission Specialist astronaut exemplified the ethnic diversity of the contemporary officer corps, as well as NASA's eagerness to please its largest single shuttle customer, the Air Force.

Judy Resnik was a quintessential new American woman. Not only was she an electrical engineer, a profession that traditionally did not attract women, but she had a doctorate in this discipline. Just a decade before, the press would have noted that she was divorced; now this was no longer newsworthy. And no one seemed to find it unusual that Ron McNair—a black from a small Deep South town—had earned a doctorate in Physics from MIT.

What was unusual about Greg Jarvis and Christa McAuliffe was their normality. While Scobee and Smith were stamped with that unmistakable "Right Stuff" cachet, Onizuka had the precise calm of a veteran flight test engineer and the three Mission Specialists all projected the physical grace of experienced flight crew, the two Payload Specialists might have been any suburban couple down the block. Greg Jarvis, like most normal American men his age, could have easily lost ten or fifteen pounds. And Mrs. McAuliffe did not exude the thin intensity and discipline of Judy Resnik or Sally Ride.

Christa McAuliffe was a little chubby, there was no arguing that. Her appearance perfectly matched her identity: a beaming, gregarious wife and mother who taught high school social studies in a small New England city. When she approached the microphones, she literally bounced with excitement.

There was a masquerade quality to Christa this afternoon, as if she was dressing up as an astronaut for Halloween. Her shoes set her apart from her crewmates. The "real" astronauts wore black, shin-high flight boots. Christa McAuliffe wore stubby gray running shoes. Her sky-blue flight suit looked new, slightly baggy, the sleeves too long. Her auburn hair hung in girlish curls. She grinned, and all the reporters grinned back with warm affection. They recognized that she was one of them, an average person elevated by chance to unusual prominence.

"No teacher," she bubbled, "has *ever* been better prepared to teach a lesson."

The families filed around the back of the Gulfstream jet to join the crew for more pictures. Jane Smith held a bunch of bright flowers; her stylish high heels wobbled in the grooved tarmac pavement. Cheryl McNair embraced her husband with unfeigned warmth: the crew had been training hard the past week, spending more time in the Houston shuttle simulator than at home. This was a valid reunion, conveniently enacted before the whining Nikons and minicams of the assembled press.

But the astronauts knew this scrutiny went with the job. For months before the mission they had made the mandatory public appearances at science fairs and colleges, at contractor dinners and hometown celebrations. The space shuttle might have become mundane in the eyes of many Americans, but astronauts were still good for NASA public relations. Christa's husband, Steve McAuliffe, carried a bunch of New Hampshire T-shirts, which he proceeded to pass out to his wife's crewmates. Clowning for the press, Dick Scobee held a T-shirt up to his broad chest and joked that he'd need a larger size. The cameras buzzed and clacked. Everyone smiled in the sunlight. Watching this wholesome tableau, it was easy to rely on NASA press releases.

* * *

But as with the space shuttle itself, there were hidden stresses and tensions beneath the surface of this smiling crew. They had all worked hard to be here, and, with the exception of Dick Scobee and Mike Smith, each crew member's assignment was the result of political considerations transcending their individual skills and experience.

In the case of Judy Resnik, gender was the key. Although she would never publicly admit that the feminist groundswell of the sixties and seventies played a major role in her selection as an astronaut in 1978, Dr. Judith Resnik was clearly a beneficiary of this social revolution. Her class of astronauts was the first to include women, and each of the six female members brought with her such obviously superior credentials—medical, science, and engineering doctorates, for example—that they were briefly idealized by the news media. They continued to receive more media scrutiny than their male colleagues; their dating habits were considered suitable subjects for articles in serious newspapers and magazines, as were their tastes in clothes and food. In short, the first group of American women astronauts, to which Judy Resnik and Sally Ride belonged, was subjected to the same vapid prying by the collective American *paparazzi* as the first male astronauts, eighteen years earlier.

This media attention engendered pressures within the group. The women were serious, mature professionals, not talk-show hostesses or fashion models. NASA Public Affairs saw in the women astronauts a rich resource for bolstering public support for the space shuttle. And the breathless media debate over the selection of America's first woman in space served the goals of Public Affairs. But this needless pressure grated on the women themselves. Inevitably factions formed and internal politics mushroomed within the Astronaut Office.

Resnik found the process very distasteful. She was an intelligent, hardworking, and deeply private person who eschewed the facile glitter of the thirty-second TV interview. When Dr. Sally Ride was selected as the first woman to fly, Judy Resnik was relieved to be spared the hysterical probing by the media that Dr. Ride had to endure. After that, Resnik became increasingly reluctant to accommodate the requests for personal appearances and interviews.

She saw herself as a scientist, not a walking, talking publicity stunt. And as the politicians forced open the ranks of the Astronaut Corps, she became even more opposed to the use of the shuttle for publicity purposes. Referring to the increasing intrusion by nonastronauts, she once voiced her frustration to a close friend: "What are we going to *do* with these people?"

Now as she spoke her brief piece to the press, her manner was serious, almost stern. This would be her second flight after eight years of training. She stressed the importance of the TDRS satellite she would help deploy and betrayed nothing of her excitement. For Dr. Judith Resnik, the space shuttle was a serious endeavor, not a toy.

Ron McNair and Ellison Onizuka were both too intelligent and sophisticated to deny that racial considerations had played a key role in their selection as Mission Specialists. They also felt the tension in the Astronaut Corps when they were named to their first, then their second shuttle flight assignments. Their advantageous status as equal-opportunity pioneers continued beyond selection, to the distress of some of their colleagues. No one, however, ever accused Onizuka or McNair of personally seeking advantage because of his race.

But they were also both acutely aware that their assignments imposed unusual obligations. Ron McNair was from South Carolina; El Onizuka was raised in a Japanese-Hawaiian community in the sugar fields of the Kona Coast. McNair had transcended the cultural poverty of segregated schools to receive a doctorate in physics from MIT. His wife Cheryl and their two small children, Joy and Reggie, were more important to him than the "Today" program or the Phil Donahue show. For McNair, a deacon at his Baptist church in Houston, traditional morality offered the best channel for his message: black families staying together and working hard could overcome the still-prevailing racism in America and enter what he called the "modern age" of opportunity.

Lieutenant Colonel Ellison Onizuka used a similarly traditional conduit to carry his message of expanding opportunity. He grew to maturity in a small farming town called Keopu on the big island of Hawaii. There scouting offered one of the few outlets to the wider world beyond the sugar fields. And Ellison Onizuka excelled in the discipline of scouting, rising to the rank of Eagle Scout in only four years. Much later, as he advanced in the demanding discipline of flight-test engineering at Edwards Air Force Base, he would credit his earlier scouting experience for giving him his sense of direction.

Throughout his eight years with NASA, Onizuka made repeated visits to his home community to work with local scouting and 4-H groups. He was a proud American Air Force officer and astronaut. In one generation he had transcended the wartime contempt and suspicion to which his people were subjected following the attack on Pearl Harbor. Like McNair, he felt an obligation to the young people of his home community.

Another, less obvious, political agenda had assured the selection of Greg Jarvis. By 1983 it became obvious to NASA's leadership that the "operational" space shuttle was not going to meet its increasingly ambitious schedule of commercial satellite launches. The agency then decided to help promote satellite-launching business through other means than a firm flight schedule and subsidized rates. One method chosen was to appeal to corporate pride by offering prestigious Payload Specialist assignments to the agency's best—and most cooperative—customers. This lure proved very attractive, and several satellite corporations and national consortia applied, including the Arab Satellite Communications organization, the Mexican Morelos Satellite group, RCA, and the Hughes Aircraft Company's Space and Communications group.

Greg Jarvis became the Hughes Payload Specialist in July 1984 and was named to the 51-D Discovery mission, scheduled for launch in March 1985. As with other guest Payload Specialists, Jarvis soon realized that his assignment was largely symbolic: he would have nothing to do with the actual deployment of the Hughes Leasat satellite. But the color photos of him, weightless on the shuttle middeck, watching the big Hughes satellite spin away into the sunlit vacuum, would make a nice addition to the company's annual report.

He also realized that—like the other customers' Payload Specialists—his supernumerary status was technically usurping the place of a career Mission Specialist astronaut who might have been training for a shuttle assignment for six or seven years. The simple fluid dynamics experiment designed to test the properties of liquid fuels, which he was given as his flight task, could have easily been conducted by a regular astronaut. But Jarvis was very popular among the astronauts, and no one ever faulted him for his privileged status.

As Greg Jarvis discovered, however, being assigned to a mission and actually flying were two different things. After several months of training with Commander Dan Brandenstein's crew, the supposedly "fixed" flight manifest went through yet another spasm: the Commander, Pilot, and Mission Specialists slots were reassigned, but the two Payload Specialist slots were still open. One went to McDonnell-Douglas Engineer Charlie Walker, who operated the company's innovative CFES orbital pharmaceutical purification equipment. It would have made sense for Greg Jarvis to keep the second slot, since one of the mission's principal payloads was a Hughes satellite.

But politics intervened. NASA gave in to the lobbying of Senator Jake Garn, and this chairman of an important Senate subcommittee secured the second Payload Specialist assignment on the 51-D mission. Privately Hughes executives were furious, but they held their ire in check, fearing Garn's wrath. After the Challenger accident, however, the Rogers Commission specifically cited the "late addition" of Senator Jake Garn and Congressman Bill Nelson among the problematic changes in the 1985 manifest that upset the overly ambitious flight schedule.

These problems included changes to flight software and wasted simulator training time, which had to be repeated with the new crew members present. In testimony to the Commission, veteran astronaut Henry Hartsfield spoke with understated bitterness about the impact of such political manipulation of the shuttle flight schedule. When a Payload Specialist was reassigned, his onboard experiment would often be assigned to another flight late in the mission-planning process and upset delicate mass-and-propellant calculations. Such late additions to a mission's cargo and crew, Hartsfield said, changed the computer software that controlled many critical flight functions, including ascent, descent, and abort trajectories. All of this new software had to be tested by the flight crew in the shuttle simulator. When a politician bullied his way on board a flight late in the mission training process, it upset this intricate process. "We have had cases," he testified, "where the actual flight software was delivered within a week of the flight." He added that many astronauts felt this was "just too doggone close to the flight to see the final software."

Other veteran astronauts such as Paul Weitz and John Young echoed Commander Hartsfield's concern in their testimony to the Commission.

Privately John Young said that the entire space shuttle simulator system had "gone downhill" in the sustained rush to meet the increased 1985 and 1986 flight schedules. He said it was common practice for the simulator software to be inadequate for specific mission situations. "We would get in there, and they would give you this green card (to place over an instrument) and say this is what you're supposed to see on the scope." Young admitted that the primary mission simulator in Houston has never had a proper simulation program for every shuttle main-engine contingency. Given the complexity of this system, Young stated, a revamped simulator would require a real infusion of money. "You've got to have more resources to do more work. That's just common sense. But it certainly wasn't looking that way in 1985. We were just going like gangbusters. It looked to me like an impossible job."

Greg Jarvis was bumped not once but twice by political shuttle junketeers. When he arrived back at Houston to begin training for his new mission—the 61-C flight—he learned that Congressman Bill Nelson (whom "the Lord" reportedly had destined for space flight) had taken the open Payload Specialist slot. However, Jarvis was given a compensation, a definite assignment to the 51-L flight in January 1986.

The background of Teacher-in-Space Christa McAuliffe's assignment was even more politically charged. The Reagan administration, with the full concurrence of NASA, originally planned to fly an American journalist as the first private-citizen "spaceflight participant" aboard the shuttle. But then the 1984 election campaign intervened. Although Reagan campaign strategists felt confident that the President and Vice President Bush held a considerable lead over the Mondale-Ferraro ticket, Republican Party polls showed the administration vulnerable on several issues. And one of the most important was education.

According to a former Democratic National Committee speech-writer, Mondale planned to hammer hard on the administration's education record, in the hope of wooing young middle-class parents and women voters away from Reagan. Mondale began his attack early in the campaign. On April 26 he campaigned across Texas, a state proud of its schools and universities. Mondale pounded Reagan's mediocre support for public education, accusing the President of "second-rate leadership" that produced "an appalling record" of educational failure, the inevitable effect of an "antiintellectual administration."

At several campaign stops, Mondale distributed what he called his "report card" on Reagan's educational policy. The President got F's in all subjects except sports and dramatics. Predictably the college audiences responded with standing ovations, giving Mondale one of his few obvious tactical victories on the spring campaign trail. The White House was interested but not yet concerned.

On the Fourth of July the National Education Association, the nation's largest and most militant teachers' union, met in Mondale's hometown of Minneapolis. The meeting resembled a political convention, with banners and placards saluting Mondale's education policy and the Democratic Party. The NEA's formal endorsement of Mondale's candidacy made him sound like the savior of America's public school system. The White House was concerned but not yet worried.

Then, in early August, the news media made much of a Gallup Poll that showed a large majority of Americans believed Walter Mondale would be more likely than President Reagan to improve public education. Clearly the Democrats' strategy was working; they finally had an issue on which they could attack the popular President. Now the White House was worried.

It took the Reagan administration less than a month to counterattack, and when they did, they advanced on a wide front, all guns blazing. Friday August 27 was Education Day in the Reagan reelection campaign. Someone in the campaign committee decided that Washington's Jefferson Junior High School would be the perfect place for Reagan's big speech on education, apparently forgetting that it was summer and that there would therefore be no kids around. In any case, enough kids were reassembled from wherever they were spending their summer vacations to hear the President speak eloquently about his administration's continual support for "excellence" in public education. That afternoon the President named new members to his Advisory Council on Education. The White House press release on the new panel made it clear that Selma Morrell, a black woman appointee, had served "as a member of the National Education Association."

As a final volley in the President's counterattack, he made public the choice of America's first citizen passenger on the space shuttle. "Until now," the President said, playing out the announcement to build excitement, "we hadn't decided who the first citizen passenger would be. But today I'm directing NASA to begin a search in all of our elementary and secondary schools and to choose as the first citizen passenger in the history of our space program one of America's finest—a teacher.

"When the shuttle lifts off," President Reagan added, "all of America will be reminded of the crucial role that teachers and education play in the life of our nation. I can't think of a better lesson for our children and our country."

One year later, New Hampshire high school teacher Christa McAuliffe was selected from over 11,000 applicants to be America's Teacher-in-Space. The official White House announcement pointedly noted that she was a member of the National Education Association.

*   *   *

With Mrs. McAuliffe's selection, of course, came the status as a media superstar. She was photographed, videotaped, interviewed, and carted around parade routes and conventions almost continuously during the next six months. Simultaneously she was obliged to undergo Payload Specialist training at the Johnson Space Center in Houston.

There were the inevitable strains and stress of dislocation from her family; her husband, Steve, a successful attorney in Concord, New Hampshire, was given the full responsibility for their two children, nine-year-old Scott and Caroline, five. Christa became an infrequent commuter between New England and Texas.

The pace and complexity of training increased as launch date approached. Ideally a shuttle crew might total four: the Commander and Pilot to fly the spacecraft and two Mission Specialists to work the Remote Manipulator System robot arm during satellite deployment. This size crew could be safely seated on the flight deck, and the problems of "emergency egress" during aborts, ditching, or landing mishaps were greatly simplified. But with a crew of seven seated on two decks, considerable simulator time was required so that each member could learn by rote—and demonstrate that learning to the trainers' satisfaction—the complex sequence of several emergency exit procedures.

Although not trained in advanced technology like her crewmates, Christa McAuliffe was a hard worker and slowly mastered all the skills needed by a Payload Specialist. She jokingly told a fellow teacher that much of this training consisted of stern admonitions to "never touch these switches," but in reality her final weeks of training were exhausting.

Unfortunately she had to contend with additional pressures throughout her training. Having signed a contract with NASA, she was a de facto civil servant for the duration of her Teacher-in-Space tenure. However, like Sally Ride before her, Christa McAuliffe was also a highly visible role model for American women, especially for American women educators. During the seven months between her selection and the Challenger flight, she was reportedly called on to lend her endorsement to a variety of political causes and to take sides in certain public education issues. Being a naturally open person with an instinctive liberal streak, as well as a highly independent personality, Christa McAuliffe occasionally chafed at NASA's rigid prohibition against "political activity." But she valued her role as an educational pioneer and overcame her natural inclinations in order to accommodate her government sponsors.

*   *   *

When the last photographer and TV camera crew was satisfied with the shots from the Astronaut Arrival photo session, the astronauts and their families waved good-bye and headed for the waiting vans. Away to the west, the sun was setting above the mangrove marsh and palmettos. It had been a perfect afternoon. The assembled reporters were in a jolly mood as the NASA school bus jolted back to the Press Site.

One young woman education writer who was covering her first space shuttle mission was positively beaming. "They were beautiful," she gushed, referring to the crew. "They're just like . . . well, the *best* America can offer."

High on the aluminum cliffs of the VAB, the huge American flag glowed fiercely in the sunset.

The Challenger astronauts (left to right): Christa McAuliffe, Greg Jarvis, Mike Smith, Ron McNair, Ellison Onizuka, Dick Scobee, Judy Resnik.

Vehicle assembly building at the Kennedy Space Center. Mobile launch platform with solid rocket boosters is in the foreground.

Dale Myers, Rockwell's Trojan Horse inside NASA management.

George B. Hardy, Marshall Manager who was "appalled" at Morton Thiokol's recommendation not to launch.

Dr. William R. Lucas, the strong-willed
Director of the Marshall Space Flight Center. "I have never on any occasion reported
to Mr. Aldrich."

Dr. James C. Fletcher, the NASA Administrator most closely connected to the shuttle's past and future. President Reagan
reappointed him to head NASA once
again after the accident.

James M. Beggs, the NASA Administrator
who championed the "operational" Space
Shuttle. He urged NASA to "fly out that
manifest."

Jesse W. Moore, NASA's Associate Administrator, who made the final decision to launch Challenger. "The thought did not cross my mind that, for example, Rockwell was saying 'no go.'"

Arnold D. Aldrich, Director of the National Space Transportation System, who voted to launch Challenger over Rockwell's objections.

Lawrence B. Mulloy, Director of Marshall's Solid Rocket Booster Project. "My God, Thiokol, when do you want me to launch, next April?"

Stanley R. Reinartz. "For better or worse, I did not perceive any clear requirement for interaction with Level II..."

Ice on Launch Pad 39B, January 28, 1986.

Two views of Challenger on the launch pad. The picture on the left was taken .033 seconds before the picture on the right. The growing puff of dark smoke from the aft field joint of the righthand solid rocket booster is evident.

Challenger is launched on its final mission, 11:38 A.M., January 28, 1986.

THE MEN FROM MARSHALL

The predicted weather front did not pass through the Cape on Saturday morning. By nine thirty-seven, the launch time originally scheduled before the latest slip, there were widely separated thunderheads in the area but no overcast or precipitation. Half an hour later, however, one of these thunderclouds had drifted over the Shuttle Landing Facility and was dumping rain on the runway. Two miles away the VAB stood beneath a blue sky; three miles farther seaward, Challenger gleamed in bright sunlight. This isolated rain did not interfere with activities on the launch pad.

But the rain did throw a kink in the travel plans of the ten-man delegation arriving that morning from the Marshall Space Flight Center. The Marshall group, headed by Center Director Dr. William R. Lucas, was due to land at the shuttle strip in time to attend the L-minus One Day review scheduled to begin at eleven in the KSC headquarters building. Shortly before landing, however, their NASA propjet was diverted to Patrick Air Force Base, twenty miles down the coast. Cecil Houston, Marshall's resident manager at the Cape, had been waiting at the shuttle strip to meet the group with a small fleet of rented cars.

The plans had originally called for each Marshall project manager and engineer to load his bags in his car and proceed independently to the meeting, then on to his local project office or his room at the Holiday Inn in Merritt Island. It was a system that Dr. Lucas had begun early in the shuttle flights. Among other activities, Marshall's people managed the space shuttle's entire propulsion system: main engines, external tank, and solid rocket boosters. Once the L-One review was completed, their separate responsibilities would lead them in different directions. By flying on the NASA plane and being met with rental cars, no one would waste time, an important consideration for Dr. Lucas.

Now Cecil Houston had to rush off to Patrick in his red NASA van to meet the diverted Marshall aircraft. The L-One review would begin promptly at eleven. Dr. Lucas valued promptness and would not accept tardiness in subordinates. One can imagine, therefore, that normally easygoing Cecil Houston ignored the speed limit as he sped down Route 1 toward Patrick. Most people who worked at Marshall would gladly accept a speeding ticket in lieu of a dressing-down from the director. Dr. Lucas liked to do business with precision, a trait he had displayed working under Wernher von Braun when Lucas was a young staff member on the Army's guided-missile development team in the early 1950s. And when Dr. William R. Lucas had a preferred manner of doing business, his subordinates at Marshall made whatever arrangements necessary to accommodate his wishes.

Dr. Lucas had been Marshall's director since 1974 and the deputy center director for three years before that. All told, he had served almost thirty-five years in Huntsville, beginning when the facility was called the Redstone Arsenal and continuing for all its years as the Marshall Space Flight Center. In that time he had helped supervise the development of the Saturn moon rockets, the lunar rovers, Skylab, and of course the complex propulsion system of the space shuttle. Over the three decades of this service, he had received practically every medal and citation NASA could award for distinguished achievement. If NASA awarded knighthoods, Dr. Lucas would have been named a Peer of the Realm.

Like many aristocrats, however, Dr. Lucas had a certain authoritarian manner; the Washington *Post* called him "strong-willed"; reporters from other newspapers were far less charitable, privately describing him as a "tyrant." But everyone who knew him did agree that the sprawling, complex operation at Huntsville bore the stamp of Dr. Lucas's personal leadership. Ironically and contrary to popular press myth, Lucas had not acquired his "Teutonic" management style from Wernher von Braun and the "Hunsville" Germans; in fact many observers saw Lucas's leadership style as the exact opposite of von Braun's. Where von Braun had been a charismatic visionary who instilled loyalty through personal magnetism, Lucas was a coldly distant (and often rigid) master bureaucrat. He believed in doing things according to regulations. Interpreting the regulations was his personal prerogative.

According to one veteran industry observer in Huntsville, who wishes to remain anonymous, a clear indication of Dr. Lucas's leadership style could be found in an incident that had occurred a few years after Lucas became Marshall director. This incident has acquired certain mythic proportions, but the actual occurrence has been confirmed by a variety of reliable sources. On a warm afternoon Dr. Lucas glanced out of his ninth-floor office window and saw two engineers in shirt-sleeves, pitching horseshoes on the shady lawn below. He immediately summoned a subordinate and demanded an explanation. "Those men are on their lunch hour, Dr. Lucas," the man is reported to have replied. "They've finished eating, and they're just relaxing."

"If they've finished eating," Lucas is said to have retorted, "they can get back to work."

Following the horseshoe incident, Dr. Lucas issued a confidential, limited-circulation memorandum to department heads: they were to call in their section chiefs for oral briefings, and in turn these subordinates were to issue the following oral warnings to employees: since regulations called for a thirty-minute lunch break, it was logical to assume that no employee could both eat *and* participate in organized athletic activities within the prescribed period. This was especially true for the activity of jogging; no man could eat, change to jogging togs, run, then shower and change back to office clothes in thirty minutes. Henceforth, Dr. Lucas decreed, any employee seen jogging on his lunch break would be docked time from his annual leave.

According to an experienced Marshall engineer, who also wishes to remain anonymous, another version of the jogging legend holds that Lucas did not want his counterparts from the Army Ballistic Missile Agency to see NASA employees taking time away from the job. Whatever the true motive, the actual ban on jogging has been authenticated.

This edict from the director's office had an immediate result. At a time when other NASA centers were actively encouraging their hard-pressed engineers and managers to take up jogging and lunch-hour sports in order to break the stress of their heavy workloads, Lucas turned the pressure screws even tighter on his employees. But significantly he did so through confidential channels, so that he would not subject himself to outside criticism. Marshall was *his* center; he had served there man and boy, and he knew what was best for his people.

According to other experienced observers (who also desire anonymity), this autocratic leadership style grew over the years to create an atmosphere of rigid, often fearful, conformity among Marshall managers. Unlike other senior NASA officials, who reprimanded subordinates in private, Lucas reportedly used open meetings to scornfully criticize lax performance. And like many demanding task masters, he required absolute personal loyalty.

The leadership situation at Marshall was summed up in an explosive letter signed simply "Apocalypse," which was delivered to Marshall's Inspector General two months after the Challenger accident. The Marshall office sent the letter to the Inspector General at NASA Headquarters in Washington, which forwarded the letter to the Rogers Commission. From the wealth of detail in the letter, "Apocalypse" is clearly an experienced program manager (as he claims) who had suffered for years under Lucas's autocratic rule. And sources on the Rogers Commission cite the letter and the subsequent investigation it provoked as the ultimate cause of the director's resignation. This condemnation is found in the letter's second paragraph:

"The Marshall Space Flight Center is run by one man, William R. Lucas. His style of management can best be described as feudalistic. In his ten year tenure as center director, he has established a personal empire built on the 'good old boy' principle. The only criteria for advancement is total loyalty to this man. Loyalty to country, NASA, the space program, mean nothing. Many a highly skilled manager, scientist, or engineer has been 'buried' in the organization because they underestimated the man's psychopathic reaction to dissent."

This chilling condemnation of Marshall Director William Lucas was independently confirmed by four reliable sources (who must remain anonymous), with collective decades of experience dealing with the man. Dr. Lucas's dictatorial leadership produced obedience but stifled criticism.

Perhaps the most relevant section of this letter to the Challenger accident can be found in this paragraph:

"It has been apparent for some time that the Flight Readiness Review process developed by Lucas and other senior NASA managers simply was not doing the job. It was not determining flight readiness. Rather, it established a political situation within NASA in which no center could come to a review and say that it was 'not ready.' To do so would invite the question 'If you are not ready, then why are you not doing your job? It is your job to be ready.' At each Flight Readiness Review, every center and every contractor are asked to vote on readiness. It is a 'no win' situation. For someone to get up and say that they are not ready is an indictment that they are not doing their job. As a consequence, each center gets up and basically 'snows' Headquarters with highly technical rationales that no one but the immediate experts involved can completely judge. *Lucas made it known that, under no circumstances, is the Marshall Center to be the cause for delaying a launch. . . ."* [author's italics]

The Rogers Commission found that Marshall's management, under the firm direction of Dr. William Lucas, often seemed more loyal to their own parochial interests than to "common sense" cooperation within the agency. In that regard the special self-image or separate identity of the Marshall center was not new to Dr. Lucas. But his leadership exacerbated the sense of defensive isolation that had surrounded the center from the earliest days.

The Marshall Space Flight Center and the von Braun team had come into their own in the fat-budget years of the Apollo program, and their achievements were monumental. But Huntsville had not always been recognized as a center of excellence. Beginning as a backwater missile R & D station during the heydey of big manned bombers, Huntsville scientists and engineers managed to overcome indifference and obstruction to lead America into the Space Age. It was the Huntsville Jupiter missile team (which included Dr.

Lucas) under General John Medaris and Wernher von Braun that launched America's first satellite, Explorer 1, on January 31, 1958, three months after the Russian Sputnik coup had stunned the world. Had the military Jupiter team not been constrained by the Eisenhower White House—which favored the quasi-civilian Vanguard project—von Braun's people could have beaten the Soviets to this space milestone. But Eisenhower did not want America's first satellite launched by a team of German expatriates, using a ballistic missile they had designed to fire hydrogen warheads halfway around the planet.

Huntsville managers—including Dr. William Lucas—reportedly never forgot this. They saw themselves as the Free World's true space innovators, the can-do team that could overcome *any* obstacle. Over the years they grew to view the burgeoning NASA bureaucracy, located at rival centers such as Johnson and Kennedy, as naturally subordinate followers of the true Huntsville pioneers. After all, space flight was based on rockets, and Huntsville, which became the Marshall Space Flight Center in 1960, was the fountainhead of American (albeit German) expertise in rocketry. But the legacy of bitterness dating from the late 1950s lingered for decades at Huntsville. Even though Marshall engineers consistently brought forth the innovative breakthroughs that made the moon landings, Skylab, and the space shuttle practical realities, they rarely received popular credit for these accomplishments. Indeed few Americans had ever heard of the Marshall center; it was consistently eclipsed by the more glamorous Cape Canaveral and Mission Control in Houston.

The stunning success of the Apollo years did, however, solidify Marshall's collective sense of superiority, especially in its relationship to the Johnson center in Houston. And the rivalry intensified in the lean years after Apollo. Many managers at Huntsville reportedly saw Houston as an overrated, but politically well-connected competitor for the scarce funding in the early shuttle development program. Marshall designed and developed innovative hardware; Houston's role was less well defined. Over the years of inadequate budgets and protracted hardware problems that plagued the shuttle program in the 1970s, the mutual distrust between Marshall and Johnson coalesced into a garrison mentality on the part of Marshall's director.

Lucas allegedly became increasingly defensive about the problematic development of the shuttle's complex propulsion system. And under Dr. Lucas, Marshall's managers began to keep their own counsel, hiding difficulties within the center. In fairness Houston played the same game of bureaucratic turf protection. But the pattern had historical precedent at Marshall. And the autocratic leadership of Dr. Lucas, which began during the lean and frustrating years of the shuttle's early development, exacerbated the prevailing Marshall-against-the-world mentality.

*   *   *

Cecil Houston somehow managed to make it down the coast to Patrick without incurring the wrath of either Dr. Lucas or the Florida Highway Patrol. The men from Marshall jammed aboard the van and sped north along Route 3 toward the Kennedy center. And the delegation filed into Room 2201 in the Headquarters Building behind Dr. Lucas just as the L-minus One Day Review was about to begin. Although there is no official transcript or tape recording of the meeting, participants report it was a fairly routine gathering, at least on the surface. That is to say, the meeting was tense, a charade with the three rival centers warily scanning the opposition.

The Marshall team sat together on one side of an open square of tables, facing their counterparts from Houston, who were grouped around Arnie Aldrich, the director of the National Space Transportation System Program. Officially the chain of command ran upward from Marshall's three shuttle project offices (responsible for the main engines, external tank, and the solid rocket boosters), through Marshall's newly appointed Shuttle Projects Office Manager, Stanley Reinartz, to Arnie Aldrich. In turn Mr. Aldrich reported directly to the so-called "Level 1," NASA's Associate Administrator for Spaceflight, Jesse Moore, who was sitting at the head table, near the Kennedy center delegation grouped around center director Dick Smith.

There was no clear-cut function for Dr. Lucas at this review. He was officially bypassed in the chain of command. But his presence

III

at the head of the Marshall delegation gave his center stature. "Apocalypse" called these gatherings blatant deceptions, during which Marshall managers were under orders to raise no issue that might result in a launch delay. Perhaps Dr. Lucas had no direct role in the deliberations, but he could certainly observe the performance of his people as they dealt with their rivals from the Cape, Houston, and Washington.

As the meeting progressed through the typically dense agenda of "closed" and "open" items that still had to be "worked," it became clear that there was no Marshall problem that might jeopardize the scheduled launch. The men from Marshall could rest easy; compared to the nightmare of the 61-C launch, Challenger's flight was shaping up to be a piece of cake. The Marshall delegation was able to formally certify that every component within its sphere of responsibility was ready for the launch; all issues left "open" at the Flight Readiness Review were now classified as officially closed. But (as predicted by "Apocalypse") the Marshall delegation brazenly defied NASA regulations by not revealing all known problems with their hardware. As we will see later, Marshall had been struggling for *years* with a potentially catastrophic fault in the solid rocket booster joint seals. And on January 16–17, immediately after the Challenger's Level I Flight Readiness Review, a team from the prime booster contractor, Morton Thiokol, had visited Marshall to acquire final approval for an extensive redesign of these seals. But at this L-minus One Day review, the Marshall delegation remained absolutely silent about these developments.

Under Dr. Lucas's watchful gaze, they certified that the Marshall hardware was ready for safe flight. If there was to be any further delay in meeting the flight schedule, it would not come from Dr. William R. Lucas's Marshall team.

* * *

The weather, however, was still a major consideration: the threatened cold front that had caused the slip from Saturday to Sunday was stalled in Georgia, blocked by a secondary low that had unexpectedly developed. Unless that front and its accompanying heavy rain passed through in the next twelve hours, the weather could definitely influence the launch decision.

And this decision was far from a simple last-minute judgment call. Launching the space shuttle required at least eleven hours of intense final preparation, much of it centered around the complex process known as "tanking." This operation entailed the precise filling of the shuttle's huge external tank with its full flight load of cryogenic propellants: almost eight hundred tons of super-cold liquid hydrogen and oxygen. The go for tanking was not a step to be taken lightly.

Given the weather problem, it was decided to delay the final tanking decision until the Mission Management Team under Aldrich could meet again that evening to reassess the weather. With this issue partially resolved, Mr. Moore collected each delegation's formal certificates of flight readiness. Then, for good measure, he proceeded to poll the various project managers to be absolutely certain that no last-minute hardware problems had cropped up that might jeopardize the next day's launch. Stanley Reinartz spoke for Marshall: the decision was "go."

Throughout this process, Dr. William Lucas remained rigidly aloof. He did not deign to respond to someone of Arnie Aldrich's rank. As Lucas later testified to the Rogers Commission: "I have never, on *any* occasion, reported to Mr. Aldrich."

This attitude of feudal independence would have catastrophic consequences on the morning Challenger was finally launched.

*   *   *

Among the Marshall officials present that morning was Lawrence B. Mulloy, the fifty-one-year-old manager of the Solid Rocket Project. Mulloy had a reputation as a smiling Cajun who often hid his real engineering expertise beneath an affable exterior. Like many senior Marshall managers, he had served at the center most of his career and had advanced under the stern leadership of Dr. Lucas. During the long years of the shuttle's development, Larry Mulloy had been Chief Engineer on both the Inertial Upper Stage Satellite Booster Project and the External Tank Project. A mechanical engineer, he had one advanced degree and had almost completed a Ph.D. in public administration. Mulloy had run the

Solid Rocket Booster Project at Marshall since November 1982, reporting first to Shuttle Projects Manager Bob Lindstrom, and for the past four months to the new manager, Stan Reinartz.

When his turn came, toward the end of the meeting, Larry Mulloy formally stated that Challenger's solid rocket boosters were ready for launch in the morning. By so doing, he did his part in bolstering the Marshall center's recently battered reputation. For the men from Marshall, the 61-C flight had been a near disaster, and they were not about to repeat that painful episode.

A month before in this same room, Mulloy had certified that Columbia's SRB's were go for the first 61-C launch attempt. Then at T-minus fourteen seconds on December 19, a turbine problem on the hydraulic power unit of Columbia's right SRB caused a scrub; a "Marshall" component had failed, and Dr. Lucas was reportedly very displeased. Worse still, changing the SRB hydraulic unit took several days, and the next launch attempt was thus delayed until after the holidays. "Apocalypse" has stated that Lucas abhorred delays caused by Marshall failures, and it is therefore interesting to speculate about the retribution Mulloy might have received after this embarrassing failure. Then, to exacerbate this situation, on January 6, the next launch attempt was scrubbed at T-minus thirty-one seconds, due to a faulty propellant valve. For the second time in two attempts, a Marshall propulsion system component had failed at the last minute. Marshall's reputation for excellence was taking some hard knocks. Lucas's reaction to this situation is unknown.

But when the January 7 launch attempt was scrubbed because of weather, a broken temperature sensor from a piece of ground support equipment was discovered stuck in a liquid oxygen line. As "Apocalypse" points out, Columbia would have probably exploded had it been launched with this stuck propellant valve. But this was a failure of a piece of launch pad equipment, not a Marshall component. So the blame for this delay-plagued mission could then be shifted to Kennedy.

And Dr. Lucas might well have wished to keep things that way. When his team reported during the 51-L Flight Readiness Review telecon on January 15, each of the shuttle project managers had certified that his operations were go. Once more, "Apocalypse" proves the accuracy of his insights: In twenty-five Flight Readiness Reviews, he states, not a single "no" vote on launch readiness had *ever* come from the Marshall delegation.

And at this final review, despite whatever private anxieties they might have felt about the main engines or the SRB's, they again voted for launch. The word was out among the Marshall troops that two embarrassing last-minute delays due to Marshall equipment failures were more than enough. Dr. Lucas demanded loyalty from his people, and they complied. Arnie Aldrich and Jesse Moore therefore received an optimistic report on this Saturday morning. All propulsion hardware was go for launch. If the flight was to be further delayed, it would not be due to another problem from Marshall.

*   *   *

The Lucas delegation's united front at these two crucial meetings was understandable, given the leadership style of the center director and the history of the trouble-plagued main engines. The multiple problems with these engines had been a near scandal for years, a situation that reportedly made Dr. Lucas even more defensive. When NASA officials from other centers were asked about potentially hazardous shuttle hardware, they all pointed to the main engines. The history of last-second launch pad aborts, when the computers shut down the main engines just before solid booster ignition—and the nearly disastrous Abort-to-Orbit the previous summer—all underscored the unpredictable nature of the Rocketdyne-Marshall shuttle main engines.

But the main engines were not the only potentially fatal flaw in the shuttle's propulsion system. While NASA insiders worried about the liquid engines, the solid rocket boosters were every bit as dangerous. That there had also been a long history of potentially catastrophic defects in the solid rocket boosters, and that knowledge of this situation had been effectively concealed within the Marshall bureaucracy, came as a shock when the Rogers Commission began to investigate the Challenger accident. However, the investigators should have realized that it was not the habit of Marshall managers to risk additional criticism by exposing hardware problems that they felt confident could be resolved within the center. As "Apocalypse" put it, the loyalty of Dr. Lucas's men seemed irreversibly bonded to their director, not to NASA, the space program, or their country. And in this regard Larry Mulloy —the affable Cajun engineer who liked to spend weekends aboard a houseboat on the Tennessee River, shucking oysters with his friends—proved himself an intensely loyal subordinate.

By now, of course, every informed person knows about the vulnerable field joints of the solid rocket boosters and their notorious O-ring seals. Post-accident tests and the Rogers Commission investigation established beyond all doubt that the failure of this joint system destroyed Challenger and her crew. But despite its thorough effort, the Commission did not uncover every aspect of the managerial duplicity and corporate greed that had been building for years to make the accident almost inevitable. To understand why Challenger exploded that cold January morning, we must dig deeper into the siege mentality that had come to control the men from Marshall.

As manager of the Solid Rocket Booster Project, Lawrence Mulloy was responsible for all aspects of booster performance, as well as for future hardware development, project cost effectiveness, relations with Morton Thiokol, the prime booster contractor, and, of course, for flight safety issues connected to the boosters. In his capacity as Senior Booster Safety Manager, Larry Mulloy had been obliged to deal with a chronic problem that had reached serious proportions the previous spring. Two flights in early 1985 had produced alarming anomalies in the booster field joints, which even the defensive Marshall managers could no longer keep hidden within their bureaucratic walls.

As the world is now acutely aware, the monstrous pillars of the SRB's were hardly the monoliths they appeared on television. Because of the various political and budgetary compromises imposed during the shuttle's design and development, the boosters were built in reusable segments, which were filled with propellant at the Thiokol plant in Utah and shipped to the Cape, where the segments were vertically assembled in the VAB into the actual booster rockets. These segments have been compared to giant coffee cans, stacked end to end and sealed at the so-called "field joints." A circular tongue-and-groove joint system involving a protruding tang and a U-shaped groove called the clevis formed the actual joint. One hundred and seventy-seven thick steel pins connected the tang and clevis at even intervals around the booster circumference.

And this joint was protected against the high-pressure blast of the burning rocket fuel by the now-famous synthetic rubber O-rings, which were designed to extrude into machined channels in the clevis at the moment of ignition, thus forming a pressure barrier that blocked the passage of gases. The actual pressure-transmission mechanism was a thin coating of flame-proof zinc chromate putty, which lined the surface between the insulation faces at the open ends of each segment. When the boosters' solid fuel ignited with a blast of superhot gas, this putty was forced out toward the O-rings; the putty conducted the pressure pulse, compressing the air in the cavity around the O-rings. The rubbery rings sprang into place, filling any gap between the metal surfaces, and the seal was complete once the pressure inside the O-ring cavity equalled the pressure on the other side of the putty flame barrier.

When the Thiokol Corporation had proposed this system, they stated that their joint design was based on the seals used in the highly reliable solid rocket boosters of the Titan missile. And it should be recalled that NASA Administrator James Fletcher was generous in his praise of this Thiokol design. However, there were several crucial differences between the two designs: on the Titan booster, the U-shaped clevis faced downward, and the single O-ring seal was secured in its proper position by a technician before the joint was closed during field assembly; the clevis of the Thiokol SRB field joint faced up, with the dual O-ring seals on the inner face of the clevis groove. These rings had to be activated by the ignition pressure pulse. This modification of the proven technology would have disastrous consequences. In effect the Titan booster joint was simple and reliable, and the Thiokol joint was complex and unpredictable.

According to the Marshall-Thiokol design specifications, however, this dual-ring seal was fail-safe. If for some reason the first ring failed to seat properly, the secondary O-ring would have already automatically popped into place. This was the "innovative" redundant system that Administrator Fletcher had praised so highly during the contract-award controversy in the mid-1970s.

But as early as the first test firings in the 1970s, it became clear that the field joint design had dangerous fundamental flaws. A 1977 "hydroburst" test of the steel booster casings, which used pressurized water to exceed the 1,000-pounds-per-square-inch pressure of booster combustion, produced a truly surprising result. Instead of the tang-and-clevis joint being forced more tightly closed by the force of ignition, the pressure caused the unexpected phenomenon that came to be known as "joint rotation." This occurred when the metal parts bent *away* from each other, opening a narrow gap through which hot gases could leak. The steel booster cases ballooned outward during the first fractions of a second after ignition, bending the tang away from the inner clevis lip.

This rotation actually caused a momentary drop in air pressure around the O-rings instead of the anticipated immediate air compression. In other words the circular seal of highly compressed air, which was supposed to equalize the pressure inside the burning booster, would actually not exist for the several hundred milliseconds during the initial pressure surge, the "ignition transient" in engineering terms. The implications of this discovery were ominous. Without this pressure seal, the hot combustion gas could shoot through the putty and erode the O-rings. If this erosion was widespread, an actual flame path would quickly develop and the booster would burst at the joint, destroying the entire booster, and, of course, the space shuttle itself.

Thiokol's reaction to this discovery was quite calm. In their reports to Marshall, the company stated that joint rotation was a self-limiting phenomenon: the O-rings did, they reported, spring correctly into place after several hundred milliseconds into the transient, well before the entire booster case reached flight pressure at approximately 0.600 second.

To Marshall's credit, however, the center's engineers were not about to accept this argument. For three years engineers in Marshall's Solid Rocket Booster Project wrote memoranda to the Project Manager, George Hardy, strongly suggesting that the current Thiokol field joint design was unacceptable. One memo written in 1978 by John Q. Miller, Marshall's Chief of the Solid Rocket Motor branch, stated that this design was so hazardous that it could produce "hot gas leaks and resulting catastrophic failure."

But according to Rogers Commission investigators, Hardy did *not* forward these memos to Thiokol. Although the Commission does not elaborate on this omission, it should be remembered that Thiokol was generally seen among many NASA officials as enjoying unusual support from Administrator James Fletcher. And it was Fletcher who named Dr. William Lucas as Marshall center director in 1974. The political dimensions of this situation will probably never be entirely clear. But it is sufficient to note that the alarming concerns of knowledgeable Marshall engineers did not result in a redesign of the SRB field joint before flights began.

In September 1980 the Shuttle Verification and Certification Committee recommended that the SRB field joints be accepted for flight.

On November 12, 1981, the Orbiter Columbia flew the second space shuttle mission. When the SRB's were recovered, disassembled, and inspected, it was discovered that the primary O-ring in the aft field joint of the right-hand SRB had been badly eroded by hot combustion gases. This vital component was burned through a quarter of the ring's 0.28-inch diameter. The Marshall center did not report this at the Flight Readiness Review for the next flight, STS-3. Rather Dr. Lucas's people decided to keep the problem within the confines of the Marshall-Thiokol reporting channels, and away from the national shuttle office in Houston and the associate administrator in Washington.

After the first four shuttle missions, NASA introduced a new lightweight SRB: basically the same design with a thinner casing wall to save weight. It soon became obvious that the joint-rotation problem was going to be even more severe with this design, due to greater ignition-transient ballooning of these thinner cases. Booster combustion gases reaching temperatures over 5,000 degrees Fahrenheit and pressures of almost 1,000 pounds per square inch were blasting through the field joints and badly eroding the vulnerable O-rings.

As General Donald Kutyna, an outspoken member of the Rogers Commission put it, this situation was analogous to evidence that an airliner wing was about to fall off.

On December 17, 1982 (one month after Mulloy took up his duties), the field joints and their O-ring seals were reclassified Criticality 1, from their previous status of Criticality 1R (Redundant), which meant the joints were now a potential single-point failure that could result in:

"Loss of mission, vehicle and crew due to metal erosion, burn through, and probable case burst resulting in fire and deflagration."

As Project Manager, Larry Mulloy had been obliged to sign off on this reclassification. The highly touted fail-safe redundancy of these field joints had proved itself to be far from fail-safe.

But no one at Marshall called for a halt in shuttle flights until this could be corrected. Instead these NASA and Thiokol engineers convinced themselves that the problem was self-limiting. They believed that the field joint rotation and O-ring erosion were a kind of natural phenomenon which was relatively harmless. Using circuitous logic, which Rogers Commission member Richard Feynman would later describe as a kind of "Russian Roulette" mentality, the engineers came to feel that they fully understood the problem. The erosion occurred, they believed, in the first two or three hundred milliseconds of the transient; after that, the O-rings seated in their grooves and the pressure seal was complete. This certainly was not an ideal situation, but it was, they reported, an "acceptable risk."

The Marshall and Thiokol engineers decided that one certain method of insuring the integrity of the field joint seals was to pressure-test the assembled boosters' O-rings for leaks at a higher pressure than they had originally used. Their theory held that a leak test conducted at 200-pounds-per-square-inch pressure would duplicate the worst-case situation during the joint rotation in the ignition transient.

But *after* they raised the test pressure, so-called O-ring "distress" got much worse: over half the subsequent shuttle flights experienced O-ring erosion or actual blow-by of hot gases.

As Rogers Commission investigators would later clearly establish, the higher pressure leak test was actually creating "blow holes" in the sealing putty, which would give the superhot ignition gases a clear route to the O-rings. But the men at Marshall and Thiokol felt confident that they had the situation well in hand. Neither Thiokol—which was coming under increasing scrutiny as the privileged sole-source contractor for the solid rocket boosters —nor Marshall, whose main engines caused chronic flight delays and launch pad aborts, wanted to call for a shuttle flight halt.

By the summer of 1985, however, the engineers at Marshall and Thiokol most intimately involved with the boosters could no longer deny that they had a potentially catastrophic situation facing them. Analysis of the recovered boosters from the April 1985 Challenger Spacelab mission showed that hot gases had blown past the primary O-ring of a nozzle joint and badly scorched the secondary ring. Two months later, when Mulloy learned of this obvious failure of a Criticality 1 component, he was obliged to impose a formal launch constraint on the next scheduled flight. This was another Spacelab mission, also flying on Challenger, with launch set for July 12. But for some still obscure reason (or perhaps acting on pressure from above), Mulloy waived the launch constraint he had just imposed. Over the next six months Mulloy imposed then waived five more launch constraints. No one from Marshall ever brought this practice to the attention of the national shuttle office in Houston or to Jesse Moore in Washington.

But the mounting anxiety about the solid boosters was eclipsed yet again by the unpredictable main engines. Another embarrassing launch pad abort halted Challenger's July 12 launch attempt at the T-3 seconds mark, with all three main engines firing. On July 29 Challenger was finally launched. And then, less than five minutes into the flight, a faulty engine-turbine temperature sensor caused the premature shutdown of the number one engine and the near shutdown of another. Challenger was forced into the Abort-to-Orbit mode, narrowly missing disaster. Given this poor showing by Marshall hardware, it is not surprising that the center's leadership decided to keep to themselves the bad news of the five previous launch constraints and their inexplicably capricious waivers.

But there is now irrefutable evidence that both Marshall and Thiokol realized that they were risking disaster by allowing shuttle flights to continue despite the chronic O-ring erosion. At Thiokol a field joint redesign task force was assembled, charged with producing a remedy to joint rotation and O-ring damage. As we will see, however, Thiokol apparently intended to go slowly on this redesign effort, lest the problem become public and jeopardize their position in the contract-renewal negotiations scheduled for that fall. But despite Marshall's seemingly blasé attitude there is now proof of just how serious the center's managers considered the field joint problem. As New York *Times* science writer William Broad discovered in September 1986, Marshall managers had gone so far as to order new solid rocket booster case segments that included a so-called "capture feature," which was in effect a circular lip extending from the inner side of the field joint tang; this feature would grip the inner clevis face and prevent joint rotation. In July 1985 Marshall signed procurement contracts for seventy-two such new cases, to be fabricated and delivered to Thiokol by the Ladish Corporation in Wisconsin. These segments would each have approximately three inches of additional steel around the tang, so that the capture feature could be incorporated.

At a time of such severe budget constraints, a multimillion-dollar contract for new hardware would not have been easy to hide. Certainly—if "Apocalypse" is correct—Dr. Lucas would have been quite aware of this order. Although the Rogers Commission did not mention this hardware contract, it is obvious that NASA's senior management in Washington must have also been aware of it. Among Marshall engineers, the capture feature was called the "big fix." When it was incorporated, the nagging—but to some apparently trivial—problem of O-ring erosion could finally be put to rest. To many Marshall and Thiokol engineers, however, the situation was dangerous and unacceptable: it would be over a year before the capture feature could be incorporated. Yet NASA continued to authorize shuttle flights, and Thiokol continued to sign Flight Readiness Review certificates. The line engineers might be overcome with anguish, but apparently not so overcome as to buck orders from above.

Richard Cook was a NASA auditor who stumbled on the problem by chance in the summer of 1985. He sent several urgent memoranda to his superiors, warning of the "catastrophic" results of field joint failure and calling for an immediate halt to shuttle flights. There is no record that his warnings were acted on either in Marshall or at NASA Headquarters.

"The engineers knew about the big fix," Cook told William Broad. But until the new hardware could be completed and readied for flight, "they held their breath every time the shuttle took off."

*   *   *

The L-Minus One Day Review ended a little before 1:00 that sunny Saturday afternoon. At three o'clock Jesse Moore met the press and declared that Challenger was ready for flight the next morning. The only problem that might arise, he said, was from the weather.

*   *   *

Challenger's crew had awakened early that morning, anticipating a normally hectic L-minus one schedule of flight plan reviews, weather briefings, and the final preflight physical examinations. By the time they finished the physicals after lunch, however, the weather had become increasingly problematic. A slip until Monday seemed probable, so the crew remained close to their quarters on the third floor of the Operations and Checkout Building, waiting for the word.

The traditional prelaunch family beach party was over; their families were comfortably installed at local motels, and, following the physicals, the crew was in quarantine. Only spouses could visit and then only briefly. That afternoon, Steve McAuliffe came to see Christa. They reportedly talked about how excited the children were to finally be in Florida. If there was, indeed, a weather scrub, Steve McAuliffe reportedly told his wife, he would take Scott and Caroline to visit Disney World.

Late that afternoon, Challenger Pilot Mike Smith's wife Jane returned from visiting him at the crew quarters. She joined over a hundred and fifty of their relatives and friends at a festive prelaunch party in a banquet room at a Cocoa Beach resort. The room was decorated with pictures of Mike as a Naval Academy midshipman, as a Navy fighter pilot, and as an astronaut. There was one display of his impressive collection of awards and combat citations. As people drank champagne and ate canapés, the mood of decorous celebration gave way to an unabashed down-home Carolina party. They laughed and sang and hugged Jane and the kids. Everybody said how darn proud they were of Mike. After all these years of serving his country, his dream was coming true. It was just a shame he couldn't be there to help them celebrate.

*　　*　　*

As the sun set, orange and brassy across the scrub pines and palmettos, technicians at Launch Pad 39B rolled back the massive Rotating Service Structure. For the first time since arriving at the pad almost six weeks before, Challenger was unencumbered by steel pipes and girders. At 8:16 that night, the countdown was due to resume. Now darkness seemed to swell upward from the calm indigo surface of the lagoons. Challenger stood within its crystal pyramid of spotlights, silent in the warm dusk, a strangely graceful Juggernaut, seemingly invulnerable.

PART III

ACCEPTABLE RISKS

A QUESTION OF WEATHER

Saturday, 8:16 p.m.

At 8:16 Saturday night the terminal countdown team was assembled in Firing Room Three on the seaward side of the Launch Control Center. This team represented about half the personnel who would be present for the actual launch. As the engineers and technicians waited at their consoles, the quiet banter in the room tapered to silence. The men adjusted their foam-padded earphones for comfort; if all went well, they would be at their posts for the next twelve hours.

A calm voice sounded over the Orbiter Test Conductor's channel on the OIS, the Operational Intercomm System, that linked all the people at the three tiers of consoles. "Short count . . . four, three, two, one. Mark. T-minus eleven hours and counting."

On scores of console screens, tiny amber digit blocks began to pulse with life, and the mood in the room torqued one notch tighter. The twenty-fifth terminal space shuttle countdown had begun. During the years of more relaxed flight schedules, most of the countdowns had been conducted in Firing Room One, on the southern end of the broad building. Firing Room Three was the "classified" launch center, with secure communications channels for military shuttle flights. The only reason it was being used for the Teacher-in-Space mission was that the other two firing rooms were already being prepared for upcoming missions.

But the very term "firing room" had a certain military ring to it, evocative of the sunken concrete bunkers that had once lined the Cape Canaveral beachfront, close by the rusty launch gantries of the early space program. When the Apollo program triggered the monumental expansion of facilities at the Cape, the pioneering bravado was carried over into the new buildings. Hence the nostalgic nomenclature: for many NASA veterans, a shuttle mission was still a "shot," and the Orbiter was "the bird." And the firing rooms in the Launch Control Center had even retained the classic split-level layout of a Peenemunde bunker. The upper tier of management consoles was nestled inside the sloping latticework of a glass curtain wall that gave a broad perspective onto the launch pads. And these windows were protected by massive vertical concrete louvers, evocative of the blast screens on the early launch bunkers. Here stood straight rows of communications stations from which the launch director's team issued their orders. There were only a few night-shift stand-ins at these stations. But the lower level was crowded. Crescent banks of green-metal operational consoles were grouped into four open circles. Above them, three digital clocks marked Universal Time, Local Time, and Shuttle Count. The ruby digits of the shuttle clock were now counting down from 11:00:00.

But the resumption of the count produced no cheers, no bursts of exuberance. These same men had begun four such countdowns in the past forty days while they tried to launch Columbia. Many were now more wary than enthusiastic. They stared silently at the dancing polychrome data blocks on their console screens, watching for any sign of malfunction as the Test Conductor cleared his throat and began to work slowly through the thick binder of procedures that would monitor and activate Challenger's myriad flight systems.

The loading of cryogenic propellants, "tanking," was due to begin halfway into their shift, and no one wanted to make a mistake that would jeopardize that long and complex operation. The keyboards and glowing red function buttons at each console were connected through electronic ganglia to the launch pad and the shuttle. During the next twelve hours, the operators would be called on to perform a sequence of complex procedures. Issuing an erroneous keyboard command or simply pushing the wrong button could damage delicate systems aboard the Orbiter or on the ground support equipment. This definitely was not a drill, not a dry run to shake the kinks out of the system. In a few hours eight hundred tons of supercold liquid hydrogen and oxygen would begin flowing into Challenger's external tank. Simultaneously console operators responsible for the main engines, the solid rocket boosters, the payloads, and the Orbiter's thousands of redundant avionics and control components would be performing their final checks and activations.

There was much activity but almost no audible conversation. Each operator wore a headset with earphone and attached microphone. Perhaps twenty different voice channels were now active, and the men spoke quietly, reciting cryptic exchanges comprehensible only among the initiates on their particular "loops." On the elevated management tier, the wide expanse of the seaward windows reflected lights from the parking lot and security checkpoints three floors below. The windows glowed like stained glass when yellow caution lights blended with red beacons. Then the room acquired the aspect of a futuristic monastery, with each man at his console a penitent monk, devoutly chanting the long night's liturgy.

Challenger stood naked in its cone of spotlights, three miles across the black dunes.

*   *   *

Saturday, 9:00 p.m.
One floor above in the Operations Management Center, Challenger's Mission Management Team assembled to discuss the weather and the status of the countdown. With its narrow, T-shaped conference table, chalkboard, and slide screen, the Ops Center was a more intimate version of the huge conference rooms where the preceding flight-readiness reviews had been held. And although the team that met here included all the key officials involved with the final launch decision, it was smaller than the cumbersome delegations from the rival centers that had performed the elaborate ritual of readiness certification.

The team was officially headed by Jesse Moore, NASA's Associate Administrator for Space Flight. Arnie Aldrich led the group from the National Space Transportation System in Houston, Bob

Sieck was KSC's Director of Shuttle Operations, and Gene Thomas was the regular KSC Launch Director. Tonight, however, there was another official present, Dr. William Graham, the Deputy Administrator of NASA, who had been the agency's Acting Administrator for several months.

James Beggs, the Administrator, was on a prolonged leave of absence while he prepared his legal defense in a federal criminal case, stemming from his indictment for fraud while a vice president of General Dynamics, the huge defense contractor that had been bidding on the ill-fated Sergeant York antiaircraft weapon system for the Army. So Dr. Graham found himself running the agency only two months after the Senate confirmed his nomination as deputy. Graham was a brilliant scientist with doctorates in both physics and electrical engineering. A former nuclear weapons specialist with the Rand Corporation, he had spent three years as the chairman of the President's Committee on Arms Control and Disarmament before coming to NASA the previous fall. He had a reputation as a conscientious, quiet, and hardworking scientist. But he was the new boy, and this presented certain problems.

In all probability Graham was going to move up to assume the administrator position officially as Beggs's legal problems dragged on; therefore, he had to be considered the agency's permanent leader, not just a temporary substitute. But he was not yet fully "read in" on the complexities of the shuttle program, nor on the personalities of his key managers. Nevertheless he would have to write the performance reports on many of the men seated around him at the Ops Center. He, and they, knew this. At stake were the intangibles of executive relationships, which, in a government bureaucracy were always charged with a certain tension between the "Schedule C" political appointees such as Dr. Graham and the career civil servants who made up NASA's permanent senior management.

In this case, the relationship was further confused by several factors. First Dr. Graham was known as a White House man: he had been a science and arms control advisor on the President-elect's 1980 transition team. And second Graham's first close encounter with a space shuttle mission had been the embarrassing 61-C Columbia fiasco. If he had to write performance reports based solely on that operation's collective management, the men at this table were in deep trouble.

As members of the Senior Executive Service, favorable performance reports meant more to these NASA managers than simply a boost to the ego. They were all eligible for generous salary bonuses based on recommendations made by their superiors. In the past they had received very handsome supplements to their annual salary after such recommendations. For example, Marshall center Director Dr. William Lucas received a hefty $20,000 in 1980, while Jesse Moore and Arnie Aldrich each received $10,000 in 1982. In 1985 Jesse Moore was granted a bonus of almost $14,000, the highest award that year. Moore's bonus recommendation stated that he had "determined the minimum changes necessary to improve organizational effectiveness and set priorities for change"; in other words Moore had streamlined the shuttle program's management without begging for more money, a management style considered worthy of reward.

Dr. Graham had flown down that afternoon on the NASA One Gulfstream. He was here to observe his key managers in their most important roles as decision makers.

But the decision whether to proceed with the countdown for a Sunday morning launch was not at all easy or straightforward. Although obviously not part of the official Launch Commit Criteria, one prime consideration that night was political. As things stood now, Vice President George Bush was scheduled to leave Andrews Air Force Base early the next morning aboard Air Force Two, en route to the inauguration of the new President of Honduras. If Challenger was going to fly in the morning, the Vice President's plane would land at the Shuttle Landing Facility, he would greet the crew and their families, watch the launch, say a few kind words about NASA, the shuttle, and the Teacher-in-Space mission, then fly on to Central America. George Bush was the Administration's point man for space policy, a role traditionally assigned to the Vice President.

With the Vice President in attendance, television coverage of a Sunday launch would be much greater than could normally be expected. That was an important point to weigh. Conversely such intensified press scrutiny could boomerang if the launch was an on-again, off-again process ending in a scrub, as had occurred four times with the Columbia 61-C flight. And therein lay the dilemma: NASA's politically astute senior managers would have loved the favorable media attention that was bound to accompany the successful launch of the Teacher-in-Space mission attended by the Vice President. There would be great "visuals" on the roof of the launch center with George Bush surrounded by the crew's families, hooting and hollering as Challenger blasted skyward. You couldn't get better publicity if you paid for it. But the Vice President was a busy man, and his staff had to be notified *tonight* if Bush were to approve a stop at the Cape on Sunday morning, en route to Honduras.

So the unstated political considerations facing the Mission Management Team were these: if NASA could assure an on-time launch on Sunday morning, the Vice President would give the shuttle program a needed boost with his presence at the launch. But no one in the Ops Center wanted to drag George Bush out of his way to stand around in the drizzle, watching the launch window run out. And that was the kind of weather everyone expected. Chances for a launch Sunday morning were less than fifty-fifty. Normally NASA would have taken those odds. But the possibility of the Vice President's visit made the situation anything but normal. So the question here was the weather.

The cold front was driving relentlessly down from the northwest. According to Lieutenant Scott Funk, a meteorologist who briefed the managers by telecon from the weather center at Canaveral Air Force Station, the turbulent leading edge of the front was due to reach the Cape around five Sunday morning, just when tanking would be in progress. The forecast was for low ceilings and poor visibility, with fog and increasing rain. There could even be some dangerous lightning if thunderheads developed when the cold air mass encountered the warm waters of the Gulf Stream, just off shore. Satellite pictures showed the characteristic crescent of overcast of a strong cold front already touching the Florida Panhandle. Jacksonville, Tallahassee, and Pensacola were currently reporting rain, and their radar plots showed thickening overcast with predicted downpours of almost an inch. By 9:36 A.M., the scheduled lift-off time, the center of the front was due to be just north of Daytona Beach, only fifty miles up the coast. That meant the weather would only deteriorate during the three-hour Sunday launch window that lasted until 12:36.

However, the Air Force Shuttle Weather Office predicted that the cold front would move across Cape Canaveral around 3:00, and the skies would be clear by eight Sunday night, just in time to begin the terminal countdown for a Monday launch. And the forecast for Monday was excellent: a few scattered clouds and good visibility. There would be some gusty winds behind the front, though, but they would blow from the northwest, which would not create a crosswind problem for a Return to Launch Site Abort at the shuttle strip.

The weather at the primary and backup Trans-Atlantic Abort sites at Dakar and Casablanca was unchanged: Dakar was poor, due to a Sahara dust storm, but Casablanca was acceptable. This put a definite constraint on the launch window: Casablanca was not equipped for night landings, which meant the shuttle could be launched no later than 1:10 P.M., local Florida time. On the other hand, the dust storm plaguing Dakar might dissipate on Monday enough to permit use of the big French-built international airport there.

In the discussion that followed this forecast, the question of Tuesday's weather was raised. Tuesday, Lieutenant Funk told the management team, might be a problem. The air mass behind the cold front was basically a dry arctic ridge that had been up in northern Canada only a few days before. Already temperatures were dropping rapidly behind the front, as the counterclockwise wind system sucked this frigid air south. Overnight temperature predictions for Monday were for record cold: only fourteen degrees in Tampa and twenty-one in Orlando. The conditions at the Cape would be a little better, but the temperature on early Tuesday morning could break a local record, dropping to around the mid-twenties.

By launch time on Tuesday, the temperature would probably still be well below freezing. The tired men around the polished teak conference table frowned in resignation. They explained to Dr. Graham that the space shuttle launch operation involved the use of water for multiple functions: fire hoses on the Fixed Service

Structure, troughs, and fountains that dampened the powerful acoustic shock waves from the solid boosters reflecting off the steel plates of the Mobile Launching Platform, and high pressure suppression hydrants that could extinguish the residual hydrogen flares around the main engines in the event of a launch pad abort. But the normal contingency for such a hard-freeze forecast was draining the pad's entire water system so that the unprotected steel pipes would not burst.

Almost exactly one year before, on January 23, 1985, the 51-C mission of Discovery was scrubbed for twenty-four hours due to a similar problem with freezing weather. The overnight lows then had been in the high twenties, and the pad crew had been obliged to hustle to get the complex plumbing of Pad 39A drained in time to prevent damage. This problem last winter had not received much play in the press, however, since the Discovery mission was the first classified flight completely dedicated to a Defense Department payload. But the men seated around the Ops Center conference table this Saturday night were acutely aware of it. Even with the one-day slip of the Discovery DOD mission, the overnight low in the early hours of January 24 the year before had been thirty-four, damned close to freezing. The launch team had been obliged to add antifreeze to the water troughs and keep a trickle dripping through some of the pipes on the service structure. Since then, a more elaborate freeze-protection plan had been evolved but had not yet been tested under really cold conditions.

Now this same issue exacerbated the already complex—indeed confusing—considerations that affected the decision the team had to make at the meeting. With the unacceptable weather of the approaching front threatening a Sunday launch—to the point where it was ill advised to invite the Vice President to attend—and the freezing conditions making Tuesday look unacceptable, Monday was shaping up to be a very important day. Obviously any slip for whatever reason after Tuesday was going to have a major impact on the timing of the March ASTRO mission. And no man in the Ops Center that night had to be reminded of the importance of that particular mission to NASA's image and the administration's prestige. If they could beat the Soviets at their own science propaganda game by scooping them on Halley's Comet coverage, the agency would have gone a long way to justifying the shuttle, both with the White House and the American public. Therefore the launch of Challenger on Monday, January 27, was essential.

Again, Jesse Moore questioned the project managers. If they did slip until Monday, he asked, were there any problems that would prevent a launch within that morning's window?

Weather was the only open question. If Dakar did not improve, lift-off would have to occur before darkness closed Casablanca as the primary TAL site. Also the winds Monday afternoon were expected to back around to the west and freshen, and they could exceed the RTLS crosswind limits.

Otherwise there were no payload or hardware constraints to a Monday morning launch.

Jesse Moore conferred briefly with his top managers and with Dr. Graham. The launch of Challenger's 51-L Teacher-in-Space mission would be scrubbed until Monday morning at 9:37 local time. The management team would meet in this room tomorrow at two in the afternoon to reassess the situation.

Shallowly submerged political considerations had been as relevant as the more obvious engineering and weather criteria. If there had not been such political considerations involved, the management team probably would have opted for tanking Saturday night, and taking a chance with the weather on Monday morning. But 61-C had taught everybody the frustrations of that approach, and no one wanted the Vice President at the Cape for such a scrub.

There was also the question of the fatigue of the launch and flight control team. If they did work all the way through a countdown tonight, in the hope that the weather would favor them in the morning, the men in the firing room here and a similar team in the Mission Operations Control Room—the so-called "MOCR" in Houston—would have been on duty for a full twelve hours. Then, after the scrub, they would have to grab some sleep and come right back to their consoles to begin the countdown again Sunday night. That route led to fatigue and mistakes. And Jay Greene's flight controllers in Houston could not afford to make any wrong calls during the crucial first minutes of the ascent phase. For twenty years this awkward division of labor between the Cape and Houston had been the source of irritation and confusion. Now, with the shuttle taking off and landing at Kennedy, many people there felt that Mission Control should revert back to Kennedy, where it should have been all along. For the moment, however, pork-barrel decisions twenty years ago shaped the practicalities of shuttle flights. "Press on" bravado at the Cape might result in dangerous exhaustion in the Houston MOCR. So they would be pleased in Houston that the scrub had come early enough to allow them all a good night's sleep.

Dr. Graham arranged to inform Vice President Bush. Gene Thomas and Bob Sieck contacted the launch team in the firing room and on the pad. The clock would be recycled to the T-11 hours and holding point. Within minutes the pad crew would roll back the Rotating Service Structure to give the Orbiter some protection from the heavy rain everyone expected to start falling before dawn.

A call was made to the O & C building: if the crew weren't already asleep, let them know it's a scrub for tomorrow. They could sleep in.

In the Press Dome, Information Officer George Diller drafted his announcement on the scrub, which would be recorded for release on the KSC's broadcast news service. When he got to the paragraph on the impact of the weather on a possible Tuesday launch, Diller used the kind of honest and straightforward language that had been the center's hallmark since the days of Apollo:

> "On Tuesday the weather will turn much colder with a low temperature forecast of 21 degrees in Orlando and 14 degrees in Tampa. This would be a constraint to launch."

Here Diller was referring to the formal Launch Commit Criteria constraint that read:

> "Ambient Temperature Restrictions:
> The shuttle will not be launched if the ambient temperature is less than 31 degrees F. or greater than 99 degrees F."

In other words, NASA would never permit a shuttle launch in freezing conditions.

Contacted by reporters, Jesse Moore commented on the delay. "We'll sit on the ground until we all believe it's safe to launch."

Out on Pad 39B, Challenger's white curves were cut by a web of shadow as the Rotating Service Structure rumbled back into position around the Orbiter. It was a warm, windless night, with a bright, subtropical moon hanging above the calm ocean. Away to the north, the sky was clear and starry. There was no sign of the approaching front.

*   *   *

Sunday, 7:00 a.m.

As Saturday night wore on, the sky remained clear at Cape Canaveral. The firing room emptied; launch pad personnel secured the vehicle and departed, leaving behind a skeleton crew and just a few cars in the parking lots around the VAB and Launch Control Center. Once the spotlights were extinguished on the pad, the moon reasserted itself. Still, the horizon remained clear to the north and west.

By dawn Sunday it was obvious that the approaching front had stalled in the Florida Panhandle. The sun rose like a blood orange from the sharp blue line of the ocean. Overhead a few feathery clouds caught the sunrise and glowed. The morning was warm and windless. Had there not been a weather slip the night before, the crew would be at breakfast, about to enter the Astrovan for the drive to the pad.

But there had been a slip. The decision had been made, and there was no way to revoke it.

In the crew quarters at the Operations and Checkout Building, Pilot Mike Smith rose a little before seven and opened the blinds of his room. The sunlight was bright and hot. Smith would later tell a friend that he was not amused by the sight of a warm, sunny morning. He was an experienced Naval aviator whose professional expertise included a deep understanding of weather dynamics. Although the stalled front would pass through the Cape later than expected, he realized, it definitely would move south. And when it did, the inevitable bad weather could well interfere with the launch on Monday morning.

Smith had spent his entire adult life working in bureaucracies, both military and civilian. He knew that decisions made for political reasons by hard-pressed bureaucrats like those on the Mission Management Team often brought ludicrous results, but the decision to slip made the night before—apparently so the Vice President would not be inconvenienced—really took the cake.

Since Columbia's multiple weather scrubs in December and early January, Mike Smith had studied the long-range weather patterns for the period of his own flight with special intensity. You didn't have to have a Ph.D. in meteorology to track the jet stream pattern and approaching storm systems a week in advance. Therefore, he was especially alarmed the night before he left Houston to observe the ominous storm building in the Pacific Northwest. Even though he was in quarantine in the JSC astronaut quarters, Smith was so alarmed about the weather that he slipped home so that he could use the telephone in privacy. He called Challenger's flow director, Jim Harrington, at the Cape. Mike had learned of the Astronaut Office T-38 that Harrington had dispatched to Edwards for spare parts from Columbia. Jim, he said, the weather looks terrible for early next week. You've got to do everything you possibly can to install those spares and finish out the work on Challenger and get us launched by Saturday, Sunday at the latest.

*   *   *

Sunday, 8:30 a.m.

As the sun rose at the Cape Canaveral Air Force Station, the Shuttle Weather Office was already busy. Like meteorologists all over the world, whose forecasts influenced operational decisions, these men and women sometimes felt unfairly judged. Military commanders and NASA managers were constantly demanding forecasts based on hard data, but meteorology is a science of probabilities, not absolutes.

The satellite photos and teleprinter messages, clipped on sagging lines like so much wet laundry above the plotting boards, now revealed a different picture from that of only twelve hours earlier.

An unexpected secondary low had developed overnight in southern Georgia, and its air flow was blocking the progress of the strong cold front. The low would probably ride up the face of the front, filling as it moved, and be absorbed in the maritime low-pressure trough centered below New England. In fact the front was already showing signs of its southeastern movement again. But the low ceilings and rain that should have reached the Cape before dawn would not arrive until afternoon.

In other words the weather at the Cape would remain perfect for a space shuttle launch throughout the original three-hour launch window Sunday morning.

But the stalled cold front presented graver concerns than simply the press ribbing that was sure to follow the weather scrub decision. As the arctic air ridge filled in behind the front, cold temperatures and higher than normal winds could be expected for launch time on Monday. Currently the predicted temperature for the 9:38 T-0 point, lift-off, was only forty degrees, down almost fifteen degrees from earlier estimates. And the record lows predicted for Tuesday were now a near certainty.

The tired weather officers hunched over their computer terminals, patiently tapping in data entries, trying to solve the four-dimensional puzzle of the atmosphere for this particularly turbulent and unpredictable corner of the planet for the next fifty hours. Whatever the outcome, their effort would no doubt prove a thankless task.

*   *   *

Sunday, 9:40 a.m.
At his office in the LCC, Launch Director Gene Thomas called the Air Force weather office and received the updated forecast. He was not pleased with what he heard. Outside the wide office windows, the sun beat down on the lagoons and palmetto scrub. The sea was chalky blue.

With a subordinate and a man from Public Affairs, Thomas cut through the fourth-floor offices and climbed the stairs to the broad observation deck on the roof. The sun was a dazzling weight on the white paint of the concrete deck. Across the road the flat mirror of the barge basin reflected the vertical mass of the VAB. From this perspective, Challenger was clearly visible within its web of RSS scaffolding out on Pad 39B. It was just after nine-thirty, the original launch time. Thomas leaned back and squinted in the sunlight.

"It looks to me," he said with soft irony, "like we could have made it." The two men beside him nodded. There hadn't been such a pretty morning for a launch since last fall. But the decision was made, and they would just have to live with it.

*   *   *

Sunday Afternoon

That afternoon Challenger's crew spent the obligatory hour or two reviewing the flight data files that they had already studied over all the months in Houston. They were still in quarantine after their final preflight physical examination, so they were limited in close contact to their spouses and the immediate members of the Astronaut Office staff who had accompanied them from JSC. There had been a certain amount of subdued and almost wholesome ribaldry about these "conjugal visits," because the astronaut quarters were more evocative of a thin-walled college dormitory than a hotel. Dick Young, of the KSC Public Affairs staff, described the decor as "early Holiday Inn."

Whatever the quality of the furnishings, the third floor of the O & C building certainly was not the most comfortable or relaxing place to wait out these launch delays. Originally the crew had anticipated being there Thursday and Friday nights and flying on Saturday. Now, if they were lucky, they would fly Monday morning, only two days later than scheduled.

But Mike Smith was not sanguine. Once more his experience as a Naval aviator told him that the approaching front was going to cause some real headaches. He had spent two tours at the Naval Air Station in Pensacola, and he'd learned to fly as a kid on the coast of North Carolina. He understood only too well what these strong arctic cold fronts did to flying conditions. If the front spawned yet another secondary low nearby, the system could stall right here at the Cape and prevent launching all next week.

In Vietnam he had flown the "all-weather" A-6 Intruder off the carrier U.S.S. Kitty Hawk on scores of combat missions during an eleven-month tour. And he had become wary of weather forecasts made by men at computers, forecasts that influenced the lives of men in the cockpits of aircraft. But Smith kept his own counsel that morning as he watched the sky. By noon he saw some high cirrus to the northwest, the first signs that the approaching front was moving again.

Smith and Dick Scobee spent several hours that afternoon flying the Shuttle Training Aircraft, the modified Grumman Gulfstream whose flight deck duplicated the controls of the Orbiter. As they practiced the steep, fast shuttle landing approaches, the high cirrus clouds rapidly thickened to solid overcast, and the heavy cloud deck hunkered lower. By mid-afternoon it was raining steadily, and they had to abandon plans to fly aerobatics in the more nimble T-38s, the traditional way astronauts worked off their prelaunch nerves and sharpened their already well-honed flying skills.

They drove back to the O & C Building in a steady drizzle, in time to join the rest of the crew to watch the Super Bowl. Before their early dinner, the crew were joined by their spouses, and they all sipped soft drinks before the wide color television screen, watching Refrigerator Perry crash through the Patriots' line.

It was still light when dinner was served, and no one seemed especially hungry. After dessert and coffee, Ron McNair fetched a shopping bag that his wife, Cheryl, had brought from her motel. He ceremoniously removed a magnum of champagne that had a reasonable approximation of the space shuttle etched on the green glass bottle. Ron even had an etching pen, and the crew took turns etching their signatures into the glass. Back home in Houston, they said, we're going to have one heck of a party, and this champagne will kick it off.

When it was time for the families to leave, Mike Smith took Jane aside and confided that he still felt frustrated by the seemingly inexplicable decision the night before not to tank the shuttle and carry out the countdown in anticipation of a weather break. They had never just scrubbed like that before, *anticipating* bad weather, as far as he knew, and the decision had him edgy.

Perhaps the other crew members shared his frustration. Perhaps it was the unnaturally early dinner, but Christa McAuliffe couldn't sleep. Around sunset she knocked on Greg Jarvis's door and the two set out for a walk around the KSC industrial area. Down in the O & C parking lot, they found a couple of delivery bicycles, so they borrowed them for a ride farther afield. A local TV van spotted them on Route 3, pedaling merrily through the twilight toward the floodlights of the VAB.

Christa smiled and waved for the camera. "Don't come real close," she warned, "we're in quarantine."

On the station's videotape, her face looks clear and rested, her eyes have a liquid gleam. There is no sign of fear.

* * *

Sunday, 8:30 p.m.
That night Mike Smith called his friend Bill Maready in Winston-Salem, North Carolina. Bill was an attorney who had flown his family down on his Beech Baron on Friday to see the launch. But after the scrub, he returned to North Carolina on Sunday afternoon. Before he left, Maready told Smith he'd give him a first-hand report on the weather conditions in that approaching front, since he'd be flying right through it en route to North Carolina.

Mike pressed Bill Maready for details on cloud types and thickness, wind strengths, turbulence and precipitation. Smith seemed especially concerned about the freezing conditions behind the front.

But the weather down here, Mike said, had been perfect—Visual Flight Rules all morning. There was no doubt about it, they should have flown today. He sighed and vented his frustration. "You know, Bill," Mike said bitterly, "you've got people making decisions down here who've never even flown an airplane before."

* * *

As the two men spoke on the telephone, the launch team assembled once more in Firing Room Three. The Orbiter Test Conductor gave his short count, and the red digits of the shuttle clock began clicking again, backward from the T-11 hours mark. Out on

Launch Pad 39B, the Rotating Service Structure rumbled back once more, exposing Challenger to the chill northwest breeze. Overhead the overcast of the retreating front shredded beneath the coldly distant moon.

SCRUB

Monday, 1:30 a.m.

As the moon rose above the scudding clouds, the wind steadied off, a chill fifteen knots from the northwest. Out at Launch Pad 39B the men working among the intricate piping of the cryogenic farm felt the cold on their hands and faces. Up on the Fixed Service Structure, the breeze began to keen in the struts and girders. It was a chilly night, but the front was finally past, the sky was clearing well, and there was work to do.

In Firing Room Three the launch team finished their initial tests and activations on schedule. The acting Lockheed Test Director, the LTD, verified the master checklists, polling the console operators to be certain of Challenger's onboard fuel cells—the Orbiter's electrical power source—were producing the correct voltage and amperage. The fuel cells were go, so one access arm to the Orbiter was retracted, and the LTD gave the order to evacuate the pad prior to tanking.

An operator on the main floor of the firing room requested permission to begin the purge of the payload bay and engine compartments with inert gaseous nitrogen, a routine that minimizes the risk of fire when the volatile "cryos" start flowing into the external tank.

At 1:17 Monday morning, as the moon rose higher, the LTD gave the order to begin "chilldown" of the propellant lines. Liquid hydrogen fuel and liquid oxygen oxidizer began to seep into the pipelines from the huge insulated igloo tanks on either side of the circular launch pad perimeter. The pad was completely evacuated during this hazardous operation, which was fully controlled from the consoles in the firing room.

Over the next three hours, the supercold propellants continued to flow, filling the big rust-colored external tank with five hundred thousand gallons of fuel—over eight hundred tons, more than one third of the shuttle's total weight. This tanking operation proceeded smoothly, even though the equipment on Pad 39B was being used for its first shuttle launch. The long hours of rehearsal and computer simulations were paying off.

*   *   *

Monday, 4:20 a.m.
Just before 4:20 that morning, the countdown clock reached the planned two-hour hold that coincided with the end of tanking. The external tank was in the "stable replenish" mode, with only enough propellants piped in to replace the slight evaporation loss. As the false dawn paled on the ocean horizon, the wind persisted. The early morning darkness was cold, just above the freezing mark. Wispy oxygen vapors puffed from vents on the shuttle and launch pad, and were instantly dispersed by the rising wind.

On the termination of tanking, two NASA vans climbed the long concrete incline to the base of the pad and parked near the edge of the concrete abutment, in the deep shadow cast by the Mobile Launching Platform. Above the vans the massive bulk of the space shuttle rose in its cold white mantle of floodlights, an almost surreal presence that always affected the men who climbed down from the vans, no matter how often they saw it.

One van carried the closeout crew, who would prepare the Orbiter to receive the astronauts, and the other bore the ice and debris inspection team. Their job was to carefully inspect the launch pad for windborne debris that might damage the Orbiter or be sucked up into the nozzles of the SRB's at the moment of ignition. Next they would inspect the external tank and the Orbiter for any signs of dangerous sheet ice that might have built up during tanking. With the cryogenics at temperatures hundreds of degrees below zero, and the prevailing humid coastal conditions at the pad, icing was usual. The Ice Team's task was to make certain the frost on the tank was not so thick that the chunks that fell during the blasting roar of lift-off would damage the Orbiter's fragile tiles on impact.

The team was led by Charlie Stevenson and Billie K. Davis. Both were veterans of many shuttle launches. They set to work quickly and quietly, one group moving through the shadows below the launch platform, while the other headed for the elevators at the foot of the Fixed Service Structure.

The closeout crew was made up of both NASA and Lockheed Space Operations Company—"LSOC" in Kennedy jargon—personnel. Their work station was the so-called "White Room" at the end of the Orbiter access arm, 195 feet up the Fixed Service Structure. One NASA member of the closeout crew was the "ASP," the Astronaut Support Person, Sonny Carter. Among many other tasks, his job would be to prepare the flight deck and mid-deck communications equipment prior to the arrival of the crew. Bill Campbell from LSOC was in charge of two other Lockheed technicians, Paul Arnold and Joe Sullivan. Their responsibilities included closing and sealing the circular crew-access hatch and then pressurizing the crew compartment.

NASA suit technician Al Rochfort was in charge of the crew's personal flight equipment, their helmets, Personal Emergency Air Packs—"PEAP's"—and their life jacket harnesses. The final NASA team member was Johnny Corlew, the Quality Assurance Inspector, who would approve every phase of the operation and affix his NASA inspection stamp on the closeout form to guarantee each step had been performed correctly.

While the Ice Team disappeared in the darkness, the closeout crew loaded their gear aboard elevator number one and mounted to level 195. The wind was brisk and chilling out on the exposed steel walkways, and the men had to brace themselves as they carried their equipment down the long open catwalk to the White Room. From this height the entire space center was visible, webs of twinkling lights among wide lakes of darkness. The white mass of the Orbiter stood like an icy cliff within the framework of the service structure.

An almost full moon hung cool and chalky on the western horizon. As the men ferried the bundles of flight equipment and tool boxes down the catwalk, the eastern horizon flared candy pink with sunrise. It looked like a beautiful morning for a shuttle launch.

In the Launch Control Center, the night crew had now "handed over" to the first team. The senior NASA managers under Launch Director Gene Thomas occupied the first row of consoles in Firing Room Three. One row down were the working countdown supervisors, including Ken Jenisek, the Lockheed Test Director, or LTD. Beside him sat Roberta Wyrick, the OTC or Orbiter Test Conductor. Jenisek had overall responsibility for all aspects of the countdown, while Wyrick supervised the final preparation of the Orbiter and crew for launch.

As the closeout crew prepared the White Room to receive the astronauts, Sonny Carter entered the Orbiter and climbed the short ladder to the flight deck. The Orbiter was in the vertical launch position, of course, so the crew seats faced upward, more like couches than chairs. Carter hauled himself to the flight deck gingerly, placing his hands and feet only on prearranged spots inside the crew compartment. A misplaced step or faulty handhold could result in serious damage to flight controls or instruments. Once in the commander's seat on the left side of the flight deck, Carter contacted Roberta Wyrick on the ground-to-air radio channel, and they began working through their long checklist. For the next forty minutes, they would verify dozens of instrument readings—the voltage meters of the fuel cells, the propellant pressures in the orbital maneuvering system engines, and many more. Every one of the several hundred toggle and slide switches on the flight deck had to be properly configured for launch. They worked slowly, patiently, with calm precision.

The White Room's thin aluminum walls rattled lightly in the wind, but the closeout crew were too busy to take much notice. With the circular Orbiter hatch open, they inserted a wide orange cabin ventilation hose, so that the air inside was constantly circulated. The open end of the White Room that abutted the Orbiter held an inflated cushion collar, similar to the skirt of an airport jetway that snugs up against an airliner. This collar helped seal the enclosed White Room from the invisible stream of gaseous nitrogen that was escaping from the nearby payload bay door on the top of the Orbiter. Nitrogen itself was not a toxic gas, but it was slightly lighter than oxygen and could cause rapid asphyxiation if it displaced the air in the overgrown closet of the White Room. Working together, Al Rochfort and Johnny Corlew hung the crew equipment from hooks on the left-hand wall. The crew would enter the White Room to dress for launch in the sequence they entered the Orbiter, Commander Scobee and Pilot Smith first, followed by Mission Specialists Ellison Onizuka and Judy Resnik. Then the mid-deck crew would board: Christa McAuliffe, Greg Jarvis, and finally Ron McNair, who would be seated immediately inside the access hatch. Working with the same patient precision as Sonny Carter, the two NASA technicians verified the name tags and hung each flight harness in proper sequence, then arranged the customized launch helmets in a straight line.

On the television monitor in the firing room, the white-suited closeout crew looked almost like surgical nurses preparing an operating room.

The sun rose, cutting hot orange slashes in the cloud banks out to sea.

*　　　*　　　*

Monday, 6:15 a.m.
On the third floor of the O & C Building, Challenger's flight crew were eating their traditional launch-morning breakfast of steak and eggs. They smiled dutifully for the NASA cameras and made convincingly lighthearted small talk. Before them on the long table stood a centerpiece of two dozen red and white roses arranged with small American flags and a big square cake decorated with their mission emblem: Halley's Comet, the Orbiter, and a bright red apple for the teacher.

After breakfast they changed out of their white polo shirts and slacks, and into their black boots and sky-blue flight suits. In the common room of the crew quarters, they waited a few moments for the televised weather briefing from Houston. Despite the gusty winds at the Cape, conditions were looking good at the TAL sites, at Edwards, and at White Sands. Mike Smith's earlier apprehensions seemed unfounded.

He certainly appeared relaxed and happy during the "Astronaut Walkout," the ritual exit from the side door of the building and the short Indian-file march past the television cameras and still photographers to the waiting Astrovan. Each of the crew waved and smiled; their eyes shone with excitement in the floodlights.

The narrow alleyway where the van was parked was protected from the wind, but overhead the scattered clouds were moving fast from the northwest. As they boarded the van, Dick Scobee and Mike Smith each looked up, veteran pilots checking the sky signs that sometimes predicted the local flying weather better than a computer.

*   *   *

Monday, 7:20 a.m.
During the shiny Astrovan's ritual progress toward the launch pad, LTD Ken Jenisek polled his launch team to be certain there were no violations of the formal Launch Commit Criteria. Every operator was go. Jenisek next called Bill Campbell and gave him formal approval for the crew to enter the Orbiter. To laymen this process might have seemed unnecessarily cumbersome. But NASA mission planners had carefully considered the question of crew fatigue when they formulated the countdown procedures. With the Orbiter in the vertical launch position, the crew would be lying on their backs, strapped tightly into their seats; the seats themselves were hard and narrow, nowhere near as comfortable as the couches of the Apollo capsule. If the countdown dragged on for hours, the astronauts could suffer cramped limbs that could inhibit them in the event of an emergency. So the Lockheed Test Director was obliged to be absolutely certain there were no launch constraints prevailing before he committed the crew to enter the Orbiter.

The Astrovan drove up the long ramp to the base of Pad 39B just as the rising sun broke free from the ocean cloud banks and flooded Challenger with warm light. Al Rochfort and Paul Arnold met the van and escorted the astronauts up in the number one elevator. On the walkways of level 195, Dick Scobee was exuberant, pointing out the clear pattern of the retreating cold front clouds, far out at sea to the southeast.

"What a beautiful day to fly!" he exclaimed.

He and Mike Smith were the first to cross the narrow catwalk of the access arm and enter the swinging "saloon doors" of the White Room. While Al Rochfort and Joe Sullivan helped Dick Scobee with his harness and flight helmet, Mike Smith stood to one side, softly reciting the checklist for the auxiliary power unit startup sequence he would have to perform later in the countdown. This was a habit he had acquired as a carrier pilot, one which had stood him in good stead during all those combat missions over North Vietnam. He cleared his mind with memory exercises, and his precise intellect was able to focus completely on the task at hand.

Scobee and Smith each stooped to kneel on the raised step at the lip of the hatch, then carefully pulled themselves inside and mounted the ladder to the flight deck. Ellison Onizuka entered the White Room next, followed by Judy Resnik. In smooth sequence, each of the crew donned their harnesses and helmets and crawled into the hatch. On the mid-deck, Sonny Carter helped Christa strap in, then check her communications links on the Orbiter's intercom and on the two radio channels to the Launch Control Center. After he repeated the process with Greg Jarvis and Ron McNair, Carter left the Orbiter, and the Lockheed crew carefully closed the hatch.

The closeout team was running well ahead of schedule. The next item on their Operational Maintenance Instruction (OMI) checklist was the latch and lock sequence for the access hatch. This was a straightforward but vitally important step in the countdown. The thick circular hatch was one of two regularly used openings in the pressurized crew compartment, the other being the airlock to the payload bay. Because the hatch was on the side of the Orbiter fuselage, it was covered with black and white heat tiles in a mosaic that looked like a dartboard. The hatch provided both pressure integrity while in the vacuum of space and thermal protection during reentry. To verify that the hatch was fully closed and locked in the properly sealed position, the technicians relied on two microswitch indicators that could be read on an electrical panel on the wall of the White Room.

After the Lockheed team carefully slid the hatch in place and used a T-shaped driver tool to engage the locking mechanism, Johnny Corlew checked the panel to make sure the microswitches read latched and locked. One switch read correctly on the Ohms meter, one did not. It was just after 8:30, and the long morning's troubles were beginning.

While Bill Campbell called in the problem to the LTD, Corlew inserted a lighted mirror into the narrow pressurization port in the center of the hatch. Using this tool, he could verify that the locking mechanism was correctly seated. The trouble had to be from a malfunctioning switch. Probably just needs a little adjustment, Corlew thought. But it was too late in the countdown to start tinkering with delicate microswitches. Corlew repeated his inspection with the mirror light, then gave Campbell the tool and let him see for himself. Dutifully Bob Campbell called in the news to the LTD. The latches were clearly in place, but the switch didn't show locked on the panel.

In the firing room the news provoked considerable discussion among the Orbiter teams. Everyone was concerned about the ominous ramifications of a bad hatch seal. They could live with a malfunctioning indicator switch, but no one wanted to approve a launch if the hatch-sealing mechanism were actually faulty. The hurried consultations spread outward from the firing room in ripples of phone calls and impromptu telecons, finally reaching the Rockwell orbiter support room in Downey, California. While the engineers worked, the countdown clock clicked ahead to a planned T-20 minutes hold. And there, indeed, it held.

In the White Room, the closeout crew waited impotently for word from the firing room. All they knew for the moment was that the LTD was "working" the problem. The wind was up and they could feel its force on the flimsy White Room walls.

*   *   *

Monday, 8:30 a.m.

At the Shuttle Landing Facility, four miles from the pad, a team had gathered to man the caravan of ground equipment. They were here to support the Return to Launch Site Abort (RTLS) capability, and one of their concerns was weather. Specifically they were becoming anxious about the wind. As the sun rose higher, the average wind speed also increased, and the wind was definitely backing around to the west. The shuttle runway was oriented northwest, southeast, to take advantage of the prevailing wind directions at the Cape. According to the Air Force weather briefing given to the Mission Management Team the previous afternoon, today's winds were to be generally moderate from the northwest, with a chance of stronger westerly winds later in the day, as the center of low pressure to the north tracked up the coast toward Cape Hatteras. But the wind was already swinging west and beginning to gust above fifteen knots.

And that was the problem. The weather section of the formal Launch Commit Criteria detailed acceptable surface winds for Orbiter landing, including RTLS landings. A headwind of no greater than twenty-five knots was permitted, but the maximum allowable crosswind for a runway landing was only fifteen knots. With the wind periodically swinging over to an azimuth of about 290 degrees and gusting just above fifteen knots, the present conditions were only marginally acceptable.

In the firing room, the frustrated launch team were beginning to see the dimensions of their problem. The longer they waited for the teams of supporting engineers to analyze the hatch-locking malfunction and to recommend a safe course of action, the greater the chance that unacceptable crosswinds would prevail at the SLF. Yet if they simply ignored the problem of the apparently malfunctioning microswitch, they were risking a catastrophic decompression of the Orbiter during ascent. No one would even consider such a course. Unlike earlier space flights, on which the crew had pressurized space suits, shuttle astronauts wore simple flight coveralls and helmets that were open to cabin atmosphere. These helmets would not protect them in the event of an explosive hatch failure in space; the helmets' primary function was to provide breathable air from the PEAP's during an emergency evacuation involving smoke or toxic fuel leaks. In effect the integrity of the space shuttle's highly touted "shirt-sleeve" environment depended on a series of small alloy latch pins and, indirectly, on the microswitch system that was currently proving just how sensitive it was.

Explosion of Challenger.

Mission Control Room in Houston. Flight Directors Alan Briscoe (left) and Jay Greene. "No downlink."

The evolution of the shuttle booster joint

How NASA applied safety feature to designs for new booster casings.

1970's	1982	1985	1986
Original Design	Filament Casing	Revised Steel Casing	Latest Proposal

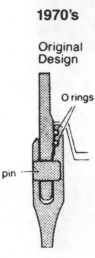

O rings

pin

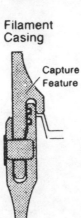

Capture Feature

Third O ring

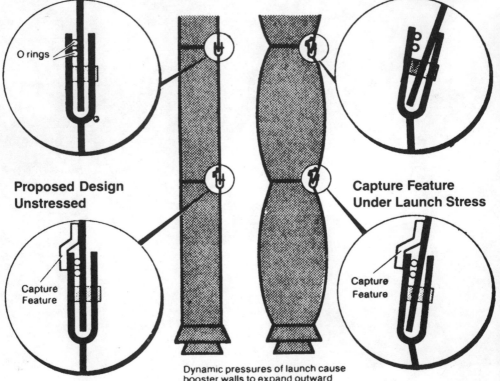

Original Design Unstressed

O rings

Original Design Under Launch Stress

Proposed Design Unstressed

Capture Feature

Capture Feature Under Launch Stress

Capture Feature

Dynamic pressures of launch cause booster walls to expand outward between seals.

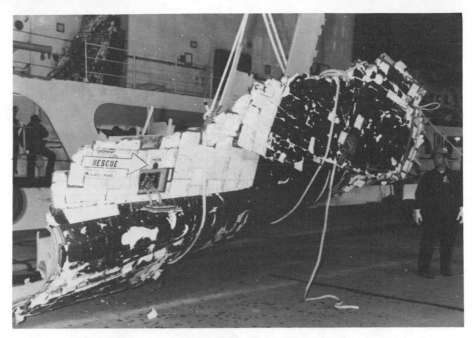

Wreckage of Challenger recovered from the Atlantic.

Challenger's crew remains are airlifted from Kennedy Space Center, April 29, 1986.

Professor Richard P. Feynman, member of the Rogers Commission. "It flies and nothing happens. Then it is suggested therefore that the risk is no longer so high for the next flight. We can lower our standards a bit because we got away with it last time. It's a kind of Russian roulette."

Dr. Sally K. Ride, member of the Rogers Commission.

Neil A. Armstrong, Vice Chairman of the Rogers Commission.

William P. Rogers, Chairman of the Rogers Commission. He ruled that the decision to launch was "clearly flawed."

Mike Smith. "You've got people making decisions down here who've never even flown an airplane before."

Christa McAuliffe.

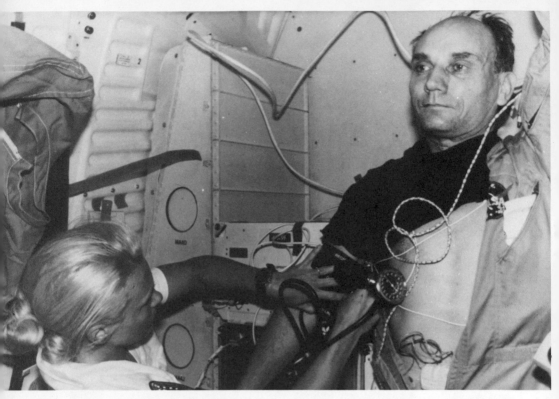

Senator Jake Garn undergoing medical experiment aboard space shuttle Discovery in orbit.

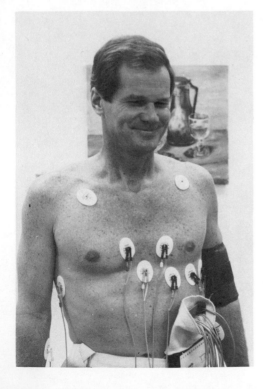

Congressman Bill Nelson training for his space flight. "Yet I had confidence that the Lord had brought me to this point for a reason and I think that is to fly."

Monday, 9:30 a.m.

After a considerable delay, Bill Campbell received the word from the LTD that a safe verification system had been approved. The technicians were to use the T-handle to open and close the hatch-locking mechanism, while astronaut Ron McNair—who was seated beside the hatch—would bend down to watch the pins actually fall into place. This operation was not as simple as it sounded, however. First there was the awkward communications loop, with the White Room technicians passing their instructions to McNair through the LTD in the firing room. Then there was confusion as to exactly what the technicians wanted Ron to look for. Like the other astronauts, he had been thoroughly trained in the operation of the hatch, but he had never been shown how to verify visually the correct movement of the locking latches. Finally McNair found that he could not lean close enough to the inside hatch handle to see the locking pins because his bulky flight helmet struck the lip of the porthole.

More time passed. The men in the White Room began to pace with frustration, then stopped, acutely aware of the television camera inside its small glass window on the padside wall. Everything they did was being recorded on videotape. If things went well, few people would even remember seeing them; but if they didn't solve this problem soon, they might end up in starring roles on the "CBS Evening News."

By now the crew had been lying on their backs for over two hours. Commander Dick Scobee called for status reports several times and was told the closeout crew was working the problem. There was a certain amount of ribald chatter over the Orbiter intercom about various portions of the anatomy becoming numb. The wind shook the White Room as the technicians bent down to squint into the narrow confines of the hatch mechanism.

Ron McNair indicated that he could just distinguish the pins in place. Johnny Corlew used his lighted mirror again: everything looked good. The microswitch still indicated the latch was unlocked, but the word came from the firing room to proceed. Corlew placed his NASA quality-assurance stamp on the closeout sequence form, and the men hurried to complete their work.

Although the removal of the so-called "milk stool" external

hatch handle had not yet come up on the closeout checklist, the men decided to go ahead with the procedure in order to save time. Unlike airliner hatches, with external aluminum skins, the space shuttle's crew hatch was covered with fragile thermal protection system (TPS) tiles. Therefore, the hatch could not simply be pushed tightly closed by hand while the locking mechanism was turned, nor could it be swung open in the same manner. The TPS was so delicate that even a fingernail could scratch the tile surface. To overcome this design difficulty, Rockwell had developed a hatch handle that was anchored directly to the aluminum shell of the hatch through three openings in the TPS tiles. A three-legged aluminum tube frame—not unlike a short milking stool in an old-fashioned dairy barn—connected to the hatch with three so-called "captive fasteners" made of hard Inconel alloy. Using the milk stool handle, technicians could safely move the bulky hatch without fear of damaging the tiles.

In theory the handle could be put in place and removed in less than a minute. The technicians inserted a long hexagonal-head wrench into the first two legs of the milk stool and loosened the captive fasteners. But when Joe Sullivan tried to turn the third fastener bolt, the wrench spun in his hand.

"Hey, Corlew," he said over his shoulder, "we got a problem. This thing's loose."

Johnny Corlew stepped over and took the wrench. "Let me see it a second."

Corlew had been a Navy aviation metalsmith for twenty years and had spent three tours aboard aircraft carriers off Vietnam. He knew as much as anyone about improvising repairs under difficult circumstances. He slipped the tool into the tube, felt the hexagonal head engage the slot on the bolt, then backed the tool carefully counterclockwise. The fastener spun without much friction; obviously the threads were stripped. "All this thing is doing is spinning," Corlew said. "We've got problems."

Because they still had a few minutes before hatch removal would appear on the closeout checklist, the men tried various tricks to make the stripped bolt threads catch in the nut plate inside the hatch. First they tightened down hard on the two other fasteners, so that the milk stool wouldn't rotate against the hatch and damage the tiles. Then they applied pressure to the third leg, pulling it this way and that, while angling the wrench, hoping to make at least one thread catch. They had no luck; the fastener simply spun as before.

Corlew realized the scope of the situation. "Call the LTD," he told Bill Campbell. "Tell him we've got a problem here, that we've got a captive fastener that won't come out."

Campbell reported over his headset and was advised that the launch team would "work the problem." While the men in the White Room waited, Johnny Corlew tried to figure out a solution. "About the only way we're going to get this thing out of there is to drill the head off this captive fastener," he said, shaking his head in frustration. "Tell them to send us a drill and a hacksaw."

After a few moments of conversation, the LTD told Campbell that a battery-operated drill and a hacksaw were en route to the launch pad. Because of the constant hazard of gaseous hydrogen leaks, only nonsparking battery-operated power tools were allowed on the launch pad once the external tank was filled. And the men in the White Room were keenly aware that they were only a few feet away from eight hundred tons of explosive propellants.

When the drill had not arrived after fifteen minutes, they began trying again without it. They jammed a long screwdriver down the tube to squeeze the nut plate against the metal hatch frame, then tried angling the hex-head wrench once more, praying for the threads to catch. The fastener spun uselessly. Before the drill finally arrived, each man had tried his luck with the balky fastener. But there was no luck to be had this morning.

During the wait, Commander Dick Scobee spoke with the OTC and was told about the stripped hatch bolt. He took the news reasonably well, but he did ask about the wind conditions. The crosswinds at the SLF were still marginally acceptable.

Forty-five minutes after the call had gone out from the White Room, a van arrived with the tools. The men worked as quickly as they could unloading the equipment. The drill was a standard Black and Decker handyman drill with a rechargeable battery mounted in the plastic handle. Campbell fitted a drill bit with an eight-inch shaft, and they set to work drilling out the bolt head. Almost as soon as the bit contacted the Inconel, however, the drill's high screech dropped to a hum, then a ragged buzz. The battery was too weak to make headway against the hard alloy of the bolt.

Corlew bent over the milk stool, then turned to Campbell. "Tell the LTD we're going to have to cut this milk stool off in order to get at the fastener. Tell him we need more batteries, too."

Waiting for the batteries, the men took turns with the drill, trying to coax a little more energy from it. The problem was two-fold: a battery that had sat out in a cold tool box all night losing its charge, and the tough alloy of the fastener. Also, the eight-inch bit was not really long enough; the drill chuck kept butting on the lip of the tube, further reducing the drill's power. And using such an awkwardly long drill bit so close to the Orbiter was a problem in itself. If the bit skipped off the hard alloy bolt head and punched through the thin aluminum leg of the milk stool, they might actually drill a hole in the Orbiter's pressurized crew compartment, thus provoking an automatic scrub that would probably entail a total cancellation of the mission.

A final problem was the nitrogen hazard close to the hatch. The men were warned not to spend too much time up there because of the proximity of the gaseous nitrogen payload bay vents. And they did not have to be warned twice. They all remembered the two workers who had died inside Columbia's engine compartment, asphyxiated by nitrogen during the preparations for the first space shuttle mission, five years before.

Almost half an hour later, another van arrived with nine replacement batteries. Once more, the closeout crew worked as quickly as they could. But the first battery was even weaker than the original one. In angry frustration the technicians tested all the batteries. Only one of the nine had much charge in it. The rest were flat. But again the battery-operated drill was not strong enough to make any headway against the tough alloy fastener.

They called the LTD and formally requested permission to use a stronger AC drill or, if that didn't work, to cut the leg off the milk stool with the hacksaw. While they waited for this permission, they could feel the wind rising around the exposed Orbiter access arm and the White Room.

In the firing room the Lockheed team conferred with the NASA managers and with the airframe specialists from Rockwell. Time had suddenly become a key factor. There were less than ninety minutes left in the morning's launch window, and the wind was definitely blowing west-northwest and gusting above fifteen knots. The senior NASA managers on the top row of consoles were acutely aware that they might be facing yet another scrub, this one triggered by a stripped bolt that was worth perhaps five dollars, even at inflated government contract prices. The nightmare sequence of scrubs that had plagued the 61-C mission for over a month was now threatening the Challenger mission. A scrub today because of hardware problems and a scrub tomorrow caused by the predicted freezing weather would mean their March ASTRO mission would almost certainly be delayed.

It was quickly determined that the actual explosion hazard from a sparking AC drill was negligible at that position on the Orbiter because of the masking influence of the nitrogen from the nearby payload bay vents. And of course on such a windy day, venting hydrogen from the engines would be dissipated long before it reached the 195-foot level. NASA managers cut the knot of indecision and authorized using the power drill. But as with the battery-operated drill, the bit was neither long or strong enough to gouge off the bolt head. The closeout crew reported their failure and asked again for permission to use the hacksaw.

While the experts conferred, Johnny Corlew felt the frustration tighten inside him. Why was it taking so long to come up with a decision to cut off the milk stool? Surely they weren't trying to save a few dollars by not damaging this piece of equipment. The milk stool was just welded aluminum tubing; he could have put together a replacement back at the OPF. If they did scrub, the wasted propellants in the external tank alone were worth over $500,000. So saving the hatch handle was not the reason for the delay. More likely the engineers were debating what kind of stresses the sawing procedure would place on the hatch itself, especially on the multiple seals and hinges. In the early days of the shuttle program, there would have been a NASA orbiter engineer right here in the White Room during closeout, a man who could have made his own decisions. Since Lockheed had won the shuttle processing contract, however, the role of the NASA engineer had been filled by a lead technician. And this technician always had to defer to a licensed engineer when problems arose.

This management arrangement was instituted as one of many similar economies that had helped Lockheed win the coveted shuttle processing contract. But the new procedure had often provoked delays. And today this process seemed especially cumbersome. Twenty minutes after they had requested permission to use the hacksaw, word still had not come down from the LTD. Johnny Corlew decided they had waited long enough. "Look," he said to Campbell, "just go ahead and cut it."

As Johnny spoke, Campbell held up his hand, signaling that he was getting a message on his headset. "The LTD says we've got permission to cut the milk stool."

They had the hacksaw ready, and it did not take very long to hack through the aluminum tube and the hard alloy fastener. As soon as they cut the bolt shaft, they loosened the other two fasteners and the milk stool lifted neatly away. The severed end of the fastener slipped back inside the nut plate of the hatch. Johnny Corlew determined that the tiny stub of the bolt would not cause any problem in there, and he was finally able to approve the closeout sequence form for hatch removal.

They hurried to install the TPS plugs in each fastener hole and to test these plugs for fit and adhesion. Once more, Johnny Corlew was able to affix his NASA quality-approval stamp. The men were working as fast as they could, within the limits of safety; they certainly did not want to damage any component and cause yet another delay. Cabin pressurization was the next item on the checklist. They attached the pressure hose and started the flow. Campbell stood stiffly at his station, listening for confirmation from the flight crew that cabin pressure had reached sea level. Once word came, they quickly unscrewed the air-hose nozzle and spun the large B-nut until it was hand-tight over the pressure inlet.

They were almost home. Johnny watched as they safety-wired the nut, then closely inspected the wire itself. Once more he stamped his approval. The Lockheed technicians affixed the TPS plug—the size of a pie plate—over the B-nut, and Johnny Corlew checked it for proper seating.

They were ready to ease away the White Room skirt in preparation for swing back of the access arm. With almost an hour remaining in the launch window, the men were now feeling a lot more confident. The final item on Johnny's checklist was a visual inspection of the TPS around the hatch, to be certain no tiles had been cracked or gouged during crew ingress. The tiles were clean. Two hours behind schedule, the closeout crew was ready to depart.

But they would not receive the order to leave the pad until the LTD was ready to resume the count at the T-minus twenty minutes mark. And that resumption could not occur with the launch constraint now in effect. While the closeout crew had been working, the westerly crosswinds at the shuttle landing field had risen to a steady twenty knots.

The closeout crew waited in the White Room, their toolboxes packed. The flight crew waited on their stiff, aching backs inside Challenger. The launch team waited in tense frustration in the firing room.

And the crew's immediate families waited in Launch Director Gene Thomas's office on the fourth floor of the LCC. It had been almost three hours since they arrived, and the small children were getting fussy. They played with cutouts and coloring books on the carpeted floor; their families sat tiredly in chairs around the director's conference table, staring out the broad windows at the white dart of the space shuttle, immobile on the launch pad, three miles away.

In the VIP grandstands near the press mound, all of Mike Smith's large contingent of family and friends waited in the cold wind, squinting at the stationary digits of the countdown clock. Christa McAuliffe's parents sat on the bleacher seats, smiling gamely for the photographers. Some of the press waited in their own grandstand, but the experienced reporters had stayed inside the Press Dome, out of the wind.

Chief astronaut John Young flew a series of approaches in the shuttle training aircraft; the gusty crosswind was clearly unacceptable. And still the wind rose, peaking above twenty-five knots, flattening the saw grass along the wide shuttle runway.

As the delay dragged on, several of the weary reporters in the crowded Dome got a little punchy with coffee nerves and general disappointment. They began scratching parodic *National Enquirer* headlines on their note pads and passing them around the bullpen. "Blade Wielding Scientists Slash Space Mom's Ship" was one of the more wholesome. Several were downright obscene.

A little after noon, with the wind still gusting hard from the west, Gene Thomas asked Commander Dick Scobee if the crew were up to waiting the optional half hour beyond the 12:37 expiration of the formal launch window. Scobee polled his crew and came back with a strong "Yes, sir."

But T-minus twenty minutes in the countdown actually included a built-in ten-minute hold before the automatic Ground Launch Sequencer computer program would begin. So by 12:36 P.M. there was no longer enough time in the window, even counting the thirty-minute optional extension.

Roberta Wyrick broke the news to Scobee. He replied that tomorrow would probably be a better day.

* * *

Monday, 12:50 p.m.
As the tired, aching astronauts climbed stiffly from the hatch, the men of the closeout crew apologized for the long hassles with the hatch that had eaten up so much of the launch window. Dick Scobee drew himself wearily up to full height and shucked off his life jacket harness.

"Geeze," he said, grinning warmly, "we didn't know what was going on down here at first when we heard all that drilling." He pointed to the open hatch. "Sounded like a bunch of termites."

Johnny Corlew shook his head and began to apologize all over again. Scobee patted him on the back. "Hey," he said, "forget it, Johnny. That's the way things go sometimes. We'll just try it again tomorrow."

CHAPTER ELEVEN

JANUARY 27, 1986

PRESS ON

Monday, 1:00 p.m.

Although most of the people in Firing Room Three were probably not aware of it, the term "scrub" has a colorful derivation. The expression to "scrub a mission" had slipped into the jargon of American rocketry from the Air Force during the early days at the Cape, testing V-2's after the war. The Air Force had adopted the jargon from the RAF, which had inherited the expression from its World War I predecessor, the Royal Flying Corps. At British aerodromes on the Western Front, operational sorties were chalked up on a blackboard the night before; if weather or mechanical problems aborted the missions, an orderly "scrubbed" the blackboard clean. If conditions were marginal, the commander might decide to "press on." And the term, of course, had crept into the vocabulary of the early military aviators from their earthbound predecessors, the cavalry. Its meaning was clear: do not be timid; analyze the risks, accept them, then move ahead.

So in the early afternoon of Monday, January 27, it would not have been unusual for the tired and frustrated engineers hunched at their consoles in the firing room and the various support centers at Kennedy, Marshall, and Houston to be discussing the earlier decision to scrub and the probable subsequent decision to "press on" for a twenty-four-hour turnaround. They could not yet "stand down"—another inherited cavalry term—because the numerous technical teams had to be polled about the feasibility of a fast turnaround. While teams of technicians swarmed around the launch pad, "safing" ground support equipment and the shuttle's potentially volcanic propulsion system, the various project managers polled their technical support personnel about a one-day turn-around.

But cold weather threatened the complex operation. This is the Tuesday launch weather forecast that Air Force Lieutenant Scott Funk gave the NASA managers immediately after the Monday scrub:

"Situation—Strong cold air advection as arctic high pressure moves into southeast U.S. Generally clearing skies and lessening winds as gradient lessens. Freezing temps expected for approximately 11 hours with expected low of 23 degrees F.

"Forecast—Clear skies, good visibility, winds northwesterly 10 to 18 knots, low temperature expected to be 23 degrees F. with slow warming through launch window."

In other words, the managers could anticipate one of the coldest nights of the winter. And they had to decide if this cold was an acceptable risk, if they should press on for a Tuesday launch.

One of these managers was Larry Mulloy, the head of the Solid Rocket Booster Project at Marshall. From his console in the Mission Support Room, Mulloy called over the booster channel of the OIS communications network, working down his checklist as he contacted every member of the widely dispersed support staff. Some were at the Cape, some at Marshall, and others out at the Morton Thiokol Wasatch plant in Utah. Mulloy's concerns centered on the cold temperatures predicted for launch time Tuesday morning, not on the overnight lows. Specifically Mulloy wanted to learn if the cold weather would trigger any violations of the formal Launch Commit Criteria (LCC), the body of rules that governed launching a shuttle mission. Mulloy was aware that these rules had become rather elastic with the increased flight rate, since he himself had been writing launch constraints and automatic waivers to them for the past six missions. Therefore, polling for potential launch-commit violations had become something of an empty exercise, but no Project Manager would openly admit this. Instead they bent the LCC's law to serve operational necessity.

*   *   *

During the countdown the night before, an especially flagrant example of rule bending had occurred. As the sky cleared Sunday evening, the cold air mass behind the front exerted itself; after midnight, temperatures dropped toward freezing, and by early Monday morning this cold had begun to cause problems.

The greatest concern was over the nose cone vent of the external fuel tank. Liquid oxygen was stored in the upper portion of the tank. The tank's nose cone contained a vent for gaseous oxygen to boil off and be safely carried away by the so-called "beanie cap." Launch Commit Criteria ruled that there could be "no visible ice buildup on the nosecap fairing exit area . . ." and the "redline" minimum temperature for the nose cone was 45 degrees F. To maintain this minimum, the tank was equipped with electrical heaters. However, engineers at the firing room consoles had discovered that the heaters could not keep up with the cold, and the nose cone temperatures were sliding toward the redline. They expected the temperature might actually fall as low as 30 degrees Monday morning before the sun warmed Challenger again. Instead of calling a halt to the countdown, however, NASA managers under KSC Director of Engineering Horace Lamberth simply wrote a waiver to the LCC nosecap temperature rules, which read: "For STS-33 (51-L) Min. LCC acceptable is 28 deg. F. [previously 45 degrees F.] Ullage transducers are acceptable down to 28 deg. F. [previously 40 degrees F]."

These transducers were vitally important instruments that measured the gas pressure in the oxygen tank and controlled the amount of helium needed to bring the tank to flight pressure for proper engine function. By toying with the acceptable temperature redlines for these transducers, Lamberth's men were taking yet one more "acceptable risk" with disastrous potential. Without accurate ullage pressure readings, they were risking premature main engine shutdown, a hazardous launchpad abort that had occurred (for different reasons) twice before in the program.

Their rationale for writing this illogical waiver was that the LCC temperature minimums could be safely bypassed so long as there was no visible ice on the exit fairing and the launch team had accurate pressure readings from the tank. But such accurate readings depended on functional transducers, and these instruments were only calibrated to work correctly at temperatures between 40 and 140 degrees F.

The launch team leaders were perfectly aware of this on the morning of January 27. The tape of the OIS engineering channel reveals the following exchange between Horace Lamberth and an engineer named "Mac":

MAC: "Hey, are you guys reading this LCC that the consequences of exceeding the nose cone temp redline? The sheet we have over here says that we will get inaccurate ullage pressure readings."

HORACE LAMBERTH: "Okay, Mac, we understand. Thank you."

And after the scrub on Monday, the KSC engineering staff discussed the almost certain inability of the tank's heaters to keep up with the extremely low temperatures predicted for Tuesday morning. One unidentified voice on the OIS channel specified the engineers' collective concern:

"You got it [the tank heater] full blast. You're gonna be down to eighteen to twenty degrees tomorrow on the nose cone. And the waiver we wrote today said we're only good down to twenty-eight. That was today's . . ."

Lamberth listened to the concerns of his technical support staff, made no immediate effort to address them, then proceeded to report in the formal postscrub meeting that the predicted temperatures for a Tuesday morning launch were a matter of some concern but would be within acceptable limits. There is no record of his degree of explicitness about redline waivers at this meeting.

* * *

According to his testimony before the Rogers Commission, Larry Mulloy polled all the solid rocket booster support staff and found only two temperature-related concerns that could possibly jeopardize a twenty-four-hour turnaround for a Tuesday launch. If temperatures at launch time were down around thirty-one degrees, he was told, the batteries that powered the radio beacons of the SRB recovery system might not function; that would be a violation of the LCC redlines. Also, and much more serious, such low temperatures would probably violate redlines for the nitrogen purge system of the hydrazine fuel supplies in the hydraulic power units that swiveled the boosters' nozzles and helped steer the shuttle during ascent. He requested a more detailed analysis, based on the fact that the temperatures at launch *had* to be above 31 degrees because that was the overall redline minimum temperature for the entire shuttle system. His people came back on the net to say the redlines would not be violated at higher temperatures. "It was concluded," Mulloy testified, that "we did not have a problem. . . ."

According to his testimony, there was no concern raised at this point about the effect of the low temperatures on the booster field joints or their vulnerable O-ring seals.

*   *   *

At one that afternoon, less than half an hour after the scrub, Mulloy joined Lamberth and dozens of other managers and engineers in the large conference room directly across from Firing Room Three. This room, 3-R-22, was normally used for the big meetings known as Weekly Assessment Reviews during which the myriad elements of the complex shuttle flow process were discussed. But the room was also large enough to hold all the participants in a typical postscrub conference. As the tired, disappointed engineers and managers took their assigned places, there was a nasty sense of *déjà vu:* they had attended four such conferences in the past month during the launch problems of 61-C.

Arnie Aldrich and Jesse Moore sat at the head of the long open rectangle of conference tables; the sides were occupied by the Senior Technical Project Managers, and the supporting engineers and contractor representatives took chairs around the sides of the room. The mood was quiet, somber. And the KSC people, including the Lockheed reps, seemed especially subdued. There is no record of any acrimony passing between the senior NASA managers and those on the Lockheed launch team responsible for the fiasco of the dead drill batteries and the long-delayed permission to use the hacksaw on the milk stool, but no one was smiling.

Aldrich polled all the managers as to what they had learned from their technical staffs concerning a twenty-four-hour turnaround. One by one the men spoke up, voicing their assessments of the cold weather's impact. The consensus seemed to be that although the cold would bring clearly marginal conditions, and some redline limits might be stretched, there were no unacceptable risks involved in proceeding with a minimum turnaround. One area of concern not related to the weather was propellants, but it was quickly determined that the cryo farm at Pad 39B had adequate supplies for another launch attempt on Tuesday morning.

The biggest worry was the launch pad itself. If the overnight temperatures really did drop to the low twenties, such a hard freeze would almost certainly cripple the pad. One year earlier a similarly cold night had forced a weather slip of the 51-C launch. The multiple water systems on the pad's service structures and launching platform were not insulated against such cold. In January 1985 the solution had been to drain the entire water system on Pad 39A or risk burst pipes and a dangerous drenching of the Orbiter; then, a day later when the temperature climbed above freezing, the systems were refilled and an emergency plan put into effect. The launch proceeded. For that second launch attempt, the Kennedy Space Center had developed a freeze-protection plan that entailed bleeding steady streams of water through the emergency showers and fire extinguisher systems, out through the pad's drains and downspouts on the northwest side of the Fixed Service Structure. Several thousand gallons of antifreeze would also be added to the sound-suppression troughs beneath the solid rocket boosters. In theory this procedure would protect the pad from burst pipes during the hard overnight freeze without resorting to the time-consuming process of draining the system, which would have entailed an automatic one-day slip.

The freeze-protection plan was a Kennedy solution to a Kennedy problem; Dick Smith and his people recommended the procedure wholeheartedly. Like their counterparts from Johnson and Marshall, no one at KSC wanted to be responsible for a system-endemic failure that would explode the carefully nurtured myth of the operational space shuttle. The shuttle was meant to fly *on schedule,* winter and summer, and here was a test of NASA's "mettle" worthy of James Beggs's challenge the year before.

Huge charts covered the walls of Room 3-R-22, intricately detailed bar graphs ten feet high and fifty feet long. These were the Integrated Operations Assessment charts that tracked each of the four Orbiters through the OPF and VAB for the next several months. The charts were dense with small magnetic tags symbolizing deadlines and milestones in four simultaneous shuttle flows, the progress toward meeting the manifest. But no one in the room —least of all the men from Kennedy—needed this graphic reminder to be aware that 1986 would be a frantically busy year for the space shuttle program. The politically important Columbia ASTRO mission in March and the two planetary science missions in May had inflexible launch windows. The men in the room all knew how the multiple delays of 61-C had in turn delayed the launch of Challenger's 51-L mission; and today the frustrating hassles with that hatch handle had eaten up a perfectly good launch window. A successful launch this morning would have put the program back on schedule. But it was not too late to salvage the year's manifest: the shuttle flow experts at KSC had made a firm assessment that if the Challenger flew by January 28, the ASTRO mission might still be launched by the original March 6 date and beat the Soviets to the Halley's Comet coverage. But if Challenger did not fly the next morning, the ASTRO Halley's mission would undoubtedly be delayed. And no one wanted to be responsible for that.

Before the men left the conference room, the senior managers admonished them to continue the surveys of their technical support staffs. In half an hour the Mission Management Team would meet to assess in detail the possible constraints to a one-day turnaround. Right now, conditions appeared marginally acceptable, but the managers needed more information. The subordinates were to contact their supervisors if they came across any problem whatsoever—especially weather-related problems—that would threaten another scrub. NASA wanted desperately to launch tomorrow, but they certainly wanted to launch safely.

The senior members of the Mission Management Team had a few minutes for a sandwich and another cup of coffee before they convened again in the fourth-floor Ops Center. There was still the possibility that they would call for a slip. But the unofficial word now was: Press on.

*   *   *

Monday, 1:30 p.m.

One of the senior NASA officials in the firing room during the Monday morning countdown and scrub was Shirley Green, the agency's Director of Public Affairs. Ms. Green was a political appointee who had worked for Vice President Bush for seven years. She was a newcomer to NASA, still feeling her way among unfamiliar personalities in the agency's top management. Her responsibilities included liaison with the White House press office, keeping Larry Speakes and Pat Buchanan informed about NASA's newsworthy activities. Ms. Green dutifully telephoned the White House press office after it had been decided at the postscrub meeting to go for a twenty-four-hour turnaround. The launch of Challenger, she told her White House contact, Rusty Brashear, was now scheduled for 9:38 Tuesday morning. This was also the Tuesday in January on which President Reagan would deliver his State of the Union Message.

When Ms. Green's staff drafted NASA's input to the speech in early January, it was assumed that Challenger would be in orbit and that Christa McAuliffe would have already delivered her first lesson from space by the time of the speech. But the delays had changed all that. And Ms. Green was anxious to learn how the agency would be mentioned in the final version of the message. On her arrival at the Cape two days before, Shirley Green had called her White House press office contact (she later could not recall if it was Rusty Brashear or Denny Grizzly) and asked about NASA's inclusion in the upcoming State of the Union Message. She had heard that the speech was going to be short this year and was worried her agency had not made the cut. In her interview with a Rogers Commission investigator, here is her version of the call:

"Did NASA make the State of the Union? And I was told, 'Yes.' And I said, 'Good. Did we also get the recommendation on the Space Station?' He said, 'Yes, you did, also Space Science and the Aerospace Plane.' And I said, 'You know, that's terrific. Did they tie it to the Teacher-in-Space being up?' And he said, 'No, there's no mention of the Teacher.' And I said, 'I'm sorry to hear that because it's going to be a big media event, I think. But on the other hand, the significant and important programmatic areas would be in the State of the Union.' "

If this is an accurate description of that conversation, several important questions remain unanswered. First, did Ms. Green simply not ask whether the President might reconsider mentioning the Teacher-in-Space flight, should Challenger be launched the next morning? Second, did Ms. Green not pass on this news to any senior NASA managers at the Cape (which was certainly part of her normal responsibilities)? And third, was it not obvious to Ms. Green and other NASA officials that the President was bound to mention Christa McAuliffe, once the flight was up? A President so astute in manipulating symbols and imagery for political gain could hardly be expected to pass up such a rich opportunity to score points with women and the education establishment. It was common sense to assume that President Reagan would have found room to pencil into his prepared speech a reference to Christa McAuliffe, had Challenger been successfully launched that Tuesday morning.

But it is equally sensible to assume that this was not a burning priority for the President or his Chief of Staff, Donald Regan. If NASA did succeed in launching Challenger, the President could capitalize on the opportunity; but if the flight was scrubbed again, he obviously had to have replacement language prepared. Since the Challenger accident, there has been widespread speculation in the press that White House officials "pressured" NASA to launch Challenger on Tuesday, January 28, so that the President could refer to the Teacher-in-Space in his speech, the basic theme of which was the bright future promised by the advancement of American science and technology. The White House has repeatedly denied this charge, calling it a vicious rumor perpetrated by the press.

In their denials White House officials have taken pains to emphasize that there was no mention whatsoever of the Teacher-in-Space mission in the speech *as prepared for delivery* on January 28, which is probably true. This, of course, does not address the obvious point that President Reagan would have looked foolish to praise NASA's achievements in his speech while simply ignoring the Teacher-in-Space mission, especially given the fact that excellence in education was a major theme of the message.

The full details of NASA's contact with the White House concerning the Challenger flight and the State of the Union Message will probably not be known until members of the current White House staff write their memoirs. However, it is now clear that the White House is extremely sensitive about this issue and that they are putting up a very effective barricade to further investigation.

For example, Democratic Senator Ernest F. Hollings of South Carolina officially requested that the White House release its outgoing and incoming telephone logs for the offices of the Chief of Staff, the Cabinet Secretary, and nine numbers elsewhere in the White House for the period from midnight January 20 to noon January 28. Hollings's assertion was that someone at one of these numbers might have called NASA officials at the Cape or in Houston and insisted they launch Challenger in time for the speech, or that NASA officials might have called the White House to discuss the timing of the flight. One of the nine White House numbers Senator Hollings listed was 456-2100: the number of Albert R. "Rusty" Brashear.

In his reply to Senator Hollings, Presidential Counsel Fred Fielding stated that the White House telephones were not equipped to automatically record the numbers called, but that AT & T long distance records indicated there were no outgoing calls between these numbers and NASA officials, and a review of the individuals involved also revealed no record of such communication. In the best tradition of the Teflon Presidency, Fielding added:

"While we consider such information to be confidential, as a matter of comity between the branches and in order to put this issue to rest, I can advise you in this instance that our review disclosed no record, recollection, or indication of such communication."

Obviously Shirley Green's powers of recollection were greater than those of Mr. Brashear or her other contacts in the Press Office.

The Rogers Commission conducted its own investigation of these rumors. Commission investigators interviewed twenty-three NASA officials (including Ms. Green) and collected twenty-eight

National Aeronautics and
Space Administration
Ames Research Center
Moffett Field, CA 94035
(415) 694-6453 FTS 464-6453
Mail Stop: N-233-14
ARPAnet: eugene@ames-aurora.arpa
UUCP: {hplabs, hao} ! ames ! aurora ! eugene

E. N. Miya
Software Engineering

t there had been no outside pressure on NASA
h Challenger. Associate Administrator Jesse
as to tell investigators that he did not even
y, January 28, was the day scheduled for the
Message.

's findings are summarized in the report: "The
ded that the decision to launch the Challenger
the appropriate NASA officials without any
or pressure."

mmission also concluded in its recommenda-
"relentless pressure on NASA to increase the
essure was most keenly felt by the managers of
, men like Jesse Moore, Arnie Aldrich, and
nates. And it is probable that—after Shirley
Green's calls to the White House—certain of these managers were
aware that launching Challenger on January 28 might guarantee
favorable mention by the President in the State of the Union Message. They certainly would not have been very astute senior bureaucrats if they were *not* aware of this situation. Just how much
that awareness weighed in the final decision will probably never be
known. At the least the coincidence of the speech and the launch
appears to have had some impact on the managers' determination
to press on with preparations for the Tuesday launch; the White
House understands this and is justifiably sensitive about the issue.

*   *   *

Monday, 2:00 p.m.
There is no record that the Mission Management Team meeting,
which began at two that afternoon in the Ops Center, included a
discussion of the State of the Union Message. They had much
more immediate and pressing concerns. One of the first items of
business was to arrange a telecon with Lieutenant Scott Funk, who
was at the weather forecast facility on the Canaveral Air Force
Station. The managers needed a more detailed estimate of temperatures and winds for Monday night and Tuesday morning, especially for the hours of the Tuesday launch window. Accordingly,

Lieutenant Funk provided this precise update to his earlier forecast:

Situation—Rapidly cooling temperatures as arctic front reinforces recent cold front passage with cold, dry arctic air. High pressure is located in Central U.S.A.; will move into Southeast U.S. Expect high pressure to be centered over Florida by Tuesday, 28 January, afternoon.

Clouds: Clear

Visibility: 7 miles

Wind: 340 / 10 kts, gusts 18 kts

15-hour Temperature Forecast:

Time (local)	Temperature	Wind
2400 E.S.T.	33 F.	340 / 12G20
0100	32	" "
0200	31	" "
0300	30	" "
0400	28	" "
0500	26	" "
0600	24	" "
0700	23	" "
0800	24	340 / 10G18
0900	26	" "
1000	28	" "
1100	29	" "
1200	34	" "
1300	39	360 / 10G15
1400	44	" "
1500	46	" "

This forecast provided dramatic evidence, if any were needed, of just how cold Tuesday morning would be. A hard freeze was predicted for two in the morning until past eleven, probably until noon. Jesse Moore and Arnie Aldrich led the discussion of the problems this unusual cold would cause. KSC Director Dick Smith sat opposite Dr. William Lucas, quietly listening to the discussion. At the earlier meeting the shuttle hardware project managers and the launch team had stated that the conditions would be marginally acceptable. But everyone understood there was no question of actually launching the shuttle in freezing conditions.

The formal Ambient Temperature Restrictions forbidding launch at temperatures below 31 degrees F. had never been broken, and no one was proposing they do so now. For one thing there was no way to keep the pad's water systems operational at those temperatures, even with the new freeze protection plan. This procedure allowed the launch team to maintain water in the system overnight without the pipes bursting, but the ambient temperature had to rise above freezing before the water systems could be brought up to full operating specification.

The implementation of this elaborate freeze-protection plan for Pad 39B was going to be the main area of concern during the meeting. Before the discussion began, however, the managers again polled the various project heads to be certain no weather-related hardware constraints had arisen since the one o'clock conference. Each project manager stated that his components would be ready for launch in the morning.

As the KSC people proceeded to detail the new freeze-protection plan, some concern was voiced about expected ice buildup on the pad's Service Structure. The dry air would probably mean there would not be excessive ice on the external tank. But allowing water to trickle through the fire hoses, the emergency showers and eye washes, and the platform deluge system was going to bring a lot of water in contact with cold steel during freezing conditions. Ice on the service structure, of course, could be considered dangerous debris at the moment of engine ignition. Therefore it was agreed that the ice inspection team under Charlie Stevenson would be placed on special alert for this hazard.

When the freeze plan was fully discussed, the managers agreed once more that the situation was marginally acceptable. They could pick up the countdown that night at the T-minus eleven hours mark. Obviously if Lieutenant Funk's forecast proved accurate, they would not be launching at 9:39 on Tuesday morning. But the temperature would probably climb above the freezing point before noon. And the Mission Management Team was determined to be ready.

Before the meeting broke up, Aldrich and Moore again told their people to keep a close eye on the hardware and to immediately report any cold-temperature problems that would affect the launch decision in the morning.

*   *   *

Monday, 2:00 p.m.
While the Mission Management Team met in the Ops Center, hundreds of other engineers and managers were discussing the implications of the approaching arctic air mass on the 51-L mission. In the Operations Support Center at Marshall, Lawrence Wear, the manager of the Solid Rocket Motor Branch, had received word from KSC soon after the scrub that all technical personnel were to research in detail any possible launch constraints that the predicted cold weather might trigger.

At this stage in the shuttle program the hardware contractors had become responsible for maintaining the detailed technical information about space shuttle components. Therefore Mr. Wear went to the Morton Thiokol Booster Manager at Marshall, Boyd Brinton, and asked him to follow up on the query.

Brinton did not have the data from cold-weather tests on the solid rocket boosters, but he knew there was a team of engineers at Thiokol's Wasatch plant in Utah who had been working on this problem. So Brinton made a series of phone calls to the company plant in Utah, first contacting Arnold Thompson, the supervisor of the rocket motor cases section. In turn, Thompson called Robert Ebeling, the manager of the booster's ignition system and final assembly, passing him the query and asking for a fast follow-up.

It was late morning at the sprawling Morton Thiokol plant outside Brigham City, Utah, a cold winter day on the high desert; the nearby Wasatch Mountains were plastered with fresh snow. Ebeling had been following the progress of the 51-L launch, among other matters, but now he realized he must devote his full attention to the questions raised by Marshall. Thompson had arranged a preliminary meeting at which the engineers with hands-on experience with the solid rocket motors could analyze the impact the cold Florida weather would have on the Thiokol booster.

For the Thiokol engineers with intimate knowledge of the problematic booster field joints, the meeting would be an occasion for them to finally impress management just how serious the situation really was.

*   *   *

Monday, 4:30 p.m.
Back on the East Coast, the afternoon wore on.

At the Cape, technicians worked steadily to prepare the multiple water systems of Pad 39B for the coming night.

In network television studios in New York, the anchors wrote their scripts for the first rehearsal of the evening news taping. Dan Rather's opening would hit NASA managers a hard, embarrassing blow: "Yet another costly, red-faces-all-around space shuttle delay," Rather wrote. "This time a bad bolt on a hatch and a bad-weather bolt from the blue are being blamed." Further uptown, Peter Jennings prepared the opening of his show: "Once again a flawless lift-off proved to be too much of a challenge for the Challenger."

All three networks would use NASA videotapes of the White Room crew wielding their hacksaw as the visuals supporting these headlines.

In the O & C building, the crew's spouses met them for an early dinner. The mood was somber and unusually quiet. Mike Smith tried to reassure Jane that everything was all right, but she could see he was still bitterly disappointed they hadn't flown the day before, when the weather at launch time had been perfect. Late Sunday afternoon, he had phoned Jane's mother, Mrs. Jarrell, to discuss whether she should stay at the Cape for the launch attempt on Monday. Mike advised her that she could return to her work for at least three days without fear of missing the launch. Given the impending cold weather, he said, there was no way they'd be able to fly until Thursday.

RECOMMENDATION TO LAUNCH

Brigham City, Utah, Monday Afternoon
The Thiokol booster engineers, convened by Arnold Thompson and Robert Ebeling following Larry Wear's call from Marshall, met in the colorfully painted buildings of the company's Wasatch Division, sixty miles north of Salt Lake City. The Wasatch Operations plant of Morton Thiokol is located on a rolling shelf of the high desert rim overlooking the desolate valley of the Great Salt Lake. The rocky 20,000-acre track lies beneath the Blue Spring Hills, a subrange of the massive Wasatch Mountains, which stand like a snowy wall across the Utah Valley to the east. Brigham City, twenty miles from the plant, was an outpost of the early Mormon pioneers. Until Thiokol came along in the 1950s and built this rocket plant, the town was in a postwar economic slump common to many arid western farming communities. But Thiokol changed all that. As the Defense Department awarded the company a steady series of contracts for solid rocket motors, the sage and juniper scrub around the old Mormon settlement mushroomed with subdivisions. Fast-food franchises and shopping centers sprang up among the salt bush and creosote. The prosperity of Cold War preparedness had arrived with swarms of local Utah workers and out-of-state engineers.

Within ten years Thiokol had won contracts for the solid rocket motors of several tactical and strategic missiles, including the Minuteman ICBM and the Poseidon and Trident submarine-launched ballistic missiles. When Thiokol received the multiyear NASA contract for the space shuttle's solid rocket motors, the company became the largest industrial employer in the state, with 6,400 workers at the Wasatch plant. Almost as important as the dollar value of the contract was its civilian nature. In becoming the sole source of the shuttle's solid boosters, the Thiokol Chemical Corporation had the potential of a *guaranteed* lucrative government contract—immune from the vagaries of the defense budget—well into the next century.

This prosperous corporation grew from a serendipitous laboratory discovery. In 1926 a Missouri chemist named Dr. Joseph Patrick was trying to perfect a nonalcoholic industrial antifreeze when he produced the first form of synthetic rubber. He called this compound Thiokol, from the Greek words "thio," for sulfur, and "kol," which means glue. By World War II the company was producing a variety of exotic man-made chemical compounds, including the solid fuel for artillery rockets that helped the country win the amphibious war in the Pacific. During the general pork barrel dispersion of defense contracts and contractors after the war, Thiokol established its solid rocket operations in Utah, where there was a good labor market of hard-working, clean-living Mormons who traditionally eschewed labor unions.

By 1982, when the shuttle was declared operational, it was obvious just how lucrative Thiokol's booster contract would become: the rapidly expanding flight schedule meant a sharply increasing demand for boosters. That July, Morton-Norwich Products, the parent company of Morton ("when it rains, it pours") Salt acquired the Thiokol Chemical Corporation. This acquisition looked like one of the smartest business deals of the decade. Morton Thiokol's fiscal 1985 profits reached a record of almost $198 million on sales of just under two billion dollars. The company's aerospace division accounted for almost half these record profits and sales, with the bulk coming from the shuttle booster contract. The space shuttle booster contract was so vital to overall corporate health that the company placed on the cover of its 1985 annual report a powerfully evocative original painting of the shuttle blasting skyward. The caption read:

"Twin Morton Thiokol solid propellant rocket propulsion motors have performed flawlessly for nineteen Space Shuttle flights."

As we have seen earlier, the field joints of the solid rocket boosters had performed anything but flawlessly and had been a source of mounting anxiety since the beginning of the program. The phenomenon of "joint rotation" was poorly understood at best, either by Thiokol and Marshall engineers or by their managers. By 1985, however, both organizations agreed that joint rotation at motor ignition produced the alarming related phenomenon of O-ring erosion and the momentary escape, or "blow-by," of superhot gases past the poorly sealed joint. This situation was so serious that a sweeping redesign effort was required, the so-called "big fix" that would permanently correct the faulty original design.

NASA and Thiokol engineers, led by Marshall's Larry Mulloy, had briefed Level I management on the problem during a Flight Readiness Review at NASA Headquarters in Washington on August 19, 1985. They also described a series of tests that would lead to redesigned hardware. This briefing was a product of the same concern that had sparked the order for seventy-two new steel booster casings, to be forged with an additional three inches of metal on the end lips, which would eventually incorporate the redesigned field joint. At the August 19 briefing for senior NASA managers, the Marshall and Thiokol engineers had made a detailed presentation on all the cases of O-ring erosion up to that time. They recommended an "accelerated" effort to find a new design that would eliminate both joint rotation and seal erosion. But they did not, however, recommend grounding the space shuttle fleet until this solution could be found. "It is safe to continue flying the existing design," they stated, "as long as all joints are leak-checked with 200 psig [pounds per square inch gas] stabilization pressure, are free of contamination, and meet O-ring squeeze requirements." In other words, flying with the present design was an acceptable risk.

The next day Thiokol's Vice President of Engineering, Robert Lund, established the seal task force. This group would have the responsibility of developing a safe new design for booster field joints as quickly as possible.

Between the end of August 1985 and Challenger's launch five months later, the space shuttle flew five missions. And four of those flights experienced serious O-ring erosion; three had actual blow-by.

However, the Thiokol task force and Marshall could not even agree about the nature and scope of the problem, to say nothing of a mutually acceptable redesign. The months passed, and the shuttle flew. Thiokol and Marshall exchanged memoranda, but there appeared to be a stronger-than-normal degree of organizational inertia at Thiokol. It suddenly seemed as if basic tests and engineering analyses that had been performed many times earlier in the program were now difficult to arrange. Marshall's engineers grew increasingly impatient with Thiokol's foot dragging. On September 5, Marshall Director of Science and Engineering James Kingsbury wrote to Mulloy, complaining about Thiokol's slow progress. "I have been apprised of general ongoing activities," he concluded. "But these do not appear to carry the priority which I attach to the situation. I consider the O-ring seal problem on the Solid Rocket Motor to require priority attention of both Morton Thiokol/Wasatch and MSFC."

There is no record that Kingsbury took this sense of alarm outside the tightly knit Marshall organization.

At Thiokol frustration was also mounting over the slow pace of the redesign effort. Roger Boisjoly was an engineer on the Thiokol seal task force. In a status report on the group's progress he wrote, "Even NASA perceives the team is being blocked in its engineering efforts to accomplish this task."

The Rogers Commission quotes Boisjoly's report, including his scathing conclusion:

"Finally, the basic problem boils down to the fact that all MTI problems have number one priority, and that upper management apparently feels that the SRM program is ours for sure, and the customer be damned."

Roger Boisjoly and his colleagues on the task force were both frustrated and deeply alarmed. As Boisjoly later told a Rogers Commission investigator, Thiokol and NASA had irrefutable evidence that the O-ring problem was potentially catastrophic. After the 51-B mission in April 1985, investigators discovered that a nozzle joint primary O-ring had been badly eroded and blown by and that there was serious erosion on the secondary O-ring. ". . . the erosion was considerably more than we had ever seen before. There was probably eighty percent of the [primary] O-ring gone, the entire section was actually vaporized. So at that point we said, 'My God, if that ever happens in a field joint, we've bought the farm because the secondary seal might not be capable of holding it and sealing.' "

With this degree of urgency in mind, Boisjoly threw himself into the task force's efforts, but his sense of alarm was not shared by Thiokol's managers. "This so-called 'seal team' was, for all intents and purposes, nonexistent," he told the commission investigator. "So I said, 'Oh no, they ain't going to do this to me. I ain't going to take this load on my shoulder. There ain't no way.' So I wrote my memo, my company private memo, and I says, 'Folks aren't going to say that they're not aware of this because I'm going to get action.' And that's why I wrote that, because I was scared to death that we were just going to take an extended period of time to fix this problem, and in the meantime this same thing could happen on a field joint that happened on this nozzle joint and we'd buy the whole thing."

Bob Ebeling, another Thiokol task force engineer, was equally concerned. In a message to Allan J. McDonald, Thiokol's Director of the Solid Rocket Motor Project, Ebeling began with the now notorious exclamation: "HELP!" He echoed Boisjoly's complaints that Thiokol was starving the task force for personnel and support. The company seemed very reluctant to release anyone to work fulltime with the seal team. Obviously Ebeling was at the point of desperation. He concluded his report: "We wish we could get action by verbal request, but such is not the case. This is a red flag."

Although the Rogers Commission raised the issue in the hearings, their final report avoided the sensitive question of Thiokol's commercial relationship with NASA. One major reason behind the company management's foot dragging might well have been the delicate state of Thiokol's negotiations with NASA for the second phase of the lucrative shuttle solid rocket booster contract. In the 1970s contracts, Thiokol was assigned the production of the first thirty-seven sets of boosters. Given the increased flight schedule, that number would be used by the end of 1986. Therefore, Thiokol was actively negotiating for the second-phase contract that would cover the next sixty sets of boosters, a procurement award worth a billion dollars. However, other aerospace companies had been lobbying Congress for at least two years to force NASA to break Morton Thiokol's monopoly on producing the SRB's. In the fall of 1985 Thiokol's management was acutely aware of this lobbying effort, which Congressional staff members called a "full-court press," by Thiokol's competitors. These companies included two which lost out to Thiokol in the original 1973 contract: United Technologies and the Strategic Propulsion Division of Aerojet. It might be reasonable to assume, therefore, that Thiokol was hesitant to have its engineering task force act too quickly on the booster redesign and by so doing expose the inherent weakness of the original field joint design to hostile Congressional scrutiny. For whatever reason, it is clear that the managers of Thiokol's aerospace division did not perceive the redesign effort with the same sense of urgency as engineers like Bob Ebeling and Roger Boisjoly.

The company was even able to successfully petition NASA to affect formal "closure" of the O-ring problem—i.e., its elimination from Marshall's monthly Problems Reports. The Thiokol request was based on strange logic: tests leading to a safe redesign were underway; therefore, the problem was being addressed; therefore, it was no longer an "open" problem. The incredible request worked. At Marshall, the bureaucratic papermill was so cluttered that the company's closure message was somehow processed to become official policy. Only five days before the Challenger accident, a Marshall message indicated that the "problem is considered closed."

But Thiokol's engineers were still aware of the dangerous situation. On the afternoon of January 27, 1986, the company's engineering experts amassed their test data about the effects of cold temperatures on O-ring performance and the functioning of the booster field joints. They would have another chance with NASA. When Thiokol's managers learned of the urgent query from Marshall later that afternoon, they reacted differently from the engineers. While Roger Boisjoly and his engineering colleagues saw this request for data as an opportunity to reemphasize their concerns about the vulnerable field joints, the senior management of the aerospace division apparently viewed the situation with alarm. They feared that NASA would scrutinize the inherently weak hardware design at an inopportune moment. If Thiokol hardware was so tender that it could not stand up to the rigors of the "operational" schedule, which of course included winter flights, how would the company be viewed during contract renegotiations? Boisjoly felt that management was so confident of retaining the contract that they could "let the customer be damned," but the managers themselves seemed more worried than Boisjoly believed them to be.

In any event there developed a definite schism between the Thiokol engineers and their managing vice presidents later Monday afternoon and evening, a conflict that would have tragic consequences Tuesday morning.

*　　*　　*

Titusville, Florida–Brigham City, Utah,
Monday, 4:00 p.m.
Allan McDonald, Thiokol's director of the Solid Rocket Motor Project, was not a typical aerospace engineer. Among engineers (as with physicians and academics) expertise in a narrow professional specialty is often the hallmark of success; if an engineer knows all there is to know about an arcane subject such as electrical resistance or the behavior of springs under pressure, he wins the respect of his colleagues. He becomes the man who can provide the data when they are needed, and in the profession of engineering, quantifiable data are sacrosanct.

McDonald, however, had the reputation of being an iconoclast and a loner because his intellectual interests transcended narrow specialties. He was trained as a chemical and administrative engineer, but his personal and professional concerns ranged far beyond chemistry and administration. And such a personality often causes conflict in traditional engineering circles. Harold W. Ritchey, a former Thiokol president, gave the Washington *Post* his assessment of Allan McDonald: "I have the highest regard for him as a professional and as a man. His integrity cannot be questioned, but he is not a conformist and sometimes that can be a cause of trouble in a large organization."

In Allan McDonald's case, his questioning had lead him to the conclusion that Thiokol and NASA were flying a booster with an inherently dangerous joint seal design, one that had proved itself especially vulnerable to cold weather. Following the evidence of O-ring erosion in the nozzle joint of the 51-C flight in January 1985, McDonald and Roger Boisjoly were summoned to Marshall to discuss their findings with NASA management. According to Boisjoly, the hidebound and protective bureaucracy that flourished in the center under Dr. Lucas prevented them from properly impressing NASA with the seriousness of the situation. Their conviction that cold weather might provoke a catastrophe on a future flight was watered down to a "nonissue" by the time it reached Lucas.

But McDonald and Boisjoly remained convinced that flying the solid rocket boosters in unusually cold conditions exacerbated the chronic problem of poor O-ring performance and that the problem had catastrophic potential. Simply stated, cold temperatures made the synthetic rubber O-rings less elastic, and they took longer to spring into their proper grooves and seal the joint. Therefore, McDonald was alarmed when Bob Ebeling called him at four Monday afternoon to discuss the issue of the predicted cold weather and the booster field joints. Al McDonald was at the Titusville home of Carver Kennedy, a Thiokol vice president in charge of booster-stacking operations in the VAB, with whom McDonald usually stayed during shuttle missions. Out in Utah, the engineers were preparing a detailed analysis of the weather's impact on the boosters, and Ebeling needed a more accurate assessment of the temperatures. All they had to go on at the plant was an ominous prediction that the overnight low would be eighteen degrees.

This was the first McDonald had heard of the unusual cold. And the news shocked him. Eighteen degrees would be a record low. Carver Kennedy called the launch Ops Center and received the hour by hour temperature forecast that Lieutenant Funk had provided earlier. With this information in hand, McDonald called Ebeling in Utah to spark him into action. In an unpublished interview that McDonald gave the Rogers Commission, he stressed his sense of alarm. "I told Bob Ebeling at that time that this was a very serious situation and I have got some real concern, and to make sure that he gets all of the engineering people together to review this and assess what the impact is, and to make sure that it is an engineering decision. In fact I told him to make sure that the vice president of engineering, Mr. Bob Lund, was involved in this, and that we just can't come back and present some concerns, to be in a position to come back with a recommendation for an actual temperature that we would recommend for the launch."

McDonald next contacted Marshall's resident manager at the Cape, Cecil Houston, to inform him of the concerns about the impact of the predicted cold. Houston decided that this was an issue requiring a telecon discussion among all the parties involved at the Cape, Huntsville, and at the Morton Thiokol plant. He spent the next half hour arranging that telecon, which was scheduled to begin at 5:45 (E.S.T.). In Huntsville, Judson Lovingood, Larry Mulloy's deputy in the Booster Project Office, tried to round up his colleagues at the Cape to participate. Mulloy had gone to dinner, but Lovingood managed to reach Stanley Reinartz, Marshall's Manager of the Shuttle Projects Office. Lovingood also contacted George Hardy, Marshall's Deputy Director of Science and Engineering, who had already reached his home in Athens, Georgia. Although Mulloy was missing, the other key Marshall managers were ready to hear Thiokol's case.

So approximately two hours after McDonald received word of the company's concern, Thiokol's engineers were prepared to discuss the issue with the Marshall managers. Unfortunately the vagaries of contemporary telephone technology prevented a thorough discussion of the boosters' space age technology: George Hardy could not hear the discussion on his home phone, and the Thiokol engineers grouped around their conference phone speakers in the plant's Management Information Center could not hear the participants calling from the Holiday Inn on Merritt Island near KSC. Altogether, the abortive telecon proved a waste of time. But it became clear that Thiokol's initial recommendation was that NASA delay the launch until afternoon, when temperatures would be much higher. The Thiokol engineers were worried that their temperature data base for O-ring performance only went down to 53 degrees F., the estimated seal temperature for the 51-C flight the previous January. Transmitting this information over the precarious telephone loop proved impossible. So the participants reached the conclusion that the issue was too complex and too serious to address at an impromptu teleconference. Therefore, it was resolved that all the responsible Thiokol engineers and NASA managers would "meet" again in a formal telecon at 8:15 P.M. (E.S.T.), to be conducted from the conference rooms at the Cape, Huntsville, and the Thiokol plant. These facilities were equipped with four-wire teleconference phones and telefax document-transmittal machines. In the interim Thiokol was to prepare a formal presentation with detailed charts of engineering data, transmit those charts by facsimile machine, and be ready to address every aspect of the situation.

Following this first teleconference, Lovingood called Reinartz at the Holiday Inn and suggested that he invite Dr. Lucas and Jim Kingsbury, Marshall's Director of Science and Engineering, to participate in the teleconference. From the tone of Thiokol's original presentation, it was clear to Lovingood that the company might recommend against launching. Therefore, Reinartz would probably want to involve Lucas as well as Arnie Aldrich, the Level II director of the National Space Transportation Program from Johnson. In Lovingood's official postaccident report on the Marshall-Thiokol discussions that night, he summarizes his concerns in this manner: "I called Reinartz at the motel and told him if MTI persisted in their recommendation at the 7:15 [8:15 E.S.T.] meeting, we should not launch. I suggested he advise Aldrich of our meeting to prepare him for having a meeting with Level I to inform them of a possible recommendation to delay."

* * *

Merritt Island, Monday, 7:00 p.m.
Stan Reinartz was naturally reluctant to involve Lucas. Although he had worked at Marshall most of his career, Reinartz had only been in his current position for four shuttle missions, and he was leery of provoking the notorious wrath of Dr. William Lucas by annoying him with minor administrative matters. Reinartz did not request that Lucas and Kingsbury attend the teleconference. At around seven that night, Reinartz and Larry Mulloy visited Lucas who was with Kingsbury in Lucas's room at the Merritt Island

Holiday Inn, where the Marshall contingent was staying. Even though this meeting was pivotal to the outcome of later events, the Rogers Commission gave it little scrutiny. Questioned by Dr. Alton G. Keel, Jr., Executive Director of the Commission, and by Chairman William Rogers, this is how Reinartz recalls the conversation with Lucas and Kingsbury:

> DR. KEEL: And did you discuss with them Mr. Lovingood's recommendation that the two of them, Lucas and Kingsbury, participate?
> MR. REINARTZ: No, sir. I don't recall discussing Mr. Lovingood's recommendation. I discussed with them the nature of the telecon, the nature of the concerns raised by Thiokol, and the plans to gather the proper technical-support people at Marshall for examination of the data. And I believe that was the essence of the discussion.
> CHAIRMAN ROGERS: But you didn't recommend that the information be given to Level II or Level I?
> MR. REINARTZ: I don't recall, Mr. Chairman, making any statement regarding that.

Although the Commission was aware at the time of this testimony of reports that Dr. Lucas dominated his subordinates, no one pressed Stanley Reinartz for more details. Yet this conversation between Lucas and Reinartz was of vital importance. At the Mission Management Team meeting that afternoon, Aldrich and Moore had *officially* requested that everyone in their reporting channels bring forward to them any concerns about the impact of cold weather on the scheduled Tuesday morning launch. Jud Lovingood had followed that request; after meeting with Lucas, Reinartz did not. And it must be remembered that Stan Reinartz was in the direct reporting channel which ran from Larry Mulloy through him to Arnie Aldrich, then to Jesse Moore. This channel did *not* include Dr. Lucas. It should be further noted that the management team requested reports of all worries and concerns, not simply hard, quantifiable data.

Dr. Lucas, however, had a reputation for not considering unquantifiable worries and concerns; he only dealt with hard fact. If a Marshall hardware component was going to be the cause of a delay, those proposing the delay would have to justify their recommendation with complete and accurate data. At seven o'clock, Reinartz did not have that data. So he knew he had no way of convincing Lucas about the seriousness of the situation.

Thiokol's Al McDonald and Roger Boisjoly had been faced with an almost identical situation one year before when they reported their concerns about the 51-C O-ring erosion to the Marshall managers. In an unpublished Commission interview, this is how Boisjoly described the situation:

"It was our feeling at the time that nothing gets presented to Dr. Lucas unless the people that are doing the presenting are absolutely sure that all bases have been covered technically and that they have all the answers to all the questions that potentially could be asked, and this was a case where clearly there were no answers available because it was just a question of observation as to what we were presenting.

"I have been personally chastised in flight readiness reviews at Marshall for using the words 'I feel' or 'I think,' and I have been crucified to the effect that that is not proper presentation because 'I feel' and 'I expect' are not engineering-supported statements, but they are just judgmental. And so when people go in front of Dr. Lucas, they know full well that if they use words like that or if they use engineering judgment to try to explain a position, that they will be shot down in flames. And for that reason, nobody goes to him without a complete, fully documented, verifiable set of data."

Even if the reader were to discount the accusations against Lucas in the "Apocalypse" letter, Boisjoly's summary of the Marshall director's managerial style goes a long way toward explaining Stanley Reinartz's actions in the next twelve hours.

*   *   *

Pad 39B, Monday, 8:00 p.m.
The full moon rose above the cold black sea. After sunset the wind had come up again, but with less intensity than the near gale that had blown at midday. On the walkways of the service structure, the pad workers had finally completed the long process of implementing the freeze-protection plan. Water trickled into the drain

pipes from fire hoses and the emergency rinse showers. The sound-suppression troughs beneath the solid rocket boosters were murky green with thousands of gallons of antifreeze. As the men boarded the elevators for the ride down, they stamped their feet and beat their hands against their legs. Although the cold weather of the previous January had been called the cold front of the century, it now seemed likely that the hard freeze tonight would be even worse.

With the Rotating Service Structure rolled back, the chill north-west wind hummed around the pillars of the solid rocket boosters and across the ocher silo of the external tank. Nine hours later, when the tank was filled, the northwest wind would move over the supercold surface of the tank and swirl around the thick base of Challenger's right booster.

*   *   *

Recovery Ship **Liberty**, *28° 36'N, 78° 42'W.*
Monday, 8:00 p.m.
NASA's Retrieval Operations Manager Jim Devlin had spent thirty-three years at sea and had been on all twenty-four shuttle booster recovery trips, but he had never seen conditions like these outside of a hurricane or a winter gale on the North Atlantic. The high winds that had howled across the launch pad that morning had become a dangerous gale where the cold front collided with the warm Gulf Stream flow, 120 miles east of the Cape. Overhead the sky was completely overcast, with no hint of the full moon. The gale blew from the west, northwest, a solid fifty knots of wind with long gusts as high as seventy-two knots. The seas were steep, close together and crashing, with wave crests above twenty-five feet, and a few rogue waves above thirty. By eight that night the solid rocket booster recovery vessels *Liberty* and *Freedom* were in trouble.

The two shallow-draft steel vessels wallowed in the deep troughs and were pounded by breaking seas on the crests. Both vessels had reduced speed, but with the following sea they were in danger of broaching. As the two ships struggled eastward toward their re-covery station, it became obvious that the prudent course of action was to turn back into the gale to take the dangerous breaking sea head on. In nautical parlance, this was the "survival mode."

And Devlin realized they were rapidly approaching such survival conditions. On the bridge of the *Liberty,* he was wedged into a corner, clinging to a grab rail while the deck plates groaned and shuddered beneath his feet. Fist-sized chunks of spray battered the bridge windscreen. The white-crested waves bearing down on them seemed unusually menacing, but Devlin knew this was an illusion brought on by the dark night. Unfortunately the thirty-footers, higher than the stack, were becoming more frequent, and they were no illusion. Beside him on the bridge was Anker Rasmussen, another veteran seaman who headed recovery operations for Thiokol. The noise of the storm increased, and both men could see astern that the following sea was beginning to do some real damage. The large spool winches that reeled in the booster parachutes were being bent by the force of the waves. And on the afterdeck, the thick timbers used as dunnage for the booster nose cones were coming adrift and crashing around in the darkness.

"Hey," Devlin yelled to Rasmussen, "we've never been off station for a launch yet, but I'm afraid we're going to have to be this time."

* * *

Brigham City, Utah, Monday Afternoon and Evening
It was mid-afternoon in Utah when the senior managers of Thiokol's Wasatch Operations learned of their engineers' concern about the weather in Florida and about the first teleconference, scheduled to begin at quarter to four their time. Calvin Wiggins, Vice President and General Manager of Thiokol's Space Division, and Jerald Mason, Senior Vice President of Wasatch Operations, were at the Tactical Division of the plant when they got a call alerting them to the situation. They quickly finished their business and headed across the desert complex to the space booster offices. In the Management Information Center, they found Joe Kilminster, Vice President, Space Booster Programs, and Robert Lund, Vice President, Engineering, busy organizing their engineers for the first teleconference. There was an atmosphere of tense resolve.

Because Wiggins and Mason rarely worked directly with engineers and were not fully conversant with the problems at hand, they took chairs as observers and waited to hear the teleconference.

Bob Lund worked closely with his engineers and was obviously well versed in the minute details of O-rings, joint rotation, and the booster ignition transient. He had set up a kind of command post in the MIC and received a continuous flow of engineer specialists, who brought him their draft inputs, some in the form of presentation charts and computer graphics. Lund himself hand-printed the presentation charts in large block letters.

While Lund organized his people, Wiggins and Mason conversed quietly with Kilminster. If Thiokol's engineers were going to recommend against a launch, the senior managers wanted to understand the rationale as well as they could. These managers had every reason to be concerned about a possible recommendation not to launch. They were fully aware of the pressures on NASA to "fly out that manifest," and they no doubt remembered well that the first hardware scrub of the 61-C mission had been provoked by the Thiokol booster. Since the previous August, the company's executives had grown increasingly anxious about keeping their lucrative contract. Eighty House members had lobbied NASA to consider accepting the bids of other contractors. Although Thiokol was assured of a short-term extension of its contract, NASA had stunned the company the day after Christmas by proposing to develop procedures for a second source for later procurement. The previous three weeks had been a period of intense negotiations between Thiokol and NASA over the terms and duration of the extension. According to Representative Robert G. Torricelli, a New Jersey Democrat on the Science and Technology Committee, "There was mounting pressure on Thiokol because of the imminent possibility of real competition. They had established themselves in a secure and highly profitable position, and they were defending that."

The negotiation meetings and long telephone conferences that had dominated the first three weeks of January were reaching a pivotal point. And there was a major negotiation session scheduled for Tuesday, January 28, 1986, a few hours after the planned launch of the space shuttle Challenger.

*   *   *

Kennedy Space Center, Monday, 8:15 p.m.
The long Monday night teleconference has acquired mythical proportions since the dramatic testimony of the Rogers Commission
hearings. Many people have come to view the conference as a tense
and acrimonious battle of wills between callous bureaucrats on one
side and greedy capitalists on the other, with a virtuous group of
engineers forming a Greek chorus of alarm, which the villainous
managers on both sides scornfully ignored. This would be good
drama; real life is more complicated. Neither the Marshall managers nor the Thiokol executives were ruthless enough to consciously
gamble on flight safety. Senior bureaucrats and corporate vice
presidents achieve their positions through cautious perseverance,
not casual disregard of hazards. If any decision maker that night
had actually believed he was risking the destruction of the space
shuttle, he would have acted differently. Pride and arrogance, not
the gambler's consciously reckless bravado, motivated the participants.
    At 8:15 P.M. (E.S.T.)—a quarter past seven in Huntsville and an
hour earlier in Utah—the three groups sat down before their
speaker phones to begin the telecon. Cecil Houston, the Marshall
resident manager at the Cape, ran the master phone console in the
conference room of Trailer Complex C. Although the wide hollow
square of tables had room for thirty people, there were only five
men grouped near Houston in the corner of the room. Stanley
Reinartz, the Shuttle Projects Manager from Marshall, sat beside
Cecil Houston, and Mulloy next to Reinartz. Al McDonald and
Jack Buchanan, Thiokol's manager of KSC operations, sat side by
side on the right side of the hollow square. As the men prepared
for the teleconference, they noted that the forced-air heating system was straining against the cold night. A periodic throaty rumble signaled the thermostat's response to the arctic air mass.
    At the Marshall Space Flight Center, fifteen men were seated
around a similar open square of telecon tables in Conference
Room 411 in the Center's headquarters building. George B.
Hardy, Marshall's Deputy Director for Science and Engineering,
was the senior man; Jud Lovingood headed the Shuttle Projects

contingent, and there were engineers from the Booster Project, the Structures and Propulsion Laboratory, and other specialized technical offices. Marshall had assembled all its key experts to hear the Thiokol presentation.

In the Management Information Center at Thiokol's Space Division, fourteen senior executives, managers, and engineers had gathered for the conference. Most of the supervisors and engineers had been working since late morning to prepare the supporting data for the company's position on the effects of the predicted cold and its recommendation on the next morning's launch. Among the Thiokol engineers most concerned about the situation were Roger Boisjoly and Arnold Thompson, the Supervisor of Rocket Motor Cases.

Cecil Houston found himself the unofficial coordinator of the telecon because he ran the master console at the Cape. An electrical engineer by training, he knew very little about the long history of booster field joint problems. He had heard about O-ring erosion at flight-readiness reviews the year before, but, like so many others, he had been led to believe that the problem was minor and self-limiting, something you had to live with in a program as complex as the shuttle operation.

Therefore, Houston was not prepared for the long, detailed engineering discussion that was about to unfold. Houston hoped that this telecon would be over within thirty or forty minutes, so that he could get on with what he considered the truly serious questions to be resolved that night. He had just gotten word from the launch team that their SRB recovery vessels were in survival conditions, fighting a dangerous gale, a hundred miles out at sea, and that they were now headed back toward land at three knots and would not be on their recovery station at launch time in the morning. This was obviously a problem that would have to be discussed with Arnie Aldrich, the Level II director of the National Space Transportation Office. Aldrich would have to make the decision whether to proceed with the launch without the recovery vessels on station. As Houston understood the problem, there was a risk of losing the boosters' main parachutes, their drogue chutes, and the nosecap frustums, all of which would probably be swept away by the gale seas before the ships could return to station. He wasn't sure, but he believed there was no danger of losing the spent boosters themselves. They would float in the so-called upright "spar mode," buoyed by trapped air, until sea conditions permitted the return of the ships.

So Houston was slightly impatient for this discussion to get started and move along; it was already past eight, and he had a lot of work to do before he could go home for a few hours sleep. But the discussion was not to proceed so smoothly. As soon as the three groups came on the telecon net and identified themselves, Thiokol's Joe Kilminster began the discussion by mentioning the engineering data charts his company had prepared. Over a dozen charts were to have been telefaxed to Kennedy and Marshall to help the NASA officials follow Thiokol's presentation. Unfortunately these charts had not arrived. So the conference got off to a bad start. There was a certain amount of confusion about which telefax machines to use at both the Cape and Huntsville, and the result was a further delay of half an hour before the charts were received and photocopied for all the participants. Even then, however, the conclusion and recommendation charts were not transmitted with the engineering data. And it was after nine before the actual discussion commenced. Naturally this delay did nothing to diminish the sense of impatience some of the NASA officials were feeling at this eleventh-hour conference. Everyone was short of sleep; the last three days had been demanding and frustrating, and no one appreciated Thiokol's seeming inability to organize a proper engineering teleconference.

Al McDonald had earlier requested that his company prepare a detailed engineering presentation based on quantifiable test data that would convince NASA about the sensitivity of the booster joints' O-rings to cold temperatures. In testimony to the Rogers Commission, McDonald stated that he wanted to make sure his Vice President of Engineering, Bob Lund, was involved in the presentation to NASA. McDonald said that "this decision should be an engineering decision, not a program management decision." He himself was well aware of management's concerns about the contract renegotiations, since he had come from one of these negotiations at Marshall earlier that week.

Once the discussion got underway, Thiokol's presentation was relatively straightforward and there was surprisingly little reaction from the NASA experts. Joe Kilminster called on his engineering staff, particularly Arnie Thompson and Roger Boisjoly to lead the discussion of the detailed data charts. Several of these charts had obviously been handwritten that afternoon for this telecon; others were more elaborate computer printouts. The thrust of the company's presentation concerned the history of O-ring erosion and blow-by on earlier flights and the relationship of these anomalies to cold weather. As the discussion evolved, a mood of neutral absorption with technical minutiae prevailed. This was pure engineering, not management policy.

However, Cecil Houston would later note with bitterness that Morton Thiokol's senior executives, Jerald Mason and Calvin Wiggins, did not even acknowledge their presence in the Thiokol conference room. This was absolutely contrary to established NASA procedure, which required all persons present in a teleconference to identify themselves, whether they took an active role or not. Because Mason and Wiggins's presence was not known to the NASA officials, Houston emphasized, it was assumed that all the recommendations and conclusions emanating from Thiokol were based on engineering criteria, just as Al McDonald had earlier requested. Although the Rogers Commission did not stress this point, it seems clear that this was an important aspect of the group dynamics at work that night.

For almost an hour Thiokol's engineers worked through their meticulous presentation. They established a convincing argument that the combined problems of field joint rotation and delayed O-ring seating would be exacerbated by the decreased resiliency of the O-ring and the increased viscosity of the rings' grease packing caused by very low temperatures. The data they were working on assumed a temperature of 26 degrees F. for the scheduled launch time of 9:38 Tuesday morning. They tried to show that this low ambient temperature would result in actual O-ring temperatures below freezing. The previous coldest O-ring temperatures had been on the 51-C mission one year before when the seals were estimated at 53 degrees F. at ignition. Extrapolating from the Air

Force hour-by-hour temperature predictions, the engineers estimated Challenger's booster seals would be 29 degrees F. at nine
A.M. and would warm up to 38 degrees F. by two that afternoon.

The engineers also presented detailed data on the speed with
which the primary and secondary O-rings would seat during the
crucial 600-millisecond ignition transient. Given the combined dynamics of joint rotation and cold-hardened synthetic rubber
O-rings, there was a probability that the seal would not become
effective early enough in the transient; in fact their test data indicated that the primary O-ring had to be in place before 330 milliseconds or there was a "high probability of no secondary seal
capability." They further argued that erosion of the primary
O-ring for any length of time would increase the danger of losing
the secondary, and supposedly redundant seal. During the 51-C
ignition transient, one O-ring was eroded almost 0.04", about a
sixth of its diameter. The Challenger mission could anticipate
worse erosion.

There was a normal amount of technical banter as these charts
were discussed, but no major challenges to the data itself. After
about ninety minutes of discussion, however, Thiokol's Engineering Vice President Bob Lund presented the conclusions and recommendations. Lund's conclusions were that although temperature was not the only parameter controlling O-ring blow-by and
erosion by hot gas, cold temperatures definitely seemed to increase
this danger. Development boosters that had been fired in horizontal test beds during very cold weather did not show blow-by because the putty between the joints had been carefully repacked
before ignition to eliminate blow holes. It was impossible to duplicate these test conditions with actual flight hardware that had been
assembled vertically in the VAB. Therefore, Lund concluded, the
only temperature data Thiokol had for the effects of cold on operational boosters contained a low O-ring temperature of 53 degrees F.

As Lund prepared to state Thiokol's recommendations, the
NASA officials at the Cape and in Huntsville became very alert.
Before them on the teleconference tables lay the handwritten
chart:

RECOMMENDATIONS:

- O-RING TEMP MUST BE $\geq$ 53° F. AT LAUNCH

  DEVELOPMENT MOTORS AT 47° TO 52° F. WITH
  PUTTY PACKING HAD NO BLOW-BY
  SRM 15 (THE BEST SIMULATION) WORKED AT 53° F.

- PROJECT AMBIENT CONDITIONS (TEMP & WIND)
  TO DETERMINE LAUNCH TIME

Lund read the recommendations and commented that the predicted temperature for the morning's launch was outside the data base and that NASA should delay the launch until the ambient temperature rose high enough to warm the O-ring seals to at least 53 degrees. They might want to consider a launch late the next afternoon or perhaps a slip to a warmer day.

The reactions from NASA were swift. And they appeared surprisingly harsh to McDonald and Boisjoly. Although the teleconference was not tape-recorded, there is a consensus in the Rogers Commission testimony that Larry Mulloy's response to the recommendation was unusually heated. He spent about five minutes reviewing Thiokol's data and challenging their logic. At best, he implied, their data were inconclusive, yet they were basing very serious conclusions and recommendations on these data. He added that Thiokol was trying to establish new Launch Commit Criteria based on this 53-degree benchmark. They couldn't do that, he said, not on the night before a launch. Using such criteria, it might be spring before the shuttle could fly again. Finally Mulloy asked, "My God, Thiokol, when do you want me to launch? Next April?"

Other NASA officials commented that such an arbitrary low-temperature constraint would hamper launch operations from Vandenberg Air Force Base in California, which had a much cooler climate than Cape Canaveral. Besides, they said, Thiokol had only been able to run one series of tests in the past six months, so their data base was limited, to say the least. The mood had shifted so that Thiokol was clearly on the defensive. There was a chorus of comment to the effect that the Thiokol data certainly were not conclusive; according to the company's own charts, there had been blow-by and O-ring erosion on flights launched on very warm days.

But Roger Boisjoly would not be shaken from his position. The 51-C flight, he replied, that was launched the year before—after an extremely cold night—had experienced a degree and type of O-ring erosion not found on other flights. There was a much larger arc of soot between the two O-rings, and the soot was much blacker and had penetrated all the way to the secondary ring, which was also scorched. Boisjoly stated flatly that there was a "significant difference" with the cold-weather 51-C launch and that it was probably due to the low temperature of the O-rings.

McDonald, who had been relatively quiet during the engineering presentation, now commented on the issue of the supposedly inconclusive data from the static tests. He seconded the Thiokol engineers' earlier remarks that the horizontal static tests could not duplicate actual flight conditions because the sealing putty in the field joints of these test motors had been repacked, whereas actual flight motors were not treated in this manner.

This pointed exchange went on for several minutes before Mulloy bypassed Lund to ask Joe Kilminster for his personal opinion on the recommendation. In effect Mulloy was removing the discussion from the realm of engineering and calling for a middle-management decision, exactly what McDonald had feared would happen. Kilminster was the Vice President of the Space Booster Group, and, in theory, had a wider perspective than the working engineers with their narrow professional specialties.

But Joe Kilminster sided with his engineers. Based on the engineering data presented that night, he could not recommend launching with an O-ring temperature below 53 degrees F.

George Hardy, Marshall's deputy director for science and engineering, broke in to say he was "appalled" at Kilminster's recommendations, coming as they did so late on the eve of a launch. However, Hardy added, he certainly would not want to fly without Thiokol's recommendation.

McDonald was troubled at the tone and import of Hardy's comment. In McDonald's opinion, Hardy was one of the most even-tempered, fairest and level-headed of all the Marshall officials. To hear him using intemperate terms like "appalled" signaled a degree of stress among the NASA people that McDonald had not witnessed in other such technical discussions.

McDonald was not the only person troubled by these signs of unusual stress. In the conference room at Marshall, Wilbur Riehl, a veteran NASA engineer who was the chief of the center's Nonmetallic Materials Division, was following the discussions very closely, but not commenting. There was an unprecedented situation unfolding tonight, almost a total reversal of the normal relationship between Marshall and a shuttle hardware contractor. Usually in such a flight-safety debate Marshall officials would steadfastly insist that the contractor prove beyond doubt that it was safe to fly; tonight for some reason, they were bullying Thiokol to prove that it was dangerous. Riehl silently shook his head and wrote a note on the back of one of Thiokol's charts, then shoved the paper to the man beside him:

Did you EVER expect to see MSFC want to fly when MTI-Wasatch didn't?

Stan Reinartz was not as vociferous as Mulloy, but he also questioned Thiokol's logic. Reinartz was under the impression that the solid rocket motors were qualified for operation between 40 and 90 degrees F. And the 53-degree recommendation certainly was not consistent with those specifications.

The debate had reached a stalemate.

Joe Kilminster cleared his throat and asked for a five-minute caucus off the net, so that Thiokol could review its data.

Before the Thiokol conference phones were put on mute, however, Al McDonald spoke up again in an attempt to clarify for the men in Utah the seriousness of the predicted cold temperature's impact on the O-rings. Unfortunately, McDonald's effort was not well articulated and produced a degree of confusion among those in the Thiokol management center. McDonald became muddled about how the leak checks of the seals with pressurized gas actually exacerbated the field joints' vulnerability by forcing the primary ring on the wrong side of its groove. He added that the secondary ring was in a position to seal after this test, but exposed to erosion if the seating of the upper ring was slowed by the cold. What the people at Thiokol actually understood was the opposite of what McDonald intended. Even Roger Boisjoly, who had worked closely with McDonald on the field joint problem, was momentarily confused. And the Thiokol managers have testified that they received the impression that McDonald was somehow favoring a launch.

*   *   *

Brigham City, Utah, Monday, 10:30 p.m. (E.S.T.)
The five-minute caucus Kilminster requested stretched on for half an hour. During this time Roger Boisjoly and Arnold Thompson, the two engineers in the room most familiar with the problem and most alarmed by NASA's stubborn response, tried desperately to convince their senior managers not to back down from the original recommendation against the launch. Jerald Mason began the caucus by saying that a management decision was required. The three other vice presidents were seated around him at the head table of the conference room. When it became clear to Boisjoly and Thompson that the managers intended to "caucus" only among themselves, the two engineers physically intervened to restate their position. Arnold Thompson went to the head table, slapped down a writing pad, and sketched the joint to impress on the managers the logic of Thiokol's original position. Boisjoly grabbed a pile of photographs showing the serious O-ring erosion from the 51-C flight and joined Thompson at the managers' table to try once more to convince them. But they did not seem responsive; his graphic proof of the danger was apparently not relevant to the decision they were about to make.

The managers seemed to believe that the O-rings, which were slightly thicker than a quarter of an inch, could be eroded up to one third of their diameter and still seat safely. Thompson gave up and returned to his seat. "I also stopped," Boisjoly later testified, "when it was apparent that I couldn't get anybody to listen."

After Thompson and Boisjoly had sat down, Mason reiterated that a management decision was required. He turned to Bob Lund and said, "Take off your engineering hat and put on your management hat."

During negotiations, managers had to consider such factors as satisfying the obvious wishes of a major customer—in this case, NASA. They also had to fathom the personality of their counterpart among the customer's management: namely, Dr. William Lucas, a man who demanded hard, quantifiable data. And Lucas's man, Larry Mulloy, had called Thiokol's presentation data inconclusive. Seen in this light, the proper management decision was obvious.

The engineers who had compiled the original data suggesting a cold-weather launch was dangerous waited silently at their table while the Thiokol vice presidents conferred. Mason polled his three fellow vice presidents; the four managers voted to overrule their engineers and recommend the launch. No one polled the engineers. Their position was well known, and their opinion was not required.

After approximately thirty minutes off the teleconference net, Joe Kilminster wrote out Thiokol's new recommendation and activated his speaker phone to call Mulloy.

*   *   *

Kennedy Space Center, Monday, 11:00 p.m.
Thiokol still maintained that the cold was a safety concern, Kilminster said, but on reassessment his people had found that the original data were, indeed, inconclusive. He then proceeded to read Thiokol's new recommendation. Their "engineering assessment" was that although it was undeniable that the O-rings in Challenger's boosters would be 20 degrees colder than ever before, that the O-rings would be harder and take longer to seat, and that there might be more blow-by and erosion than on any earlier flight, there was a safety margin because the pressure check would have seated the secondary ring in its proper position.

Therefore, Kilminster concluded, "MTI recommends STS-51L launch proceed on 28 January 1986."

Stan Reinartz asked if anybody had any comments on this recommendation. George Hardy replied that Thiokol should put their launch recommendation in writing, sign it, and transmit it by telefax to both Kennedy and Marshall before launch time. Kilmin-

ster said that they would telefax the written recommendation that
night.

The teleconference was over.

Before leaving the conference room at KSC, however, Al Mc-
Donald made a personal appeal to Reinartz. The predicted temperature for launch would definitely be below the boosters' operation specifications, McDonald argued. How could NASA
rationalize going below their *own* temperature limitations? Larry
Mulloy interrupted him to point out that the 40–90 degree qualification for the motor referred to bulk propellant temperature, not
seals. McDonald responded that this was a ridiculous argument
because the huge boosters could be exposed to subzero temperatures for long periods and the bulk temperature of the well-insu-
lated propellant would not drop very far, while the rest of the
booster would be dangerously cold. His argument did not sway
either Reinartz or Mulloy. They had their recommendation to
launch from Thiokol, and that was the end of the matter as far as
they were concerned. The data had been examined and found inconclusive. Thiokol's own engineers admitted that.

McDonald looked directly at Reinartz and Mulloy, and said
that although he might not understand the fine points of NASA's
formal Launch Commit Criteria, he still felt launching at below 40
degrees was going "outside the envelope." Neither NASA official
was swayed. "If anything happens to this launch," McDonald told
them, "I sure won't want to be the person that has to stand in
front of a board of inquiry to explain why we launched outside the
qualification of the solid rocket motor or any shuttle system."

Twenty minutes later, the formal recommendation to launch,
signed by Joe C. Kilminster, Vice President, Space Booster Programs, arrived by telefax.

*   *   *

Kennedy Space Center, Tuesday, 12:05 a.m.

Before Al McDonald left the conference room, he had tried one
last time to persuade Reinartz and Mulloy. McDonald had learned
of the recovery vessels' plight, that they were in a "survival mode"
and were returning toward shore. This flight would be the first

mission to employ a new parachute and booster nozzle ejection system; with the gale blowing at sea these components would be lost and with them valuable flight data on the modified hardware. He had also heard that dangerous amounts of ice were forming on the launch pad as the temperature dropped well below freezing. Surely, he argued, you must consider these two problems when you make your launch recommendation to Arnie Aldrich at Level II. They told McDonald that these really were not his problems and that he shouldn't concern himself with them. However, the NASA officials promised to pass on his concern to Level II.

Just after midnight McDonald delivered the telefaxed recommendation to Cecil Houston's office where Stan Reinartz and Mulloy were engaged in a teleconference with Arnie Aldrich, who was speaking from his Titusville motel room. McDonald listened while Larry Mulloy outlined the problems with the booster recovery vessels. Mulloy explained that they stood a good chance of losing about a million dollars worth of parachutes and booster nose cones, but that there was no danger of the boosters themselves sinking in the gale. He added that they had plenty of equipment in the inventory to replace the losses. That was an acceptable risk, Aldrich replied. But given these survival conditions at sea, Aldrich added, Mulloy was to make sure that the ships did not attempt to return to the recovery station until it was safe to do so.

Mulloy then raised the issue of the ice on the launch pad, and Aldrich said that this was a problem that would have to be addressed later in the morning. McDonald heard no mention whatsoever of the long, animated teleconference between Thiokol and NASA that had just terminated. As McDonald listened in angry disbelief, Mulloy finished his briefing and said good night to Aldrich. McDonald realized that the Marshall delegation was not even going to mention Thiokol's deep concerns about the cold weather launch scheduled for the morning.

During the Rogers Commission hearings, Mulloy was asked to discuss his conversation with Arnie Aldrich that night. Mulloy stated that he had given Aldrich a full briefing on the problems with the booster recovery vessels and his rationale for recommending the launch.

MR. MULLOY: I informed Mr. Aldrich of that, and he decided to proceed with the launch after that information. I did not discuss with Mr. Aldrich the conversations that we had just completed with Morton Thiokol.

CHAIRMAN ROGERS: Could you explain why?

MR. MULLOY: Yes, sir. At that time, and I still consider today, that was a Level III issue, Level III being an SRB element or an external tank element or Space Shuttle main engine element or an Orbiter. There was no violation of Launch Commit Criteria. There was no waiver required in my judgment at that time and still today.

The issue was closed. Arnie Aldrich could get a few hours sleep before the call to stations in the Launch Control Center. The responsible officials of the Marshall Space Flight Center—an institution that had inherited from the Apollo program the reputation of scientific and engineering excellence unparalleled in the world—had done their duty that night. NASA's managers could press on to the launch with confidence.

Obviously, however, the essence of the teleconference was far different from a neutral assessment of data. Mutual deception lay at the heart of the exchange between NASA and Morton Thiokol. The men from Marshall wanted their launch to proceed on schedule and would listen to no reasonable argument that recommended delay. The Thiokol managers overruled their engineering experts to satisfy a demanding customer. Then, in their revised recommendation, they deceptively described this expedient management decision as an "engineering assessment."

Yet both groups of managers somehow convinced themselves that these compromises were acceptable risks. Rogers Commissioner Dr. Richard Feynman best summarized this convoluted logic when he characterized NASA's Flight Readiness Reviews:

"I read all of these reviews and they agonize whether they can go even though they had some blow-by in the seal or they had a cracked blade in the pump of one of the engines, whether they can go the next time or this time, and they decide yes. Then it flies and nothing happens.

"Then it is suggested, therefore, that that risk is no longer so high. For the next flight we can lower our standards a little bit because we got away with it last time. . . . It is a kind of Russian roulette."

*   *   *

Challenger stood, glacial white, in the moonlight. On the exposed platforms and girders of the Fixed Service Structure, the cold wind blew spume from the overflowing drains and dripping fire hoses. Slowly, inexorably, the ice spread across the naked steel tower.

PART IV

COLD FIRE

CHAPTER THIRTEEN

JANUARY 28, 1986

DECISION TO LAUNCH

Pad 39B, Tuesday, 2:00 a.m.

As the temperature dropped and the northwest wind gusted to sixteen knots, ice spread across the Fixed Service Structure of the launch pad. Despite the addition of fourteen hundred gallons of antifreeze, thick ice was also forming in the sound suppression troughs beneath the booster blast holes in the Mobile Launching Platform. The night remained clear, the chill wind keened in the girders, and icicles formed grotesque daggers in the chalky flood-light.

After the launch team's call to stations in Firing Room Three and the support rooms in the launch center, a quick inspection of the pad by remote television camera revealed an alarming amount of ice on the structure. KSC's Director of Engineering, Horace Lamberth, dispatched Charlie Stevenson's Ice Team to the pad to assess the situation. The tanking operation had been suspended before actual propellant flow because a fire detector on the liquid hydrogen storage tank had failed and technicians were replacing the unit. This hiatus would give Stevenson time to thoroughly check the ice and report back, so that a decision to proceed with the countdown could be made before tanking actually began. That way, if the pad ice provoked a scrub, the launch team would not waste another half million dollars worth of propellant.

Stevenson began at the top of the Fixed Service Structure (FSS), at the 235-foot level. As the remote TV cameras had indicated, the freeze protection plan had run into serious trouble. But the situation Stevenson found firsthand was much worse than the cameras revealed. The plan to allow emergency showers and fire hoses to "trickle" all night to prevent frozen pipes had gone bad. This was his report back to Bob Lang over the OIS engineering channel:

STEVENSON: Okay, starting on about the 235-foot level where the top hose is, the fire hose that was draining into the shower, the hose is not really draining into the little bowl on the shower and it was spilling over. So we have a lot of hard solid ice from the 235 feet down to 195 feet where I am now. Most of it's on the west side and the north side, and about halfway in between, the floor is one solid sheet of ice about an inch and a half thick. And down on the 195-foot level, the water's on the pipe and plumbing and structure and beams all the way over to the Orbiter Access Arm [OAA]. That's as far down as we got so far.

LANG: Copy.

STEVENSON: We have some icicles about 18 inches long.

Stevenson went on to report that there was extensive sheet ice on the walkway gratings between the elevator and the emergency slide-wire escape baskets on the west side of the 195-foot level. This was the level of the orbiter access arm and the White Room. If the flight crew and closeout team had to be quickly evacuated due to a fire or fuel leak, they would have to run across this ice on their way to the escape baskets. This sheet ice covered about ten square feet between the elevators and the escape baskets, and the handrails also were coated with ice. In the event of an emergency evacuation, Stevenson told Horace Lamberth, there would be a problem. The walkway, he said, was "very slippery."

The House Science and Technology Subcommittee would find NASA's acceptance of this situation on the morning of January 28 to be highly unprofessional at best. In their report the Committee noted, "Crew safety concerns should dictate that the ice situation described by the Ice Team leader is unacceptable, and that some effort to remove the ice from the floor and handrails should be made. There is no indication that this was done. If the ice could not be removed, the mission should have been delayed until the danger represented by the ice could be eliminated."

The Committee touches the core of the dilemma facing the launch team leaders. Waiting until the sun melted the ice later that day would have delayed the launch until mid-afternoon. And this would have precluded using Casablanca as a trans-Atlantic abort site; at the moment Dakar's weather was not good. Therefore, the launch would have had to have been slipped until Wednesday or later (as Mike Smith had predicted).

But it is obvious that the "press on" mentality had taken hold of NASA's management, and they were able to accept conditions that would have surely provoked the scrub of another launch. As the launch approached there would be increasing evidence of this attitude.

An hour later, Stevenson and B. K. Davis had completed their careful inspection of the launch pad. Stevenson reported his concern that the ice on the FSS was so extensive that it posed a serious threat to the Orbiter. At the moment of main engine ignition the acoustic shock waves would dislodge a shower of long, thick icicles from the structure, which would be blown toward the Orbiter by the stiff northwest wind. Even if some did not strike the Orbiter itself, the broken ice on the Mobile Launching Platform would ricochet wildly in the cataclysmic shock waves, and some of this debris could strike and seriously damage the Orbiter's delicate tiles. Another problem with this ice debris was the so-called "aspiration" effect: when the solid rocket boosters ignited, there was a violent suction that could draw ice into the boosters with unpredictable effect.

But when launch team engineers reported this concern to Launch Director Gene Thomas, this was his reaction:

LAMBERTH: . . . Charlie's worried about it, Gene—the acoustics releasing it and it being free when the Orbiter comes by.
THOMAS: Boy, he's really stretching it.
LAMBERTH: Oh no, I don't know whether that's stretching it too much or not.
THOMAS: Well, I mean if we can ignore it, we need to feel comfortable about it. . . . We need to all know if we don't get back into tanking as soon as possible, we could possibly blow it just for that.
LAMBERTH: Yeah, we understand, Gene. . . .

The Committee would later note that a pattern emerged that night in which Launch Director Thomas repeatedly reminded engineers that there was a severe time constraint, while they were trying to assess the ice problem and that these problems could be addressed later in the countdown. By so doing, he undoubtedly contributed to the overall tolerant attitude toward this unpredictable situation. In a less harried countdown atmosphere, such time considerations would not have prevailed. The House Committee noted that ". . . the launch director was not operating in a manner the Committee would expect. Given his position as the senior official responsible for the preparation of the shuttle for launch, the Committee would expect a healthy skepticism to underlie discussions he had with members of the launch crew."

But as we have seen, Launch Director Thomas and Engineering Director Lamberth both seemed to have lost their normal skepticism during this countdown. Indeed, by signing capricious waivers to Launch Commit Criteria and by downplaying the unknown hazards of the ice debris, they seemed to have been duplicating the logic employed by the Marshall delegation in their dealings with Morton Thiokol. Rather than demanding that all those supporting the launch prove that conditions were safe, the senior members of the launch team demanded that their subordinates and the contractor representatives prove that it was *not* safe to launch Challenger.

And there can be no doubt that the launch directors did not share the same concern as their own Ice Team leader. By the end of his inspection tour Stevenson made his views quite clear to Thomas and Lamberth. The following exchange is especially illuminating:

THOMAS: Hey, we gotta come out of there [the countdown hold] when you guys [are] telling us you're pretty sure that water system's gonna work.

LAMBERTH: Yeah, you feel comfortable with what you see out there, Charlie, now?

STEVENSON: We have a lot of ice, if that's what you mean. I don't feel comfortable with what's on the FSS.

LAMBERTH: Then what choices we got?

STEVENSON: Well, I'd say the only choice you got today is not to go. We're just taking a chance of hitting the vehicle.

*   *   *

Recovery Vessel **Liberty,** *Tuesday, 4:00 a.m.*
During the eight hours the two recovery ships had been slowly steaming to windward, they had made good approximately twenty-two nautical miles. They were now safely west of the turbulent interface between the cold front and the warm Atlantic. For the first time in sixteen hours, the wind had dropped below gale force. The sea was still running at a twenty-foot level, but the wind had steadied off at thirty-five knots. The ships had escaped the dangerous conditions farther east, and the captains elected to reduce speed even more and hold station here until daylight. There was no sign of the moon yet, but farther west there was a weak, milky cast to the sky, indicating the trailing edge of the cold front overcast. Down in the damp, creaking crew compartments, the tired sailors lay wedged in their berths. Those on watch scanned the endlessly approaching ranks of white-crested swells, waiting for daylight and for the terrible weather to finally abate. As they waited, the cold seemed to seep up through their thick sea boots from the groaning deck plates.

*   *   *

Launch Control Center, Tuesday, 4:30 a.m.
NASA officials were not the only tired people to use faulty judgment during the long countdown before Challenger's launch. In the course of the complex tanking process, a contractor console technician in the firing room made a serious error, which could have had catastrophic repercussions. The operator controlled the critically important but notoriously delicate seventeen-inch liquid hydrogen disconnect valve, which separates the Orbiter main engine fuel system from the external tank umbilical. The technician broke the rules by issuing a computer command to open the valve when there was a relatively large pressure differential between the two sides of the flapper plate. The valve was held shut by this pressure for almost twenty seconds before it slammed open, a violent movement that could have damaged the sensitively tuned mechanism.

2II

If this valve had been damaged, it could have prematurely closed, provoking a sudden shutdown of the three main engines during flight. Analyses of postflight data prove that such catastrophic engine failure did not occur, but the potential was clearly there following the mishap. What is relevant to our narrative, however, is that the contractor employee decided not to report the mishap. Rather he silently continued with the tanking operation. It was only after the accident when computer tapes of the entire countdown were reviewed that the problem was revealed.

* * *

Operations Support Room, Tuesday, 5 a.m.
The top tier of Firing Room Three was partitioned at both ends into glassed-in operations support rooms. These air-conditioned greenhouses each held two rows of green metal communications consoles and featured large NASA Select color television monitors on gleaming alloy pedestals—the overall effect was Hollywood science fiction. The upper consoles of the righthand ops support room was the assigned launch station for NASA's top management, including Jesse Moore, Arnie Aldrich, and their Level I and II subordinates. On the lower row, the Marshall Space Flight Center held sway. The ops support enclosure to the left was reserved for visiting dignitaries and senior contractor executives. Shirley Green, NASA's Public Affairs Director, had her communication console in the corner of this room.

A little before five that morning, cars began to arrive in the big LCC parking lot, and the launch team members scurried through the cold wind toward the warmth of the building. The moon was low in the western sky, a cold remote presence on this frigid night. Many of the men trotting to the launch center were native Floridians who had never experienced such cold. With the wind chill of the stiff northwest breeze, frostbite was a significant hazard for the security guards and the support crews at the nearby shuttle landing facility. There was thick ice in the ditches along the roads and black, gritty ice in the parking lot potholes that had been flooded by the Sunday afternoon rain.

One of the cars to be processed through the launch-morning security checkpoints carried Dr. William Lucas and his Director of Science and Engineering, Jim Kingsbury. When they got to the Marshall consoles in the ops support room, they were greeted by Stanley Reinartz and Larry Mulloy. Reinartz presented Lucas with Thiokol's launch recommendation that had been signed and telefaxed by Joe Kilminster just before midnight. Although there is no verbatim record of their conversation, Lucas, Reinartz, and Mulloy have testified about the exchange. The essence of their testimony is that the two-and-a-half-hour teleconference of Monday night was treated as routine administrative business that required no further action by anyone from Marshall.

According to everyone who participated in or observed the conversation in the ops support room, there was never any question that a flight safety issue remained open or that the Marshall managers—specifically, Stanley Reinartz—should bring the question of Thiokol's original recommendation against launch to the attention of Arnie Aldrich or Jesse Moore. When questioned by Chairman Rogers and Commissioners General Donald Kutyna and Robert Hotz, this was Stanley Reinartz's recollection of the early morning meeting:

MR. REINARTZ: . . . Mr. Mulloy and I informed the Director of Marshall, Dr. Lucas, and the Director of Science and Engineering, Mr. Kingsbury, on the twenty-eighth of January about five o'clock of the initial Thiokol concerns and engineering recommendations, the final Thiokol launch recommendation, and the full support of the Marshall engineering for the launch recommendation, that I felt had led to a successful resolution of this concern.

GENERAL KUTYNA: Could I interrupt for a minute? You informed Dr. Lucas. He is not in the reporting chain?

MR. REINARTZ: No, sir.

GENERAL KUTYNA: If I could use an analogy, if you want to report a fire you don't go to the mayor. In his position as center director, Dr. Lucas was cut out of the reporting chain, much like a mayor. If it was important enough to report to him, why didn't you go through the fire department and go up your decision chain?

MR. REINARTZ: That, General Kutyna, is a normal course of our operating mode within the center, that I keep Dr. Lucas informed of my activities, be they this type of thing or other.

GENERAL KUTYNA: But you did that at five o'clock in the morning. That's kind of early. It would seem that's important. Why didn't you go up the chain?

MR. REINARTZ: No, sir. That is the time when we go in, basically go into the launch, and so it was not waking him up to tell him that information. It was when we go into the launch in the morning. And based upon my assessment of the situation as dispositioned that evening, for better or worse, I did not perceive any clear requirement for interaction with Level II, as the concern was worked and dispositioned with full agreement among all responsible parties as to that agreement.

CHAIRMAN ROGERS: Did I understand what you just said, that you told Dr. Lucas that the engineers at Thiokol were in accord?

MR. REINARTZ: No, sir. What I told him was of the initial Thiokol concerns that we had and the initial recommendation and the final Thiokol recommendation and the rationale associated with that recommendation, and the fact that we had the full support of the senior Marshall engineering and, as George has testified, to the extensiveness of the group of people we had involved in that telecon with the various disciplines, that those three elements made up the final recommendation.

From the tone of this testimony, one would assume that the entire issue of Thiokol's temperature concerns had not been discussed by Reinartz and Lucas before the long teleconference, that Lucas had never heard of the Thiokol recommendation to delay the launch that was made in the first, abortive teleconference. We know, however, that Reinartz and Mulloy met with Lucas and Kingsbury at the Holiday Inn and raised the issue at 7 P.M. According to Reinartz, the men ". . . had a short discussion relating to the general nature of the concerns with Dr. Lucas and Mr. Kingsbury at the motel before we both departed for the [second] telecon . . ." Further, it is highly unlikely that Lucas would have allowed the late-night assembly of his top engineering talent unless he was already well apprised of the serious nature of the situation.

Therefore, when Lucas arrived at the launch center, he had to have been keenly aware that a vital launch decision point had been resolved one way or the other in the Thiokol-Marshall teleconference the night before. Yet this is his description of the early-morning conversation about this vital issue:

DR. LUCAS: He told me, as I testified, when I went into the control room, that an issue had been resolved, that there were some people at Thiokol who had a concern about the weather, that that had been discussed very thoroughly by the Thiokol people and by the Marshall Space Flight Center people, and it had been concluded agreeably that there was no problem, that he had a recommendation by Thiokol to launch and our most knowledgeable people and engineering talent agreed with that. So from my perspective, I didn't have—I didn't see that as an issue.

CHAIRMAN ROGERS: And if you had known that Thiokol engineers almost to a man opposed the flight, would that have changed your view?

DR. LUCAS: I'm certain that it would.

CHAIRMAN ROGERS: So your testimony is the same as Mr. Hardy's. Had he known, he would not have recommended the flight be launched on that day.

DR. LUCAS: I didn't make a recommendation one way or the other. But had I known that, I would have then interposed an objection, yes.

CHAIRMAN ROGERS: I gather you didn't tell Mr. Aldrich or Mr. Moore what Mr. Reinartz had told you?

DR. LUCAS: No, sir. That is not the reporting channel. Mr. Reinartz reports directly to Mr. Aldrich. In a sense, Mr. Reinartz informs me as the institutional manager of the progress that he is making in implementing his program, but that I have never on any occasion reported to Mr. Aldrich.

Even if we accept the testimony of these two men as being both forthright and completely accurate, they seem to have exercised exceedingly poor management judgment. Using General Kutyna's analogy, Dr. William Lucas, the "mayor" of the Marshall Space Flight Center, had learned of a potentially serious fire hazard; however, apparently because Lucas wanted desperately to protect his bureaucratic turf, he refrained from alerting the fire department—in this case, Arnie Aldrich and Jesse Moore.

*   *   *

Operations and Checkout Building, Tuesday, 6:00 a.m.
Because of the hold caused by the fire detector malfunction at the pad, Challenger's crew had earned a one-hour delay in their

wakeup time. But the crew were all up and about by six. Mike Smith could see the hard blue line of the ocean horizon from his room in the crew quarters and could note that the wind was holding west, northwest. Before going to bed he had gotten an update on the predicted cold weather and the launch team's efforts to protect the pad from freezing. He was well versed in NASA's formal Launch Commit Criteria and would have realized that the space shuttle Challenger could not be launched with the ambient temperature below 31 degrees F. Therefore, Smith was almost certain that they were facing another weather scrub.

Whatever the feelings of the other crew members about this situation, they dutifully filed in to the dining room and took their places at the breakfast table. As on the day before, the table was decorated with a centerpiece of red and white roses and American flags. The cook had baked a new cake which bore the proud, albeit somewhat crowded mission logo and all seven names. Launch morning breakfasts are a NASA ritual; the menu of steak and eggs has not changed since the days of Project Mercury. But the seven people seated around the breakfast table did not resemble the lean, crewcut male fighter pilots of the early 1960s. Nevertheless, Dr. Judy Resnik did justice to the meal: when the platter was passed, she helped herself to two steaks and a generous portion of scrambled eggs. Judy Resnik had been in space before. If they actually did launch today, she'd be eating vacuum-sealed flight rations for the next seven days. Even with the shuttle's elaborate galley, the food on board was not very appetizing.

After breakfast, Challenger's crew assembled in a nearby teleconference room for their weather briefing from Johnson. The first order of business was abort sites. Low ceiling and predicted rain made Casablanca a doubtful backup TAL site. But Dakar would be well within minimums, and, equally important, Dakar had night-landing capability and could be used if the cold weather at the Cape pushed the launch toward the end of the window. Given the temperature constraints in the Launch Commit Criteria, the crew were told, they could anticipate considerable hold time on the pad, with a probable liftoff close to noon.

Following the weather briefing, they went to their rooms and dressed in their flight coveralls and boots. As Ellison Onizuka prepared himself, he folded up a warm blue flight jacket, which he sent ahead to be waiting for him in the Astrovan after Astronaut Walkout. He knew he couldn't be "out of uniform" for this media ritual, but he certainly didn't intend to freeze out at the launch pad, waiting for his turn in the White Room. Onizuka hated cold weather, and although he would have to put up with a fair amount of ribbing from his crewmates, it was better than being coatless in this weird, unnatural cold.

*   *   *

Firing Room Three, Tuesday, 7 a.m.
The coldest period of the long night came just after dawn. The temperature stood at 24 degrees F. at 7 A.M. Among the engineers monitoring the impact of this record cold, the men who had written the temperature redline waiver on the external tank nose cone the day before now had far worse conditions on their hands. Even though the external tank heaters had been going full bore all night, it was clear that the nose cone was far below the arbitrary 28 degrees F. redline written Monday morning. The following exchange was recorded over the OIS engineering channel:

ENGINEER ONE: . . . We need to send a waiver over for signatures. We're right now showing nose cone gas temps that we were discussing yesterday are down in the 12- to 16-degree range and the waiver that we wrote yesterday for 51L only gives us allowance down to 28 degrees F.
ENGINEER TWO: Yeah, we'll have to rewrite that waiver.
ENGINEER ONE: OK. You don't think we'll have any trouble getting that signed?
ENGINEER TWO: No, as long as our pressure transducers are OK.
ENGINEER ONE: OK. What number would you like to use on that, Horace? . . . We're right now sitting at 10 [degrees].
HORACE LAMBERTH: Let's hold on a minute and then we'll write the waiver; we'll probably wanna go below 10.

At this point, an unidentified engineer reiterated the faulty logic employed Monday morning:

217

UNIDENTIFIED: Yeah, we may just want to say no low and put a note on there that based on the pressure transducers.

However, this was a capriciously illogical course of action. As the House Science and Technology Subcommittee noted: "If engineers intended to apply the same rationale for waivers as that used on January 27, the argument against this decision remains. The Launch Commit Criteria backup procedure, which involves the use of the transducers as an alternative temperature monitor, was constrained to an ambient temperature range of 40–99 degrees F. Ambient temperatures at this point in the countdown were well below 40 degrees F. Therefore, the rationale was invalid."

When the countdown resumed after tanking, Launch Director Gene Thomas called Engineering Director Horace Lamberth concerning this problem:

THOMAS: OK. I understand we're in the process of writing a new waiver with a lower limit of 10?
LAMBERTH: We're still looking. We'll give you a low limit.
THOMAS: What are they running today?
LAMBERTH: It's been down as low as 10 basically.
THOMAS: Wow!

Still later, as Thomas and Lamberth worked to clear "open" items on the engineering checklist, they "closed" the nose cone temperature redline issue in the following exchange:

THOMAS: OK. The only outstanding item we have right now is the one waiver on the cone temps.
LAMBERTH: OK. It looks like we probably could say about 10 degrees and be OK on that one.
THOMAS: OK. We'll use 10 degrees then.

During the Rogers Commission hearings, the senior managers involved in the launch decision testified that Challenger's countdown was basically no different from earlier uneventful missions. One must therefore assume that equally arbitrary decisions were employed in those mission countdowns.

*   *   *

Pad 39B, Tuesday, 7:30 a.m.

In the first chill sunlight of Tuesday morning, Launch Pad 39B looked even grimmer than it had in the artificial glare of the floodlights. Charlie Stevenson and Billie Davis had returned with their Ice Team at seven when the tanking operation was complete. They were faced with an assignment of surrealistic absurdity. Under normal conditions, Stevenson's ice crew was required to inspect the external tank for frost and rime ice that might have formed when the supercold propellants froze condensation on the outside of the tank. On twenty-four countdowns the Ice Team had conscientiously reported small patches of thick frost and some clear sheet ice on the tank and overhead piping. This was to be expected, given the temperature difference between cryogenic propellants and the normally humid Florida atmosphere.

But what they found on the morning of the twenty-eighth of January flew in the face of every caution that had been instilled in them by their superiors. Normally they were to report *all* ice that could break off the tank and impact the Orbiter's delicate thermal protective system (TPS) tiles during lift-off. They were also required to remove all visible debris—pebbles, sand, even dry stems of marsh grass—that might have blown onto the Mobile Launching Platform. This morning, however, they were faced with the spectacle of a virtual frozen waterfall cascading down the west and north faces of the towering Fixed Service Structure. Some of the ice hung in thick clumps of stalactites from walkways and girders only sixty feet from Challenger's left wingtip.

Stevenson and Billie Davis might not have been top-level management, but it was obvious to them that this ice was a serious problem. As Stevenson had reported to the firing room during his first inspection, an undetermined amount of ice would break loose and fall toward the Orbiter—borne by the steady northwest wind —during the violent cacophony of engine ignition. There might be *tons* of debris on the launch platform when the solid rocket boosters ignited.

The ice team struggled with a long-handled "shrimp net" to break up and remove the thick plates of ice that had formed in the sound suppression troughs beneath the launch platform. Unless the temperature rose rapidly, this ice was bound to form again.

The antifreeze added the night before was obviously incapable of compensating for this record cold.

As his final duty in this bizarre exercise, Billie Davis trudged around the base of the external tank and solid rocket boosters. He was equipped with an infrared pyrometer—which measured the temperature of remote surfaces—roughly the size of a handheld hair dryer. The readings he registered from the external tank seemed normal enough, as did the temperature on the lefthand booster. But the temperature of the aft section of the righthand solid rocket booster was an amazing 8 degrees F. Even though Davis had never recorded a temperature this low, he was not overly concerned because there was nothing in the Launch Commit Criteria about actual hardware temperature, only the ambient temperature at launch time. However, the Ice Team did report minor frost on the tank and sheet ice on the lower segment and skirt of the lefthand solid rocket booster, which had been caused by water blowing down from the service structure during the frigid night.

Following the teleconference the night before, Allan McDonald had heatedly discussed the issue of ambient temperature, bulk propellant temperature, and the effects of the hard freeze on the booster field joints. The thrust of McDonald's argument had been the dangerously unpredictable chilling of the O-rings, their grease packing, and the flame-proof putty between the sections of propellant. Without knowing it, Billie Davis had just proven McDonald's thesis.

*   *   *

Rockwell Mission Support Room, Tuesday, 8:00 a.m. (E.S.T.)
For several hours the Rockwell International Orbiter Support Team in Downey, California, had been working hard to assess the danger posed by the ice on the launch pad. Dr. John Peller, Rockwell's Vice President of Engineering, led the effort. The team's basic problem was to quickly analyze the probable trajectories of the windborne ice that would be dislodged by the volcanic forces of ignition. They also had to estimate what was an acceptable degree of TPS damage that might occur from such ice impacts.

The television monitors in the support room graphically revealed the extent of the ice. One Rockwell engineer at the Cape, John Tribe, reported to his colleague Robert Weaver in Downey the extent of the situation:

WEAVER: . . . Looks bad, eh?

TRIBE: Ice does look bad, yeah. . . . . The big concern is gonna be the mass of ice that is on the FSS, from the 235-foot level all the way down to the MLP [Mobile Launcher Platform]. Every platform has had water running on it all night, and they're just a—some of the closeups of the stairwells looks like, uh, something out of Dr. Zhivago. There's sheets of icicles hanging everywhere. . . .

WEAVER: Sounds grim.

TRIBE: The big concern is that nobody knows what the hell is going to happen when that thing lights off and all that ice gets shook loose and comes tumbling down and—what does it do then? Does it ricochet, does it get into some turbulent condition that throws it against the vehicle? Our general input to date has been basically that there's vehicle jeopardy that we're not prepared to sign up to. . . .

WEAVER: We didn't see this when we had icing conditions before?

TRIBE: No, and they didn't run the showers all damn night before. They ran the showers this time and ran 'em, pretty heavily by the look of it, the drains froze up and they all overflowed.

While the Rockwell team ran their analyses, the company's President of the Space Transportation's Systems Division, Dr. Rocco Petrone, arrived at the Downey support room to coordinate the effort and prepare Rockwell's recommendation. Petrone polled the aerodynamicist, structural engineers, and TPS experts about the situation. He found that there was insufficient data to prove that launching under these conditions was safe. Therefore, Dr. Petrone contacted one of his vice presidents at the Cape, Robert Glaysher, and told him Rockwell's position was "we cannot recommend launching from here, from what we see. We think the tiles would be endangered." Unconsciously echoing Thiokol's Joe Kilminster, Petrone said that the company's experience, their "data base" from earlier missions, was inadequate to judge this unprecedented hazard.

*   *   *

Pad 39B, Tuesday, 8:25 a.m.

It was terribly cold at the 195-foot level of the service structure. The bitter chill even penetrated the confines of the White Room. As the crew came out of the elevator, the closeout technicians warned them about the sheet ice on the walkway to their right. A few minutes earlier, Al Rochfort, the NASA suit technician, had met the Astrovan and advised the crew to use the toilet in the vehicle because the stairs to the regular crew lavatory, one level up from the Orbiter access arm, were blocked by ice.

Commander Dick Scobee did not allow this bizarre situation to affect his cheerful and optimistic demeanor. Even if the countdown ended in another scrub, he seemed determined to keep up the morale of both his crew and the closeout team. On exiting the elevator, he took a deep breath of the cold air and smiled broadly at the blue sky.

"This is a beautiful day to fly," he said.

Johnny Corlew glanced at the ice around them. "It's a little cold though, Dick."

Scobee shook his head, still smiling. "Nah," he said. "That's good, that's great."

When Scobee and Smith entered the White Room to don their harnesses and helmets, Dick Scobee beckoned to the Lockheed Lead Technician, Bill Campbell. "Here," Scobee said, holding out a small object. "You guys might need this today. Hang on to it."

Campbell cheerfully accepted a shiny alloy bolt, done up nicely with a red ribbon. Any lingering frustration from the scrub was abolished by Scobee's friendly gesture.

Mike Smith stood by himself, slightly withdrawn, as he performed his silent mental exercises, reviewing the myriad details of the flight deck checklist.

The commander and pilot were quickly suited up and assisted to the flight deck by Sonny Carter, the Astronaut Support Person.

Ellison Onizuka came next. He wore his warm blue flight jacket over his mission coveralls. And this jacket bore the round logo patch of an earlier mission. It had been Ellison who had jokingly chided the closeout crew for their breach of protocol in not wearing 51L mission patches during the countdown rehearsal three weeks before. Now Johnny Corlew seized on the opportunity to kid his friend Ellison Onizuka.

"Ah-ha," Corlew joked. "What's this, Ellison? Don't you have the right mission patch?"

Onizuka slipped off the offending jacket and handed it to Johnny Corlew. "Well," he said with mock severity, "at least we're not on the Dan Rather show like *somebody* I could name."

The night before, Johnny Corlew had been seen across the country via CBS News, wielding the hacksaw on the stubborn bolt.

Judy Resnik and Christa McAuliffe entered the White Room clapping their arms and dancing lightly from the cold. As Judy pulled on her flight gear, she smiled at Christa as if to give her confidence. When it was Judy's time to enter the hatch, she turned to Christa and grinned. "Well," Judy said, "the next time I see you, we'll be in space."

Before the closeout crew helped Christa with her flight equipment, Johnny Corlew presented her with a big, polished Delicious apple. Christa beamed at him and held the apple before her face, then returned it to him. "Save it for me," she said, "and I'll eat it when I get back."

Greg Jarvis seemed fresh and well rested. He moved with a calm slowness, as if he were waiting in line for a bus, not about to board a two-thousand-ton spaceship. Johnny Corlew helped him with his harness.

"Well," Johnny said, "we're really going to go today."

Jarvis grinned. "Yeah," he said, "I sure hope so."

Ron McNair was characteristically patient this cold morning. While the other crew members were dressing, Johnny Corlew took Ron aside and gave him a thorough briefing on exactly what he should look for in the hatch-locking mechanism. The twenty-four-hour turnaround had not been long enough for NASA to open up the hatch lock and repair the microswitch that had malfunctioned the day before. Therefore, they would rely on Ron McNair's visual inspection to be absolutely certain the locking pins were in their proper position and the hatch was safely sealed. McNair assured Johnny that he understood what was required of him.

The process of "crew ingress" this morning was proceeding in record time, without a single problem. It was as if the difficulties of the previous day had marshalled an unconscious determination among all concerned to demonstrate perfection. Before Bill Campbell signaled the men to carefully close the hatch, they surreptitiously peeked inside to see if Christa McAuliffe had discovered her surprise. Her brother-in-law had given the closeout crew a small lacquered plaque that had been signed by her students back in New Hampshire. The plaque was emblazoned with a shooting star and bore the inscription "Reaching for the Stars." The technicians had placed the present on Christa's clipboard, just beneath the ascent trajectory sheet, and above the instructions for disassembling and stowing her seat once Challenger was in orbit. Her clipboard was held in a bracket near her right knee and the men hoped she would not grow impatient and discover the gift before the shuttle was in space.

When Sonny Carter performed his communications checks, Judy Resnik gave a loud shiver and voiced her opinion of the cold, "Cowabunga!"

True to form, Ellison Onizuka agreed about the cold. "My nose is freezing!" he exclaimed.

Strapped on their backs, wary that they might be in for another frustrating five-hour prelude to a scrub, the crew bantered back and forth about the weather. Judy shouted down to the closeout crew, complaining that the heated air pipe was too close. "Any chance you could move that blast furnace there, guys?"

The hatch was closed and sealed, and Ron McNair removed his helmet and leaned forward to closely inspect the locking pins. "Okay, Dick," he told Scobee, once he had replaced his helmet. "I gave them a thumbs-up. They look good."

It was just before nine in the morning, and Challenger's crew was sealed inside the space shuttle.

*   *   *

Launch Control Center, Tuesday, 8:40 a.m.
The crew's families entered Gene Thomas's office in a loose procession. Cheryl McNair pushed Joy, her youngest child, in a stroller and Reggie McNair trudged sleepily beside his little sister. Steve McAuliffe carried Caroline and shepherded his son Scott

ahead of him. The other children were old enough to overcome their sleepiness and were well aware that this was the second launch attempt and that they might be in for another long wait.

Gene Thomas's inner office was still decorated with the wide computer printout banner reading: "Welcome STS 51L Families from the Kennedy Launch Team." The cafeteria provided a generous selection of coffee, juice, and Danish pastries. Bob Harris welcomed the group and invited them to the inner office, where he had a videotape ready to play the launch-morning events, including crew breakfast, walkout, and the White Room activities. Harris's wife Marion was a teacher in Titusville, and she had provided an appropriate decoration for the Teacher-in-Space mission—three heart-shaped helium balloons supporting an inflated toy Orbiter. These decorations had been arranged on top of the large television monitor since the day before.

As the group entered the office, Jane Smith looked down at the balloons and saw that the space shuttle was half deflated and crumpled like a wrecked aircraft. "My God," she exclaimed, "I hope that's not an omen."

There was an instinctive chorus of strained laughter among the people in the office. Lorna Onizuka unleashed a volley of cheerful banter, laced with one-liner jokes. The families laughed at the appropriate moments, but it was clear to Harris that a somber note of tension lay beneath their good cheer.

As they watched the videotape of the ritual launch-morning crew activities, several adults wandered into the outer office with their coffee cups to stare silently at the set there, which showed a live picture of the launch pad ice. The count was now in a hold, pending the outcome of a Mission Management Team meeting convened to assess the ice problem.

The small children crawled on the floor with their toy trucks and stuffed animals, and the group dissolved into quiet family units. But Lorna Onizuka seemed incapable of mastering her nervousness. She wandered between the two offices, smiling too broadly. Dick Scobee's oldest son, Richard, a senior at the Air Force Academy, seemed preoccupied. He squatted on his heels with his back to the wall just inside the outer office doorway, staring straight ahead.

Jane Smith had recovered from her earlier bout of nerves. She sat at the secretary's desk in the outer office, answering the phone for Thomas's secretary, Barbara Rabren, who was amusing Scott McAuliffe by letting him write a letter on her computer.

Warm sunlight flooded the office. The families waited, each person coping with his own thoughts. Three miles seaward, Challenger was clearly visible, solid and white against the cold blue Atlantic.

*　　*　　*

Operations Center, Tuesday, 9 a.m.

While the crew families waited in the sunlit office, the Mission Management Team assembled in the windowless Ops Center just down the hall. The T-shaped conference table was crowded with NASA's Mission Management Team, and the raised bullpen to the rear of the room held contractor representatives, waiting to advise the managers. The purpose of this meeting was to assess the launch pad ice hazard. Arnie Aldrich had been thoroughly briefed on the problem by Kennedy Engineering Director Horace Lamberth and by NASA's Orbiter Project Manager Richard Colonna.

Charlie Stevenson had come in from the cold to present his detailed Ice Team inspection report. As with the inspection itself, the report was weirdly bifurcated: On the one hand, there was no dangerous ice buildup on the vehicle itself that would violate Launch Commit Criteria. But on the other hand, the ice on the launch pad structures was even worse than reported earlier. The Mission Management Team thanked him for his effort and told him to stand by for a possible final inspection.

A consensus on the degree of hazard was emerging among the NASA managers at Kennedy and Johnson most concerned with Orbiter safety. And that consensus was the opposite of the conclusion reached by their contractor counterparts. Rockwell's experts at Downey had stated that the amount of ice and its position on the structure presented an unquantifiable hazard. They maintained that the exact trajectories of falling ice and the aspiration effect of ice debris on the launching platform could not be calculated to any degree of certainty. Therefore, Rockwell did not have a proper engineering data base from which to form a professional judgment. Dr. Petrone and his colleagues viewed this situation as a constraint to launch.

But Colonna, Lamberth, and Johnson's Director of Engineering, Tom Moser, took the same information and formed another conclusion. This is how Shuttle Director Arnie Aldrich summed up NASA's logic for the Rogers Commission:

MR. ALDRICH: . . . Mr. Lamberth reported that KSC [Kennedy Space Center] engineering had calculated the trajectories, as you've heard, of the falling ice from the fixed service structure east side, with current 10-knot winds at 300 degrees, and predicted that none of this ice would contact the Orbiter during its ignition or launch sequence; and that their calculations even showed that if the winds would increase to 15 knots, we still would not have contact with the Orbiter.

Mr. Colonna, Orbiter Project Manager, reported that similar calculations had been performed in Houston by the mission evaluation team there. They concurred in this assessment. And further, Mr. Colonna stated that even if these calculations were significantly in error, that it was their belief that falling ice from the fixed service structure, if it were in fact to make its way to the Orbiter, it would only be the most lightweight ice that was in that falling stream, and it would impact the Orbiter at a very oblique angle.

Impacts of this type would have very low probability of causing any serious damage to the Orbiter, and at most would result in postflight turnaround repairs.

Aldrich next called Tom Moser in Houston on the conference phone and asked for the input from the mission evaluation team. Moser confirmed the detailed predictions made by Lamberth and Colonna. According to NASA, it would take too long for the heavy ice to fall, rebound from the mobile launching platform, and ricochet up to impact the rising Orbiter. Aldrich had assembled NASA's expert engineering assessment.

Like Stan Reinartz the night before, Aldrich now asked these experts for their recommendation. Colonna, Lamberth, and Moser all recommended proceeding with the countdown. Now Aldrich was in a bureaucratically advantageous position to elicit Rockwell's formal recommendation. Just as Mulloy had made it clear to Thiokol's management the night before that NASA was not receptive to arguments against the launch, Aldrich had structured the meeting in his favor. Rockwell's two vice presidents, Martin Cioffoletti and Robert Glaysher, had been obliged to sit in the Ops Center's contractors' enclosure listening to NASA's engineering assessment, which was diametrically opposed to that of their own company's engineers. Now Aldrich made them publicly show their colors.

In their testimony before the Rogers Commission, Glaysher and Cioffoletti stated that they never gave Aldrich a recommendation to launch:

MR. GLAYSHER: My exact quote—and it comes in two parts. The first one was, Rockwell could not 100 percent assure that it is safe to fly, which I quickly changed to Rockwell cannot assure that it is safe to fly. . . .

MR. CIOFFOLETTI: I felt that by telling them we did not have a sufficient data base and could not analyze the trajectory of the ice, I felt he understood that Rockwell was not giving a positive indication that we were for the launch.

Arnie Aldrich and his managers were apparently so determined to launch Challenger that morning in order to make up for previous delays and preserve the inflexible launch dates of the March ASTRO mission and the May planetary science flights that they interpreted Rockwell's position as the opposite of what it in fact was.

MR. ALDRICH: At that time, I also polled Mr. Robert Glaysher, the Vice President, Orbiter Project Manager, Rockwell International STS Division, and Mr. Marty Cioffoletti, Shuttle Integration Project Manager, Rockwell International STS Division. Mr. Glaysher stated —and he had been listening to this entire discussion and had not been directly involved with it, but had been party to this the whole time.

His statement to me, as best I can reconstruct it to report to you

at this time, was that while he did not disagree with the analysis that
JSC [Johnson Space Center] and KSC had reported, that they would
not give an unqualified go for launch as ice on the launch complex
was a condition which had not previously been experienced, and
thus this posed a small additional but unquantifiable risk. Mr.
Glaysher did not ask or insist that we not launch, however.

At the conclusion of the above review, I felt reasonably confident
that the launch should proceed.

Before the final decision was made, however, Aldrich would
dispatch Charlie Stevenson's Ice Team to the pad once more. Aldrich hoped that the sun would melt enough ice so that a more
accurate estimate could be made of the trajectory the falling ice
would take at lift-off.

*   *   *

The White House, Tuesday, 10 a.m.
After President Reagan came down from his living quarters that
morning, he received his usual briefing from his National Security
advisors and a précis of his day's schedule from his appointment
secretary. The remainder of his morning was reserved for the final
editing and a rehearsal of the State of the Union Message he would
present that night.

The White House has not revealed whether the President was
advised on the status of the Challenger launch.

However, the draft speech the President had before him contained a reference to one of the student experiments aboard Challenger. And, as Shirley Green had been advised by her White
House contact over the weekend, there was also considerable mention of NASA in this draft version. Even though presidential
spokesman Larry Speakes would bitterly deny any White House
pressure on NASA to launch Challenger in time for the speech, it
is reasonable to assume that there was a reference to Christa Mc-
Auliffe and the Teacher-in-Space mission in the draft the President
was then considering. It does not follow from this assumption,
however, that anyone in the White House pressured NASA that
morning. But it is also logical to assume that NASA's manage-

ment was aware of their agency's vested interest in having the Challenger mentioned that night by the President.

At one that afternoon, President Reagan was scheduled to have lunch with Dan Rather, Tom Brokaw, and Peter Jennings to give the three network anchors a preview of the speech. Any knowledgeable observer of Washington politics would conclude that President Reagan—the master of the relevant anecdote—would have found some way to add a reference to the successful shuttle launch to his speech and to mention the mission during his lunch with these media heavyweights.

* * *

Launch Pad 39B, Tuesday, 11:15 a.m.

The countdown clock stood at T-minus nine minutes and holding. On the launch pad, Charlie Stevenson and Billie Davis's Ice Team performed their final inspection. Although the sun was warm enough to cause considerable melting on the exposed ice formations high on the Fixed Service Structure, there was still plenty of solid ice lower down on the west face. And despite the antifreeze, ice had formed once more in the sound-suppression troughs. The Ice Team removed as much ice as they could from the troughs, checked for fallen ice debris, and left the pad.

In the Orbiter, the crew was feeling the effects of the long wait. They fully expected the Mission Management Team to terminate the countdown because of the ice hazard on the launch pad. Judy Resnik commented on the long, frustrating process. "I hope we don't drive this down to the bitter end again today," she said.

From the lefthand flight deck seat, Commander Dick Scobee agreed. "Yeah," he sighed.

A little later Judy Resnik commented again on the long delay, "After sitting like this, I can't imagine how anybody can hang in those gravity boots."

"They don't do it for four hours!" Dick Scobee replied.

A few moments later, Scobee was contacted on the air-to-ground loop and told that the countdown would proceed. The Mission Management Team had reviewed the ice situation and found no constraints to launch. "All right!" he shouted, then added with his habitual optimism, "That's great."

Behind him on the flight deck, Judy Resnik quickly calculated the new lift-off time: 11:38.

A MAJOR MALFUNCTION

Firing Room Three, 11:20 a.m.

During the scheduled ten-minute countdown hold at T-9 minutes, all the active members of the launch team went to Channel 212 on the OIS communications system. The key decision makers had to stay in constant contact. Gene Thomas conducted his final polls of Kennedy Space Center facility components. Arnie Aldrich polled his own people. One by one, the hardware and support elements came on the loop to add their recommendations to launch. . . . "Go." "Roger." "Affirmative."

Charlie Stevenson's Ice Team had fished the last slushy chunks of ice from the boosters' sound suppression troughs and photographed the ice on the service structure for later engineering analysis. Stevenson called the firing room on Channel 245 and reported what he had seen: the ice formations were still extensive on those parts of the launch pad in the shade. A voice from the firing room thanked him for his information and told him he could evacuate his team from the launch pad. Their white NASA van was the last vehicle to drive up the road beside the wide gravel crawlerway leading from the VAB to Launch Pads 39A and 39B.

Challenger stood in the chill sunlight. A dozen remote television cameras around the pad focused on different parts of the space shuttle and the service structure. In the firing room the image of Challenger shimmered on the TV monitors, making it look as if the space shuttle stood in the middle of a baking desert. In reality the temperature was only a few degrees above freezing, and the northwest breeze kept the wind chill below 32 degrees F. On the west and northwest sides of the Fixed Service Structure the thick ice formations remained intact. The ice on the sunny side of the structure had begun to drip. But in the deep shade beneath the massive Mobile Launching Platform, a frozen skin was already forming again in the sound suppression troughs.

The launch team's final weather update, however, was excellent. There were no adverse crosswinds to affect the Return to Launch Site Abort (RTLS) capability, and from the the shuttle training aircraft John Young reported no undue low-level turbulence. The T-38 weather flights had noted some high-altitude wind shear, but this was well within accepted limits. Dakar's weather was holding at the satisfactory level with broken clouds at 21,000 feet and six miles visibility in haze. The high-intensity floodlights had now been positioned around the Dakar airfield and would be activated at lift-off. In the event of a trans-Atlantic abort landing Dakar was now the primary site.

Out at the Mission Operations Control Room in Houston, Flight Controller Jay Greene polled the eleven members of his Mission Control Team for the final status report. Each of them recited the ritual "Go." Houston was ready to support the launch.

In the firing room, console operators were running their final checks on the Ground Launch Sequencer computer program that would initiate and monitor the hundreds of commands which were required in the last nine minutes of the countdown. Challenger's four general-purpose computers and the fifth backup were now racing through their own terminal systems status checks. The countdown had entered the realm of cybernetics, in which silicone-based intelligence would supersede the plodding senses and logic of the humans in the firing room. At this level of complexity, decisions were based on data analysis that occurred in milliseconds, and commands were issued in coded three-part bursts that were "distanced" by three-millisecond pauses to give the computers ample time to sort out valid commands from spurious "noise." The banks of computers in the Launch Control Center and on board the Challenger chanted an electronic fugue at speeds far beyond the powers of human perception.

As the decision point approached, the people in the firing room were becoming thoughtful observers, not active participants. Soon, their sole option would be clumsy termination of the electronic symphony which rose in silent waves within the computers. NASA's managers could only command this process to stop; they could not hope to orchestrate it. In order to prevent the disruption of this delicate operation, the doors to the firing room had been locked twenty minutes before and were now guarded by armed security officers. The countdown was reaching the point where ultimate decisions would be made.

Gene Thomas and Arnie Aldrich had run their final polls. The weather at the Cape, at the TAL sites, and at the once-around abort site at Edwards Air Force Base was acceptable. However, the weather immediately offshore was a problem. According to Launch Commit Criteria Item 1.4.2: "Offshore Recovery Area Weather Conditions," the wind and sea state from the pad to fifty nautical miles into the Atlantic were currently unacceptable. Should the Challenger attempt a Return to Launch Site Abort and be unable to make the coast, Scobee and Smith still had a ditching mode available. But to ditch the space shuttle in the Atlantic with any probability of crew survival, sea and wind conditions had to be favorable. These minimum conditions were:

- Surface winds—no greater than 25 knots.
- Ceiling—greater than or equal to 500 feet.
- Visibility—greater than or equal to 0.5 nautical miles.
- Seas—no greater than 8 feet.

The latest report from the booster recovery vessels, however, gave winds at 25 knots and seas of up to 15 feet. Visibility was poor, too, less than two miles in sea smoke: a dense fog provoked by the freezing air mass contacting the warm Gulf Stream. If Challenger had to ditch this morning, there would be little chance of crew survival.

But this ditching mode was not part of the preprogrammed abort capability; the offshore weather conditions were only guidelines, not a formal launch constraint. NASA's managers chose to ignore them.

When Thomas and Aldrich had finished their polls, their recommendation to Jesse Moore was to proceed with the countdown.

Jesse Moore has testified to the Rogers Commission and to Congress that there was no unusual pressure on him when he weighed his final decision in the firing room. He has testified that he had no knowledge of any flight safety problems provoked by the record cold. He has testified that he had no knowledge of Morton Thiokol's concerns of the night before. He has testified that no one came forward to voice alarm or to warn him not to proceed with the launch.

The Rogers Commission carefully noted his testimony. In their report the Commission cited the breakdown of communications between Moore and his subordinates as the prime example of NASA's "flawed" decision-making process.

A little after 11:25 that morning, Jesse Moore, Associate Administrator for Space Flight, joined Thomas and Aldrich at the top tier of consoles in Firing Room Three. He spoke with them quietly, examined some final paperwork, then nodded. With that simple gesture, he announced his decision. The terminal nine-minute countdown began.

*   *   *

Launch Control Center, 11:25 a.m.
In Gene Thomas's office, the families of Challenger's crew were grouped around the large television set listening intensely to the voice of NASA's Public Affairs Officer, Hugh Harris:

"One minute away from picking up the count for the final nine minutes of the countdown in today's launch. The countdown is simply a series of checks that people go through in preparation to insure that everything is ready for flight. The countdown for a launch like the 51L mission is four volumes and more than two thousand pages. . . ."

The adults looked at each other with expressions of mixed excitement and veiled apprehension. The countdown was about to resume. Somehow, NASA had found a way to overcome the overnight cold and the unprecedented ice on the launch pad. In only ten minutes Challenger would lift off.

". . . Fifteen seconds away from resuming the countdown and looking at the launch of 51L at 11:38. . . ."

They bent to zip the children's jackets, to pull up the hoods and adjust the stocking caps. In a moment they would form another procession and march to the roof of the Launch Control Center to watch the lift-off.

". . . And we are at T-9 minutes and counting. The Ground Launch Sequencer program has been initiated. . . ."

Cheryl McNair pushed Joy's stroller down the long corridors of the fourth floor, followed by almost twenty adults and children. Bob Harris was smiling broadly. It would be cold on the roof, but they wouldn't have long to wait. In the corridors of the launch center, the ceiling speakers now echoed with the terse cadence of the shuttle radio traffic. Usually, piped music was heard all day and night over the system. But the terminal countdown of a space shuttle mission took precedence over Muzak.

* * *

Press Mound, 11:30 a.m.
For this launch the VIP tent and grandstands had been erected near the barge basin on the edge of the Press Mound. Usually, the VIP's watched lift-off from their own site farther south, but that location did not offer a decent view of Pad 39B. The hundreds of invited guests who had been huddling around the coffee urns inside the striped tent crowded out to take up their places in the bleachers. This new site gave them a greater sense of involvement in the launch, positioned as they were between the press grandstand and network television platforms and the towering battlements of the VAB and Launch Control Center. Luckily the tent offered a partial windbreak and the sun provided some warmth, because most of the VIP's had not brought warm enough clothes.

But Christa McAuliffe's parents, Grace and Ed Corrigan, had been alerted to possible chill weather and wore coats and sweaters. They took their place in the center of the grandstand and tried to retain their composure as the photographers jockeyed for position around them.

Many of Mike Smith's guests had not been able to stay over the weekend and through the Monday scrub to be there. But a few had endured the delays and were now literally hopping with excitement as the countdown proceeded smoothly. In his thoughtful, meticulous manner, Mike had written to each of the guests with helpful suggestions for their stay at the Cape. The last item in his letter was his personal greeting: "Since I won't be able to see you all in person, let me say thanks for coming and have a great time, and I hope you see a good show."

*   *   *

Challenger, 11:33 a.m.

Mike Smith reached over to his right instrument bank and deftly activated the auxiliary power units starting switches in the exact sequence he had mentally rehearsed in the White Room. "APU's are coming on," he said to Dick Scobee.

Scobee nodded, his eyes fixed on his own instruments. "Got pressure on all three APU's," he confirmed. The lights on his panel registered hydraulic power on the first of the three redundant systems. "There's one up." Challenger was coming alive for flight.

Mike Smith called the Launch Control Center, "We've got three good APU's."

A moment later Dick Scobee received the order for the crew to seal their flight helmets in preparation for lift-off. "Visors are coming down," he noted, and the seven crew members lowered and locked their helmet visors.

Throughout the banter that morning, Judy Resnik and Ellison Onizuka had been the most jocular. And Mike Smith had remained somewhat apprehensive, dubious that they would actually launch. Now, as the countdown reached the final two minutes, Smith loosened up. After all of his anxieties, the weather problem had been beaten. They were going to fly.

Scobee received confirmation that Challenger's internal fuel cells were now providing electrical power. The countdown clock passed two minutes. "Welcome to space, guys," he told his crew over the intercom. A moment later, Scobee leaned to his right and craned his neck to see the liquid oxygen vent arm retract from the top of the external tank. "There goes the beanie cap," he called.

Ellison Onizuka rolled to his left to get a look. "Doesn't it go

237

the other way?" A flight test engineer with more than a thousand hours in advanced aircraft, Ellison was famous for his irreverent attitude toward high-tech hardware. The crew laughed.

Mike Smith was in a jolly mood now. "God, I hope not, Ellison."

There was nothing they could do to speed the computers, so they might as well relax. "Now I see it," Ellison called, with mock concern. "I see it."

There was no comment from the mid-deck crew. Although Ron McNair and Greg Jarvis had joined in the intercom kidding, they did not speak now. Since the first communication checks two hours earlier, Christa McAuliffe had been silent.

Dick Scobee and Mike Smith watched the automatic sequencer work through the pressurization of propellant systems. Various alarms reached sensitivity points and were verified as operational. Propellant valve heaters came on, ready for flight. The crew locked their harnesses against the anticipated jolt of engine ignition. They heard a distant whirring rumble as the Orbiter's hydraulic systems exercised the body flap, elevons, and engine nozzle gimbals.

"Fifteen," Dick Scobee called. They were fifteen seconds away from lift-off.

The amber digits blinked on the instrument panels. At T-6 seconds a whining vibration began below. The high-speed turbo pumps of the three main engines churned to life. The whine deepened to a throbbing roar as each engine reached full thrust.

"There they go, guys," Scobee called.

Judy Resnik shouted her enthusiasm, "All *right!*"

"Three at a hundred," Scobee said, noting the three main engines were firing at one hundred percent of rated power.

The roar swelled like a subway in a tunnel. As the vibration grew, they felt the Orbiter flex forward, bending toward the bulk of the external tank. This was the "twang" effect. Over a million pounds of thrust was transmitted through the vehicle to the restraining points on the skirts of the solid rocket boosters. The system was attached to the launching platform, held against this titanic force by four pyrotechnic bolts that would release a few milliseconds after booster ignition. There could still be an engine shutdown, a heart-stopping launch pad abort, as had occurred twice before when the onboard computers sensed sluggish engine performance. In the three seconds remaining before SRB ignition, the engine sensors scrutinized the main propulsion system hundreds of times on redundant channels, assessing the performance of myriad valves, actuators, and pumps. The three engines functioned perfectly.

*   *   *

Press Grandstand, 11:38 a.m.
The reporters stood at their splintery plywood desks, hunched against the cold wind, dressed in a motley combination of sweatshirts, windbreakers, and raincoats. The shuttle veterans had sheltered in the warmth of the nearby Dome until they noted the pressurization of the external tank, which signaled a trouble-free terminal countdown. But there were many reporters in the grandstand who had never seen a shuttle launch and who had been waiting out in the cold for the last hour.

On the roof of the cinderblock shed beside the grandstand, Barbara Morgan, Christa McAuliffe's backup in the Teacher-in-Space program, shivered in the chill sunlight, holding a microphone. A NASA technician beside her operated a video camera; her reaction to Challenger's ascent would be part of an educational film for the project.

". . . T-minus 10," Hugh Harris chanted over the loudspeakers, "nine, eight, seven, six . . . we have main engine start . . . four, three, two, one, and lift-off, *lift-off* of the twenty-fifth space shuttle mission, and it has cleared the tower."

Steam and smoke billowed from the launch pad; then came the glare of the solid rocket boosters. Barbara Morgan's face was rapt with joy; the experienced teacher was suddenly a small child. " 'Bye, Christa. 'Bye, Christa," she sang, waving.

The roof of the grandstand pounded with the first rolling blast from the solid rocket boosters. In the cold morning air, the noise was shocking, stronger than most reporters remembered it from previous missions. The glare of the boosters spread to a wide tail, and the volcanic smoke billowed sideways. As always there was a

239

strange optical illusion that transformed the cumbersome, earth-bound bulk of the space shuttle into a tiny dart atop a graceful, flaming rooster tail. A blazing piston, upon which the space shuttle was balanced, magically appeared from within the smoke shrouding the launch pad.

"Go!" they screamed, rookie and veteran spacehand alike.

*　　*　　*

11:38.010　T-0

Challenger's computers issued the Solid Rocket Motor Ignition Command one tenth of a second after 11:38 A.M. Igniters at the top of each booster's combustion tunnel fired a long blast of flame earthward, which instantly ignited the solid rocket fuel.

As the Rockwell experts had feared, the cacophony of ignition broke loose a shower of ice chunks from the Fixed Service Structure. Pieces of sheet ice as large as thirty-six square inches impacted near the main engines. Some of these pieces struck the lefthand solid rocket booster. Approximately one hundred small pieces of ice were sucked into the lefthand booster nozzle by the aspiration effect. Although there was no evidence of ice impact on the Orbiter, NASA's hasty analysis of the ice hazard was proved erroneous in the first seconds of the flight.

The solid rocket boosters' ignition transient occurred in the first six hundredths of a second after the igniters fired. This was the critical moment that had been discussed and analyzed in such anguished detail during the teleconference the night before. NASA's determination to launch had convinced Thiokol's managers to reexamine their engineering data. They decided that any O-ring erosion provoked by the slow seating of the cold-hardened synthetic rubber seals would be within acceptable limits.

This assessment was incorrect.

The aft field joint of the righthand solid rocket booster was the coldest spot on the booster: approximately twenty-eight degrees F. As the booster's segmented steel casing ballooned with the blasting stress of ignition, the joint rotated, expanding inward as it did on other flights. The primary O-ring, surrounded by its chilled packing grease, was too cold to seat within the first 300 milliseconds of

240

the transient. The cold-stiffened putty between the sections of solid fuel held the pressure pulse too long, then collapsed under the mounting pressure. Combustion gases at a temperature above 5,000 degrees F. blasted past the primary seal at approximately the seven o'clock position [300-degree circumference arc, facing upward] on the circular joint. Because of the joint rotation, the cold secondary O-ring was not yet in its sealed position. There was no barrier to the superhot gas. Both O-rings were instantly vaporized across seventy degrees of arc.

Eight hundredths of a second after the Ignition Command, Challenger's computers fired the pyrotechnic bolts and released the skirt restraints. The space shuttle lifted free of the Earth. With the restraints gone, the millions of pounds of energy that had been stored in the shuttle's elastic structure were released, and the "twang" effect expended this energy. Engineering cameras focused on the right side of the shuttle show a series of ominous black smoke puffs emanating from the right booster's aft field joint, near the strut attaching the booster to the base of the external tank. This smoke appeared at a frequency of three puffs a second, closely matching the vibration of the boosters. The cause of this cyclical puffing was the opening and closing of the damaged field joint clevis as the entire booster resonated. For the next two and a half seconds the cyclic smoke puffs continued while Challenger rose from the pad.

The fatal hemorrhage feared by Allan McDonald and his engineering colleagues had begun.

Even before the shuttle had cleared the tower, however, the twang vibration had been expended. Glassy aluminum oxides from the burnt propellant had sealed the charred aft field joint, temporarily replacing the original O-ring seal. The terrible pressure had been contained. The smoke puffs stopped before actual flame rushed through the damaged joint.

*   *   *

Challenger, 11:38:07
The space shuttle rolled gracefully onto its back, and warm sunlight finally reached Ellison Onizuka in his corner of the flight deck.

Dick Scobee punched his transmit button. "Houston," he called, "roll program."

Beside him Mike Smith was exuberant. "Go, you mother," he shouted.

"LV, LH," Judy Resnik called out, reminding the two pilots to reconfigure their flight instruments to "local" vertical and horizontal orientation. Then, in almost the same breath, she was overcome by the audacious surge of the moment. "Shit hot!" she exclaimed.

The noise in the crew compartment made conversation difficult. The jolting roar was like being aboard a runaway train.

Challenger swayed and shuddered. They encountered the first wind shear.

"Looks like we got a lot of wind here today," Mike Smith shouted.

* * *

Mission Operation Control Room, Houston, 11:38:22
Flight Controller Jay Greene stared at his console screen, watching the engine performance data. The Flight Dynamics Officer had just reported a good roll program. Now the so-called "throttle bucket" procedure would begin. Challenger's computers would first throttle the main engines to 94 percent of rated power, then down to 65 percent, and hold them there for the next 36 seconds while the shuttle accelerated through the moment of maximum aerodynamic stress: "Max-Q."

"Throttle down to ninety-four," FIDO, the Flight Dynamics Officer, announced.

No one spoke for the next twenty seconds. Then FIDO declared the complete throttledown to 65 percent. "Three at sixty-five."

"Sixty-five, FIDO," Jay Greene responded, searching out the proper bit of engine data on his console screen. "T-del confirms throttles. Thank you."

On the wide projection screen at the end of the room, the ruby trajectory line rose majestically, matching the nominal trace pattern. Challenger's ascent was proceeding perfectly.

FIDO announced the end of the throttle bucket. "Throttle up.

Three at one-oh-four." Challenger's main engines were now at full power.

CAPCOM Richard Covey hit his transmit switch. "Challenger, go at throttle up."

*   *   *

11:38:59.010   Max-Q

Challenger slammed through the most violent wind shear ever encountered on a space shuttle mission. To keep the vehicle's mass aligned with the flight vector and reduce aerodynamic stress, the shuttle's computers issued an almost continuous stream of commands to the Orbiter's aerosurfaces and the gimballed nozzles of the main engines and of the solid rocket boosters. The inertial guidance system was so sensitive that it could detect minor wind shifts, even as the entire vehicle blasted through Mach One, the speed of sound.

But neither the computers, the flight crew, nor the humans below detected the sudden plume of orange flame that erupted from the aft field joint of the righthand solid rocket booster. The glassy oxides that had sealed the burnt joint had been shattered by the force of the wind shear. The jolting stress of these aerodynamic forces was the final sinister element in the evolution of the accident. Had there been no high-altitude wind shear, the field joint might have maintained its precarious seal all the way to booster burnout. But with the glassy oxides crumbled, there was nothing to seal the booster's flame within the safe confines of its insulated steel casing. A second and a half later the flame plume had enlarged and was deflected downward by the slipstream to strike the external tank near the attachment point for the P-12 strut, one of three that connected the aft end of the booster to the tank.

For the next three seconds this flame acted like a monstrous blow torch, heating, then blasting through the tank's insulation to contact the naked aluminum. When the pressurized liquid hydrogen tank was breached, the volatile fuel cascaded out into the slipstream and ignited. The ruptured external tank almost instantly lost structural integrity and crumpled. Tons of hydrogen fuel ignited at the lower end of the tank. With the aft attach struts ripped free of the tank, the huge booster swiveled violently inboard around its upper struts. The nose of the booster crashed into the liquid oxygen tank and ruptured it.

Milliseconds later, hundreds of tons of propellant ignited in a huge supersonic steam cloud, a cold fire eight miles above the Atlantic.

The main engines' voracious propellant pumps continued spinning for a few moments, exhausting the fuel and oxidizer remaining in the lines. Then, on the computers' command, the engines dutifully shut down, one by one.

Challenger tumbled wildly and was instantly subjected to G forces far beyond its airframe limitations. The Orbiter was ripped apart a few moments after the structural failure of the tank. As the composite stack broke up, the righthand booster ripped across the Orbiter, and the white-hot rocket plume burned through the right wing section. Both boosters careened upward, only half of their fuel expended, creating a giant forked tongue of rocket exhaust.

A fraction of a second later, the Orbiter was in pieces, spiraling away from the swelling steam cloud. Although the Orbiter was only designed to withstand maximum aerodynamic stress of three G's, the sudden twenty-G load did not completely shred the airframe. Instead, Challenger broke neatly into its component parts, the two wings flipping in different directions, the payload bay remaining relatively intact with its satellite cargo, and the welded aluminum crew compartment tumbling free. The volatile hypergolic fuels of the orbital maneuvering engines and the reaction control system ignited on contact, giving a molten orange cast to the steam cloud.

At 11:39:13.628 on the morning of Tuesday, January 28, 1986, the last bit of telemetry data was transmitted from the space shuttle Challenger.

Six tenths of a second earlier, Pilot Mike Smith's voice was the last sound registered on the intercom tape recorder.

"Uh-oh."

*　　*　　*

Mission Operation Control Room, Houston, 11:39 a.m. (E.S.T.)
The noise of the explosion was a sudden dry rustle over the

244

CAPCOM's voice channel. Jay Greene and Alan Briscoe, his backup flight controller, turned to their left to stare at the color television monitor beside their console. The wide screen filled with a milky cylinder from which two booster plumes extended in a long smoking fork. The men spun back to face their consoles. At the top center of each screen, a bright "S" for "static data" appeared; the telemetry blocks had frozen on the screens. The quiet room became absolutely silent.

Finally the Flight Dynamics Officer spoke on the loop. "The filter has discreting sources." This was the ultimate disaster: those "discreting sources" were the broken pieces of Challenger on the Air Force radar at the Cape.

Now the Ground Communications Officer reported. "We have negative contact. Loss of downlink."

Jay Greene, normally a robust and self-assured professional, stiffened and sank in his chair. "OK, all operators, watch your data carefully." There was nothing more to say. Everyone stared at the television screen, searching for any sign that the Orbiter had flown free of the explosion.

*   *   *

Kennedy Space Center, 11:39 a.m.–12:15 p.m.
Air Force Major Gerald Bieringer sat at his radar console in the Range Safety Center, staring at the shower of diverging green blips on his screen. He turned to his right and saw the steam cloud of the explosion on his television monitor. On his radar screen the primary and alternate impact point displays for these diverging sources were jumping around wildly, indicating a tumbling debris cloud as well as several large, trackable objects in sustained flight. The range safety system computer could not differentiate between fast and slow objects. Major Bieringer was about to recommend to the Senior Range Safety Officer that they not activate the explosive charges on the external tank and boosters because the entire shuttle vehicle appeared to have already exploded. Then he observed one of the solid rocket boosters stabilize and fly toward the upper lefthand corner of his radar screen. He requested permission to "send functions," to transmit multiple coded bursts of radio com-

mands to fire the range safety explosive charges, thus destroying the errant boosters before they could swing back and menace the coast. Permission was granted. He unlocked the ARM key, triggered it, waited ten seconds, then sent the FIRE command.

*　　*　　*

The crew's families were grouped in a tight circle against the guardrail at the edge of the Launch Control Center's wide roof. It was cold and very bright, with the mid-morning sunlight harsh on the white concrete. Just before the lift-off, everyone seemed preoccupied with keeping the small children away from the edge. But as the countdown went through ignition and Challenger rose, both adults and children were mesmerized by the fierce beauty of the scene. From this perspective Challenger's glaring plume was reflected in the lagoons, and the shuttle seemed to rise from the sea itself. The roof bounced beneath their feet as the crackling booster shock waves reached them. There were cries of pride, and mindless laughter at the audacious spectacle. Then they stiffened with involuntary fear at the magnitude of the boosters' snapping thunder. Over the loudspeaker Steve Nesbitt, the Houston Public Affairs Officer, called out the trajectory.

". . . altitude 4.3 nautical miles, down-range distance 3 nautical miles. Engines throttling up, three engines now at 104 percent."

They heard the encouraging voice of Dick Scobee. "Roger, go at throttle up."

Challenger's thick white contrail climbed higher, mounting the chill blue sky. They stood, their hands shielding their eyes from the sun, swaying in the booster shock waves. The contrail thickened to a strange, creamy texture. Something pinwheeled; another object broke free. Barbara Rabren, Gene Thomas's secretary, leaned toward Bob Harris and shouted over the noise, "Look," she exclaimed, "the SRB's have already separated. Boy, this one's going really good."

Harris glared at the smoky sky. "Barbara, this is real bad," he said, nodding toward the families. "Let's go."

Suddenly the sky was silent.

The families of Challenger's crew reacted quietly at first, unaware of the true situation. Several adults whispered the word "Abort."

Then they heard the amplified voice of Steve Nesbitt on the loudspeakers.

"Flight controllers here looking very carefully at the situation. Obviously a major malfunction. We have no downlink. We have a report from the Flight Dynamics Officer that the vehicle has exploded."

The cries rose to a keening wail. Children sobbed for their fathers and for their mother. The adults were helpless to comfort them. As the escorts led the families from the roof, the cloud spread and softened in the sky. Feathery vapor trails descended, distant, steaming debris.

* * *

In the VIP grandstands Scott McAuliffe's third-grade class from Kimbel Elementary School in Concord, New Hampshire, were bunched close against the cold. They howled with joy as the booster shock waves rolled across them, louder than any Independence Day fireworks. Then the noise stopped, and the adults began to sway and moan. Instinctively the children huddled together, staring with fear at the faces above them.

Grace and Ed Corrigan, Christa's parents, were already crying at the moment of lift-off. From their perspective the contrail revealed no explosion, just a strange shimmer; then the sky fell quiet.

"Back to the buses!" an official yelled. If there was an RTLS Abort in progress, contingency plans required evacuating this area. But the crowd dispersed slowly.

The Corrigans' NASA escorts had to hold them erect as Steve Nesbitt's voice sounded across the sunlit grandstand, ". . . the vehicle has exploded. . . ."

They swayed together as if dancing to quiet music. After a few moments the escorts led them away.

* * *

In the firing room the senior managers stood at the wide windows, following the graceful contrail arching away to the southeast. Around them technicians and junior engineers whooped and hollered. This was a normal launch. All the alarmist fears and unquantified apprehensions of the previous day had come to nothing. Jesse Moore, Arnie Aldrich, Gene Thomas, Stan Reinartz, and Dr. William Lucas stared with pride at the clean white plume. Mission 51-L was underway on schedule. The year's ambitious flight manifest had been preserved. Within ten minutes, Challenger would be safely in orbit and the exhausted managers could stand down for a few hours before resuming their burdens.

The dry crackle of the explosion was clearly audible on the OIS voice channel. Men turned from the window toward the television monitors. The gray cloud billowed; the hot pinwheels spun away. They all realized what had happened.

In Firing Room Two, Cecil Houston was monitoring the ascent at an engine data console. This station was linked to "slave consoles" in the Operation Support Room where Dr. Lucas and his associates would follow the performance of the shuttle during ascent. Because the Marshall managers had requested a display of engine data, Houston was obliged to monitor the console instead of watching the launch out the window. This data channel was slow, six seconds behind real time in its update. He hunched over the screen, watching the flashing digits evolve smoothly through a nominal ascent. Someone was trying to get his attention. Houston looked up to see his colleague, Bill Trevor, whose face was drawn and white.

"Cecil," Trevor said, "it just blew up."

When Houston looked back down at his console, the data had stopped.

* * *

Jim Devlin stood on the bridge wing of the *Liberty*. Around the vessel dense sea smoke spiraled off the steep swells and was shredded in the wind. He had heard the countdown and lift-off on the radio and was now searching for Challenger's contrail to appear through a hole in the overcast. Below the bridge, most of the crew were watching the launch on television, but Devlin preferred to see what he could up here. Instead of the normal arching plume, however, he suddenly saw two boosters running a ragged parallel course.

"Anker," he yelled, "I don't know what happened, but I think we got an RTLS."

As they watched, the boosters disappeared above the overcast. There was a pounding on the steel steps from the lounge, and a sailor ran onto the bridge. "My God," the man yelled, "it just exploded."

*   *   *

In the press grandstand, Washington *Post* reporter Kathy Sawyer gazed at the burst gray sausage in the sky. The confident voice of Mission Control had abruptly stopped. Around her, people dashed down the creaking plywood stairs, yelling incomprehensible acronyms. This was Kathy's first space shuttle mission, and she couldn't understand what they were saying.

"RTLS," a man shouted. "They're coming back."

This meant nothing to her, but she realized something was terribly wrong. "Where *are* they?" she cried.

The reporter beside her suddenly sat down, his face slack, as if his legs had failed. "They're dead," he said flatly.

"You're kidding," she shouted, angry at what she thought was his ill-placed humor.

"I'm *not* kidding," he said. "They're dead. We lost them. God bless them."

A delicate web of white contrails spun down the quiet sky, pieces of the space shuttle Challenger on their final descent.

*   *   *

At the Shuttle Landing Facility, a NASA television technician stood in the chill breeze, focusing his camera on the swollen gray cloud. "Has anybody seen the shuttle?" he called forlornly. "Is the Orbiter all right?"

KENNEDY SPACE CENTER

The Press Mound parking lot shimmers in the humid August sun. There are no cars in the hundreds of slots reserved for the news media. Near the barge basin, the VIP grandstands are empty; the striped tent that had sheltered the guests at the Challenger launch has been packed away. The plywood work tables in the press bleachers swell and splinter in the tropical heat. Buzzards spiral up the thermals from the low bay roof to sail above the ramparts of the VAB. The Mission Clock is dark, fringed with Bermuda grass.

Seaward, Pads 39A and 39B stand like abandoned oil rigs.

Had Challenger not exploded on that freezing Tuesday morning, the Kennedy Space Center would now be crowded with reporters, eagerly covering the Journalist-in-Space mission. But the Cape is dormant on this stifling August afternoon.

The newly completed Logistics Facility rises behind the contractors' trailer complex, south of the VAB. Before the accident, this huge hangar was scheduled to become the badly needed central warehouse for space shuttle spare parts. It is here that NASA has assembled the recovered wreckage of Challenger. Pieces of the Orbiter are arranged on a grid pattern blocked out on the wide concrete floor. A visitor can cool off in the powerful air conditioning of the warehouse as he wanders among the tangled, barnacle-encrusted debris, like an archaeologist among amphora.

The salvage effort involving almost twenty surface vessels and submarines has recovered about forty-seven percent of the Orbiter. Working with meticulous efficiency, NASA has reassembled this debris into a skeletal facsimile of Challenger. Some parts are scorched by the booster's plume, others are pristine. The barnacles denote the length of time the piece of wreckage was submerged; little or no encrustation indicates the piece was recovered quickly, perhaps found floating by Jim Devlin's crew on the day of the accident. Altogether, several tons of Challenger debris were recovered that first day. Jim Devlin reports that the crew of the *Liberty* worked with grim professionalism, not allowing their emotions free rein until they found a section of side fuselage bearing the American flag. Then they shed their first tears.

But most of the debris was recovered from the ocean floor. Many chunks are thick with an overlapping moonscape of goose barnacles.

Behind the wreckage, wide racks of gleaming spare parts sealed in transparent plastic cocoons rise to the distant ceiling, thousands of spare shuttle parts that arrived too late to fly aboard Challenger.

The crew compartment is not on display. In March divers located the smashed aluminum pressure vessel that was Challenger's flight deck and mid-deck. The bodies of the astronauts were inside, still strapped in their seats. Pathologists worked for weeks to establish the cause of death, to determine how long the crew survived after the Orbiter broke up. The findings were inconclusive. It is known that the forces of the breakup were not violent enough to cause death or even unconsciousness. Of the four personal egress air packs (PEAP's) recovered, three had been activated and the air supply two thirds exhausted, indicating that at least three crew members were breathing during the two minutes and forty-five seconds the crew compartment fell toward the sea.

One of these air packs was Mike Smith's; it was mounted on the back of his seat, which meant Ellison Onizuka had to activate it for Mike. The other two PEAP's have not been positively identified. This evidence would suggest that the crew survived the momentary high-G-force load of the explosion and were aware of their fate. But the impact of the crew compartment with the water imposed forces in excess of 200 G's, far beyond the level of survivability.

*   *   *

Actually touching the cool, twisted shards of aluminum, the skeins of shredded computer cable, the chalky surface of Challenger's shattered tiles is a powerfully evocative experience. Here is policy made tangible. Here among the debris of the Orbiter one is forced to recognize that political compromise, bureaucratic deception, and corporate duplicity all have consequences. Handling the debris of Challenger provides an unusual historical perspective. We cannot walk inside the ruined reactor room at Three Mile Island, nor enter the concrete tomb at Chernobyl. Nor can we easily visit the new Soviet air and naval bases set up among the American-built facilities at Danang and Cam-Ranh Bay. But flawed policy inevitably produces tangible detritus. Chipping a goose barnacle from the Challenger's crumpled wing serves as an adequate reminder that political decisions involving complex technology often produce unexpected results.

Political rhetoric and image peddling are usually facile and simplistic. When John Kennedy declared America would fight any battle, defend any friend in the defense of liberty, he certainly did not anticipate the sheer technological complexity of cutting the North Vietnamese Army's supply lines on the Ho Chi Minh Trail. The politicians who promised us cheap, plentiful, and safe electric energy from nuclear power plants probably believed their own rhetoric. And a succession of presidents and NASA administrators, including Ronald Reagan and Dr. James Fletcher, probably believed that America's space shuttle would actually become the free world's omnibus space transportation system, a vehicle that would give us cost-effective "routine access to space."

The artifacts of that bankrupt policy litter the concrete floor of the logistics facility. A nation cannot simply declare its resolve to accomplish a task of immense complexity and expect the rhetoric to carry the day. Spending thirty billion dollars to send astronauts to the moon was far different from achieving cost-effective routine access to low-Earth orbit.

In an adult, the ability to differentiate between glittering image and harsh reality is a touchstone of maturity. And a mature nation must also possess such powers of discrimination. But for almost twenty years our nation chose romantic myth over a practical space policy. We seemed to prefer a circus of television spectaculars to scientific exploration and rational commercial exploitation of space. We wanted to maintain our leadership in this exciting endeavor, but we refused to pay the price. And we allowed ourselves to be hoodwinked by a duplicitous procession of politicians and bureaucrats who assured us that this leadership could be maintained at discount prices.

Perhaps it is impossible to form proper policy about complex high technology within a democratic political system such as ours. Clearly most voters do not understand modern technology. A recent poll of the National Academy of Sciences revealed that two thirds of adult Americans could not define in even a rudimentary manner the terms "radiation" and "molecule." How would such people be able to form correct attitudes about high technology in general and our space policy in particular?

But increasingly the American voter will be asked to make such judgments. If the voting public does not make its feelings known, politicians and corporate executives will shape our space policy to their own liking. Since the accident, Rockwell International and Morton Thiokol (through their supporters on Capitol Hill and in the White House) seem eager to get on with business as usual.

Space business, however, will never return to the Emperor's New Clothes normality that prevailed until January 28, 1986. The Reagan Administration finally made some difficult choices, based on reality not rhetoric. In a trip-hammer series of hard political decisions after the accident, our national leaders dismantled the myth of the operational, omnibus space transportation system. Even before the Rogers Commission had concluded that "relentless pressure to launch" had so obviously affected the judgment of NASA's managers, the Congress and the White House had decided that our remaining space assets had to be used more wisely.

Six months after the accident, a new, saner space policy was emerging. When the shuttle's poorly designed solid rocket boosters are rebuilt—with the field joint "capture feature" designed by Allan McDonald and his colleagues—and the other glaring safety deficiencies of the system are corrected, space shuttles will fly again from the launch pads at Cape Canaveral. But they will not carry junketing politicians, foreign or corporate guest astronauts, teachers and journalists, or commercial satellites at subsidized launch fees. The shuttle is no longer touted as a space truck. When it flies again, it will carry only payloads that cannot be launched by expendable booster. No longer will we risk the lives of astronauts to perform services better accomplished by twenty-year-old hardware such as the Atlas and Titan launch vehicles.

Surely this new policy is a welcome return to reality. We seem to have matured as a nation since the accident and are better able to accept practical limits while retaining our pioneering drive to explore. However, it remains to be seen whether we are willing to pay for such exploration in a period of record budget deficits.

Meanwhile, our commercial space competitors in Europe, Japan, India, and China will probably surpass us in certain corners of the space marketplace. The Soviet Union, of course, continues down the path it has followed in space for the last thirty years: massive budgetary and technical expenditures to achieve a slow, incremental advance. And it is especially ironic that the Soviet Union will probably fly their space shuttle before our own shuttle fleet is again certified for flight.

Always the technological scavengers, the Soviets have adapted what is best in our space shuttle technology while rejecting the impractical and politically expedient design compromises. While the Russian orbiter looks a great deal like ours, it differs in significant areas. The Soviet space shuttle orbiter does not carry its own main engines. Instead, the entire system is boosted into orbit using proven liquid-fuel boosters connected to a huge core booster, which takes the place of our external tank and dangerous reusable solid rocket boosters. This design allows the Russians a larger orbiter payload and the luxury of small, air-breathing engines that permit their orbiter much greater maneuverability on reentry and landing.

There is every reason to believe that this Soviet design will function with the same reliability as their tested expendable launch vehicles. And there can be no doubt that the Soviets' commitment to space will continue undiminished. Judging from their abject fear of our Strategic Defense Initiative, they recognize that space is the geopolitical high ground of the next century, and have established their space policy with this reality firmly in mind.

Unfortunately, America has never enjoyed such steady policy

direction. Nor, of course, have we suffered the economic and political stagnation of a totalitarian government. We have viewed space as either the stage for narcissistic media spectaculars or as a mundane commercial environment. Despite our bravado, we have never recognized space as a true frontier, an extension of the Earth, to be explored and ultimately colonized. But, there should be no uncertainty of where our future lies. We must recognize and accept the true cost of space exploration while we patiently await the rewards.

In the space shuttle we still have a tool to continue this exploration. The conclusions and recommendations of the Rogers Commission Report certainly appear to be a wise blueprint for the future operation of the space shuttle. However, the question of adequate funding remains. Given the reality of pork-barrel politics —especially in the megabillion dollar realm of defense procurement—is there truly a national constituency for a realistic space program? In the last decade we have allowed our politicians to convince us of the national security requirements for fifteen aircraft carrier battle groups, a fleet of B-1 bombers, a horde of MX "Peacekeeper" missiles, a score of Trident submarines, and several hundred billion dollars here and there for less glamorous military hardware.

And during that same period we starved the space shuttle program to the point where otherwise reasonable people were forced to accept the myth of the operational space transportation system.

If we continue along this path for another decade, we must be prepared to accept the consequences of a permanent second- or even third-place position among the so-called "space-faring" nations.

*   *   *

It is almost cool in the echoing cavern of the VAB. High overhead crane operators maneuver exotic hardware. On the high bay floor electric tractors tug booster section trolleys this way and that. There is still work to complete, waiting for the new boosters to be designed and certified for flight. Although there have been layoffs, the work force at the Cape is still busy. In high bay number one the Orbiter Atlantis stands attached to an external tank and solid rocket boosters. In a few days, Atlantis will be trundled down the crawlerway to Pad 39B for fit checks of the pad's new weather-protection system. The people at the Cape eagerly anticipate this event. It will be good, they say, to see "the bird" back on the pad. Certainly, they could do with a morale boost.

Although predictions that the accident would spawn a full-scale scandal involving the White House have proved wrong, the Rogers Commission and Congressional investigations did unearth many shocking revelations. These investigations provoked accusations of whitewash and cynical cover-ups. Richard Cook, the NASA budget analyst who warned of the O-rings' potential for catastrophic failure, has led the attack on the Rogers Commission. However, most independent experts on the space program consider that the Commission did an excellent job, given the time constraints and origin of its mandate. It should be noted that the more partisan investigation by the Democratic-controlled House Science and Technology Committee was harder on NASA than the Commission, but that the House investigation unearthed no evidence of an organized cover-up as Cook charges.

Senator Jesse Helms (Republican-North Carolina) has implied that the CIA investigation of possible Soviet sabotage of the Challenger flight was not vigorous enough. Few people take this seriously.

Since the accident, NASA has been battered and shaken more severely than any government institution in recent years. Reading the daily headlines after the accident brought to mind the Pentagon during the Vietnam War or the Nixon White House during Watergate. But history has taught us that such institutional cataclysms are often necessary. In the case of NASA, the casualties among the bureaucrats might well help the agency. Certainly the Marshall Space Flight Center will never be the same. Following strong criticism from the Rogers Commission, Dr. William R. Lucas retired in July. Lawrence B. Mulloy is gone; so is George Hardy. Stanley Reinartz is no longer in the shuttle program. At NASA headquarters, the personnel changes have been equally far-reaching. Dr. William Graham has returned to the White House. NASA has announced that Jesse Moore plans to take an extended "sabbatical," which many observers feel is a prelude to early retirement. Dick Smith, Director of the Kennedy Space Center, retired in the spring.

At Morton Thiokol, Jerald Mason has taken early retirement. Calvin Wiggins has been reassigned to the strategic division. Robert Lund no longer works in the solid rocket booster project. After brief banishment, Roger Boisjoly and Allan McDonald were resurrected through the intervention of Chairman William Rogers to lead the company's booster redesign team.

Despite some spirited Congressional debate, Morton Thiokol has been assured the contract for at least the initial production phase of the new booster. The White House also energetically debated the issue of a fourth Orbiter. At the end of the day, Rockwell got the go-ahead to build a replacement for Challenger. Dr. James Fletcher (who had "no commitments to Utah") and Dale Myers (whose professional loyalties were once to Rockwell) have returned, respectively, as the Administrator and Deputy Administrator of NASA.

Even with the return of these officials, it is possible that the federal government, including the Congress and the career bureaucracy, have learned an important lesson about managing dangerous and complex technology. Surely the cumulative effect of the Challenger accident, the Bophal chemical plant tragedy, and the Chernobyl disaster have penetrated the consciousness of even the most cynical pork-barreling congressman or corporate Trojan horse within government. Yale professor Charles Perrow has written with elegant insight about the problems of managing modern technology in his seminal study of the subject, *Normal Accidents, Living with High-Risk Technologies.* In his 1984 book, Professor Perrow actually foresaw the catastrophic failure of a major space mission, a nuclear power plant, and a chemical plant, two years before Challenger, Chernobyl, or Bophal.

Perrow correctly reminds us that all technology does not carry the same level of catastrophic risk. But endeavors such as space flight, chemical processing, and nuclear power production are both risky and incredibly complex. Therefore, these activities are exceedingly difficult to manage. When we add to such operations the element of "production pressure"—i.e., the acceptance of risk to achieve arbitrary operational goals, we face almost certain disaster.

*   *   *

The families of Challenger's crew have accepted their loss with a mixture of quiet dignity and outrage. Jane Smith has initiated a wrongful death lawsuit against NASA and Lawrence Mulloy. Cheryl McNair is suing Morton Thiokol. Various organizations across the country have announced plans for scholarships and memorials in the names of the dead astronauts. After a brief, intense period of mourning around the world—reminiscent of the mourning for John Kennedy—the public has accepted the death of Challenger's crew and assigned them places in the national pantheon of heroes.

*   *   *

The broad Shuttle Landing Facility ripples with heat mirage. Maintenance crews work languidly in the sun around the shuttle landing caravan vehicles. But this runway will no longer serve as a principal landing site for the space shuttle. When flights begin again, they will return to the dry lake bed at Edwards Air Force Base, which offers much greater margins of safety.

In late spring, the concrete apron that was the media stage for the ritual of Astronaut Arrival on January 23, was the scene of another, far more somber ceremony. Honor guards carried seven flag-draped caskets on board an Air Force transport. Challenger's crew was going home.

They buried Mike Smith at Arlington National Cemetery with full military honors. Beneath the etched astronaut wings on a granite headstone the inscription reads: "Michael John Smith, Captain, United States Navy, April 30, 1945–January 28, 1986, Pilot of the Space Shuttle Challenger."

Before the mission, a reporter interviewed Mike Smith about his career, a standard bread-and-butter "astronaut bio" in preparation for another routine shuttle flight. "Whenever I was conscious of what I wanted to do," Smith said, "I wanted to fly. I can never remember anything else I wanted to do but flying. To tell you the truth, it's been wonderful."

November 1986
Washington

GLOSSARY

Abort: Emergency termination of a mission

AOA: Abort Once Around

APU: Auxiliary Power Unit

Ariane: European Expendable Launch Booster

ASP: Astronaut Support Person

ASTRO: Orbiting, reusable astronomy facility carried aboard shuttle

Atlas: Expendable launch booster used by NASA and the Air Force

ATO: Abort to Orbit

Body Flap: Aerosurface beneath tail of shuttle Orbiter

CAPCOM: Spacecraft communicator

Centaur: Cryogenic Upper Stage used by NASA and the Air Force

CRIT: Critical

Cryogenics: Supercold liquid propellants

DoD: Department of Defense

Downlink: Communications and Data Transmission

EAFB: Edwards Air Force Base

Elevon: Aerosurface on shuttle Orbiter wing

ELV: Expendable Launch Vehicle

ESA: European Space Agency

ET: External Tank

FDO/FIDO: Flight Dynamics Officer

FFR: Flight Readiness Review

FR3: Firing Room Three

FSS: Fixed Service Structure

GAO: General Accounting Office

GSE: Ground Support Equipment

Hypergolic: Fuels that ignite on contact with each other

IUS: Inertial Upper Stage

Joint Rotation: Separation of metal parts in booster joint

259

JSC: Johnson Space Center

KSC: Kennedy Space Center

L—: Launch minus counts

LCC: Launch Control Center (Launch Commit Criteria)

LH2: Liquid Hydrogen

LOX: Liquid Oxygen

LTD: Lockheed Test Director

Max-Q: Maximum Aerodynamic Pressure

MECO: Main Engine Cutoff

MET: Mission Elapsed Time

MLP: Mobile Launch Platform

MMT: Mission Management Team

MOCR: Mission Operations Control Room

MSFC: Marshall Space Flight Center

NASA: National Aeronautics and Space Administration

NOAA: National Oceanic and Atmospheric Administration

O & C Building: Kennedy Space Center Operations and Checkout Building

O-Ring: Synthetic rubber "donut" ring

OIS: Operational Intercommunication System

OMB: Office of Management and Budget

OMI: Operational Maintenance Instruction

OMS: Orbital Maneuvering System

OPF: Orbiter Processing Facility

OTC: Orbiter Test Conductor

PAO: Public Affairs Officer (Office)

PEAP: Personal Egress Air Pack

RCS: Reaction Control System

Redline: Formal hardware performance limit

RFP: Request for Proposal

Roll Program: Computer-controlled shuttle roll maneuver

RSS: Range Safety System (Rotating Service Structure)

RTLS: Return to Launch Site (abort)

Scrub: Cancellation of a mission during terminal countdown

Skylab: Successful crewed orbiting laboratory flown in 1970s

SLF: Shuttle Landing Facility

Slip: Delay of a mission before terminal countdown

SRB: Solid Rocket Booster

260

SRM: Solid Rocket Motor

SSME: Space Shuttle Main Engine

STA: Shuttle Training Aircraft

Stack: To join major shuttle components vertically

STS: Space Transportation System

T—: Terminal Count minus (stops at each hold point)

T38: Two-seat NASA Training Jet

TAL: Transatlantic Landing (abort)

TDRS: Tracking and Data Relay Satellite

Telecon: Conference by speaker telephone

Telefax: Telefacsimile, a method of transmitting graphic material by telephone

Telemetry: Encoded data transmission

Titan: Expendable launch booster used by the Air Force

TPS: Thermal Protection System (heat tiles)

Transducer: Remote data transmission instrument

VAB: Vehicle Assembly Building

VAFB: Vandenberg Air Force Base, Calif.

Wind Shear: Violent wind divergence

INDEX

INDEX